Fairy Tales in Popular Culture

Description of author are "vivid"
or "blank"

6 → 5 sentences talking about what
it is in the essay (5 paragraphs or
6)

Claim
 Body 1:
  Subpoint
   evidence   ) Repeat

 Body 2:
) Repeat

 Body 3:

FAIRY TALES IN POPULAR CULTURE

EDITED BY

MARTIN HALLETT & BARBARA KARASEK

broadview press

Library and Archives Canada Cataloguing in Publication

Fairy tales in popular culture / edited by Martin Hallett
& Barbara Karasek.

Includes bibliographical references.
ISBN 978-1-55481-144-1 (pbk.)

1. Fairy tales—Adaptations. 2. Fairy tales—Adaptations—History
and criticism. 3. Popular culture and literature. I. Hallett, Martin, 1944-,
editor of compilation II. Karasek, Barbara, 1954- editor of compilation

GR552.F65 2014   398.2   C2014-900121-5

Broadview Press is an independent, international publishing house, incorporated in 1985.

We welcome comments and suggestions regarding any aspect of our publications—please feel free to contact us at the addresses below or at broadview@broadviewpress.com.

North America:
PO Box 1243, Peterborough, Ontario K9J 7H5, Canada
555 Riverwalk Parkway, Tonawanda, NY 14150, USA
Tel: (705) 743-8990; Fax: (705) 743-8353
Email: customerservice@broadviewpress.com

UK, Europe, Central Asia, Middle East, Africa, India, and Southeast Asia:
Eurospan Group, 3 Henrietta St., London WC2E 8LU, UK
Tel: 44 (0) 1767 604972; Fax: 44 (0) 1767 601640
Email: eurospan@turpin-distribution.com

Australia and New Zealand:
NewSouth Books, c/o TL Distribution
15-23 Helles Ave., Moorebank, NSW 2170, Australia
Tel: (02) 8778 9999; Fax: (02) 8778 9944
Email: orders@tldistribution.com.au

www.broadviewpress.com

Broadview Press acknowledges the financial support of the Government of Canada through the Canada Book Fund for our publishing activities.

Copy-edited by Betsy Struthers

Book design and composition by George Kirkpatrick
PRINTED IN CANADA

To my brothers Hugh and Noel, who graciously permitted me to be the third. M.H.

To Ron Reichertz and David Williams, who helped me discover the stories of once upon a time. B.K.

CONTENTS

LIST OF ILLUSTRATIONS

PREFACE

A GREAT DEAL HAS OCCURRED IN THE WORLD OF FAIRY TALE SINCE 1991, when our *Folk and Fairy Tales* anthology first saw the light of day. As we worked upon subsequent editions, we did our best to keep up with the changes but came to realize that they were happening on an ever-widening front, and since *Folk and Fairy Tales* was designed to introduce the "classic" fairy tale as *literature*, many interesting developments fell outside our purview. As time went by, however, that position became more and more unsatisfactory. With the very nature of communication being changed forever by the tidal wave of social media, concepts like "literature" and "story" and "originality" are suddenly up for grabs—and on top of that, the scene has clearly shifted away from the printed word in favor of the visual image.

To put together a new anthology that reflects the evolution of the fairy tale over the last half-century comes with its challenges. Finding recent literary retellings is not a problem; it's quickly apparent that fairy tales still cast a spell on upcoming generations of writers. Indeed, one is tempted to think that it's something of a "write of passage" to take a well-known tale and, through personal association or interpretation, turn it into something "completely different." Such a task is not without its risks because fairy tales can inspire devotion; their roots are entwined with profound and treasured memories of childhood. Sometimes, however, a radical re-visioning of a comfortably familiar tale will force the reader to take a hard look at matters well beyond the story itself; "what if" is a potent question to ask. We hope that you find our selection of tales and poems in this book stimulating, even at the cost of taking you a little out of your "comfort zone."

We then turn our attention to a variety of *still* images: illustrations that accompany a printed tale, stand-alone artworks inspired by fairy tale, even advertisements that exploit the tale's universal recognizability. Once again, we hope that our selection of pictures provides some insight not only into the relationship between word and image but also into the more complex demands placed upon the reader/viewer: What does the artist want us to see (or not see) in the story? What *other* stories is the artist telling?

The major challenge comes less in the selection of appropriate material and more in the transitory nature and sheer quantity of popular culture—witness the flood of fairy-tale movies, television series, and advertisements that shows no sign of slowing down. Like the technology that creates these fantastic images on the screen (from 3D to cell-phone size), what is cutting-edge in fairy-tale adaptation today will be history tomorrow. We make no claim to expertise in the field of popular culture *per se*; however, in examining the trail of the fairy tale over the last 50 years or so, we looked to others for guidance through unfamiliar territory. We can only hope that our good judgement did not desert us and that the discussion we offer will provide some useful insight.

Finally, in looking at the many ways fairy tales permeate our culture, we have come to realize that the proliferation of social media has provided us with an opportunity, lost with the passing of oral culture, to regain an active role in telling our stories. Thus, we have had to turn our attention back onto ourselves and examine our close and reciprocal relationship with these old tales. There is no denying that they can still surprise and entertain, whether on page, stage, or screen, but, spectacular effects notwithstanding, their appeal is more profound—it speaks to a universal need to lose ourselves in the world of imagination—to let the fairy tale transport us, even if just for a little while, into a world where not only our darkest fears are made real but also our deepest desires.

INTRODUCTION:
THE FAIRY TALE AND POPULAR CULTUR

COINED IN THE NINETEENTH CENTURY, THE TERM "POPULAR CUL-ture" is now ubiquitous, and its meaning seems obvious—except among scholars, many of whom are reluctant to provide a clear definition. Nevertheless, there is general acceptance that it stems from a "capitalist market economy" and therefore dates from the Industrial Revolution.[1] Consequently, mass and consumer cultures have become corollaries of the notion of popular culture. However, in his review of the scholarship, Holt Parker points out that to restrict the use of the term to any specific time period is "an impoverished view" since there are numerous instances in pre-industrialized societies of public events and celebrations that could by any reasonable definition be termed popular culture. He concludes that popular culture is like pornography: "we may not be able to define it, but we know it when we see it."[2] We are drawn to this more inclusive view, for who can deny that the fairy tale, with its remarkable history and current celebrity, is not popular culture?

Apart from the Bible, there is probably no body of writing that is as familiar to Western society as fairy tales, some of whose characters—Cinderella, Sleeping Beauty, Snow White—surely have the highest name recognition in the English language. Since they entered the communal bloodstream in the nineteenth century, many fairy-tale characters have attained the status of archetypes; if we are told that a young woman's life is "a real Cinderella story," we have learned a good deal about her past—and how better to describe an unimaginable distance than "east of the sun and west of the moon"?

It must be acknowledged that the number of tales that can command this level of universal recognition is limited. The collection made by the Brothers Grimm, which is undeniably the best-known source in the Western world, contains more than 200 tales, yet only a handful can be described as "classics." Just what features of a particular tale have brought about its enduring popularity is a matter of ongoing debate: Is it the romantic plot? The memorable characters? The magic? Is it something more

---

1 John Storey, *Cultural Theory and Popular Culture: An Introduction*, 5th ed. (New York: Pearson Longman, 2009) 10.

2 Parker posits that the widely attended Dionysian theater festivals in Ancient Greece and circus games in Ancient Rome qualify as popular culture of the time (Parker, 150); we would propose the mystery plays of medieval England, and even Shakespeare's plays a century later, as further examples. See Holt N. Parker, "Towards a Definition of Popular Culture," *History and Theory* 50 (May 2011): 147-50; quote p. 150.

subtle, like the psychological reassurance that comes with the happy resolution of a conflict? Or could it be the result of a successful "meme"?

The term "meme" was first coined by the evolutionary biologist Richard Dawkins in his book *The Selfish Gene* (1976)[1] to try to explain the spread of cultural phenomena such as melodies, catch-phrases, fashion, and even the making of tools. He proposed the meme as the cultural equivalent of the gene (i.e., the meme does for culture what the gene does for biology). Accordingly, the meme is a unit of cultural information that, in the process of replication, is subject to the same processes that a gene undergoes: variation, mutation, competition, and inheritance. These, in turn, affect the success of a particular meme to survive. In effect, memetics (as the field of study has been called since its inception in the 1990s) offers an evolutionary model of culture based on the principles of genetics. In accordance with memetic theory, then, certain fairy tales prospered by getting themselves replicated, while less memorable ones suffered the fate of being ignored and forgotten. Thus, the oral tales that survived for centuries, spread to cultures around the globe, and now form the fairy-tale canon may just be the result of a process of natural selection that is comparable to the one that has us walking on two legs.

In many instances, the fairy tale has also been *written down* for a long time—in Europe, for instance, as early as the middle of the seventeenth century. Important changes occur when the tale is put on paper, the most significant for our purposes being that access to the tale is thereby limited to those who can read; at a stroke (of a pen), the nature and even the meaning of a fairy tale has been changed forever. For the majority of people born between the early years of the nineteenth century and the advent of the moving picture, the written-down (or "literary") tale was the only version they would have known, and their exposure to these tales implied membership in what we might term an "exclusive" culture, available only to those who were literate.

Despite finding a permanent home between the covers of a book, often lavishly illustrated and destined for the nurseries of the middle and upper classes, the fairy tale could not be confined to the printed page, nor was it lost to the "masses." During the Industrial Revolution, it traveled with them from the countryside to the city and found a new urban setting on the stage. The pantomime, with its irreverent presentation of the "fractured" fairy tale, became the highlight of Victorian Christmas-season festivities (and the tradition remains popular in Britain to this day—see pp. 111-12). Its successor, less accessible because more expensive, was the musical, the specialty of Broadway a century later.

---

1 Richard Dawkins, "Memes: The New Replicators," *The Selfish Gene*, 30th anniversary ed. (Oxford: Oxford UP, 2006).

The twentieth century produced its own revolution—a technological one, whose breathtaking momentum continues unabated in the twenty-first. For example, it is hard for a young person today to imagine the importance of radio as a medium of communication and disseminator of culture in the first half of the previous century. Because the fairy tale was at this time the provenance of childhood, it inevitably played a central role in radio programming for children. Shows such as *Land O'Make Believe* and the award-winning *Let's Pretend*, which ran for two decades, "were an important segment of the free entertainment aired to millions of listeners on a daily basis."[1] In the words of one listener, "Radio served the same function that Grimm's fairy tales had served for children of an earlier time. It stretched our minds, it showed us the world of good and evil, honor and deceit, pain and pleasure. It sketched the story and let our imaginations fill in the details."[2] In this way, the radio had replaced the storyteller.[3]

The details that needed to be filled in by the listener in the earlier age of the storyteller and then the golden age of radio (1930s to 1950s) were soon provided by another new and exciting invention—the moving picture. The humble radio was soon overshadowed by the magic of film, and then its place in the home was usurped by the television set. Now this hitherto dominant device is in its turn threatened by the fate of the dinosaur, since we can watch the latest episode of *Once Upon a Time* or read an erotic fan-fiction retelling of "Snow White" anytime, anywhere on this year's version of a smart phone. Not only is it readily accessible, our cultural world now fits in our pocket.

It is intriguing to discover that the fairy tale's evolution—from oral to written, from visual to virtual—has had a remarkable symmetry. In its original spoken form, the folk/fairy tale belonged to everybody, since to tell a tale implies interaction with an audience. Thus, the tales were an important part of what has to be described as popular culture, reflecting as they did the common beliefs, fears, and desires of their time. This dynamic quality was largely lost when they were fixed in print by writers such as Perrault and the Brothers Grimm. At that point, they became part of bourgeois culture, falling into the new but rapidly expanding category of children's literature, where they remained until Walt Disney began the process whereby the tale has indisputably re-established itself in the popular culture of our own times.

---

1 Ray Broadus and Pat Browne, eds., *The Guide to United States Popular Culture* (Bowling Green, OH: Bowling Green State University Popular Press, 2001) 167.

2 John H. Lienhard, "Radio Days," *Engines of Our Ingenuity*, No. 1780—radio program produced by KUHF-FM Houston; transcripts available at <http://www.uh.edu/engines>.

3 It is worth noting that BBC Radio 4 continues this tradition with its broadcasts of writer Sarah Maitland's retellings of famous fairy tales.

THE ART OF RETELLING

THE TERM "RETELLING" IS CENTRAL TO THE POINT AND PURPOSE OF this book, so all the more reason to explore its meaning, which turns out to be rather more complex than one might think, not least because retelling is—and always has been—the lifeblood of the fairy tale.

From its earliest beginnings, the folk/fairy tale was told and told again; it had no other existence. It was part of an *oral* culture, which is by definition inclusive since one needs no formal training to listen. It is in this sense that we often refer to the early fairy tale as a *folk* tale, implying that it originated among and belonged to the ordinary people; it was, in fact, part of the popular culture of that time. It dealt with many issues of common concern, such as the challenges of growing up and finding one's place in the world; at the same time, it provided an escape from the hardship and monotony of daily life, and it suggested that courage and perseverance would eventually be rewarded. Because it lived in the spoken word, its survival rested upon the skill of the teller and the receptiveness of the listeners. (As an Irish storyteller of our acquaintance once observed, you keep the tales by giving them away ...) In this phase of its evolution, one would have to say that the tale was truly dynamic—a combination of news, gossip, therapy, and education, all woven together by the teller according to his or her reaction to audience feedback. In the light of that fact, it is intriguing to wonder how many good tales have been lost through poor telling—and, by the same token, how many mediocre tales were given new life by a gifted narrator.

In time, however, the literate world discovered the fairy tale, in the form of writers who, for one reason or another, were inspired to transform the spoken word into the written. For Charles Perrault (1628-1703), the intent was to provide some quaint amusement for the court of Louis XIV at Versailles; in the case of the Brothers Grimm, Jacob (1785-1863) and Wilhelm (1786-1859), their renowned collection of tales was born of their patriotic desire to celebrate their homeland. Yet we cannot underestimate the consequence of these contrasting motivations for the simple reason that now some tales at least were on permanent record; we can still read today the exact words that these men recorded hundreds of years ago. However, as highly educated members of the bourgeoisie, they lived in a very different world from that of the "folk," and their versions of these tales were inevitably colored—consciously or not—by their own preoccupations. Thus, Perrault was concerned to shape his tales to the tastes of his sophisticated audience,[1] while the Grimms saw their pioneering work strictly in scholarly terms. (It was only in response to subsequent popular demand that Wilhelm revised their tales for children.)

Once the written version of the folk/fairy tale was firmly established, the way was cleared for what may be termed the literary tale, that is, an original story that employs many of the characteristics of the folk/fairy tale. The work of Hans Christian Andersen (1805-75) exemplifies this transitional stage, since as the child of impoverished parents living in rural Denmark, Andersen would have been familiar with the oral tradition. A number of his tales draw upon older collections such as the Grimms' or the Arabian Nights; however, Andersen's fame rests primarily on his original tales, such as "The Ugly Duckling" (1843) and "The Nightingale" (1843), which have much more to do with events and experiences in his own life. So fluid was the line between traditional and "original" that the Grimms, under the impression that it was a German folktale, added one of Andersen's own tales, "The Princess and the Pea" (1835), to their collection. Although these men were in large part responsible for the annexation of fairy tales as an important part of the rapidly expanding world of children's literature, they censored the tales significantly in the process in order to make them suitable for innocent minds. Perrault appended Morals to each of his tales, the Grimms provided us with plentiful evidence of their moral concerns and criteria in the course of the seven different editions that they published between 1812 and 1857,[2] and Andersen consciously wrote to the child in all of us.

---

1 Charles Perrault was one of numerous writers (the majority of whom were aristocratic women) who frequented the literary *salons* of Paris. The tales (*contes de fées*) that they wrote were generally long, elaborate, and stylized, which explains why those by Perrault stand apart. At the same time, we should note that for many of these women, the writing of fairy tales provided a creative release from the restrictions that their social position imposed upon them; in a sense, they were early precursors of the feminist movement.

2 For instance, a review of the Grimms' best-known tales makes it clear that they were much more concerned about sexuality than violence. Interestingly, Disney shares the same perspective; his classic animations contain some memorably violent episodes.

These sanitized versions, rendered yet more respectable and anodyne in the early years of the twentieth century by the charming illustrations of artists such as Arthur Rackham, Edmund Dulac, and Kay Nielsen remained largely unchallenged well into the second half of that century.

In the evolution of the fairy tale over the last 100 years, however, nothing can match the significance of the release, in 1937, of Walt Disney's animated movie *Snow White and the Seven Dwarfs*. Such was the popularity of this and subsequent Disney fairy-tale animations that many children have grown up believing that he invented the fairy tale—an assumption bolstered by the aggressive marketing campaign that has accompanied each movie. In this instance, of course, the nature of the retelling is dramatically different. While Perrault and the Grimms took the spoken word and transformed it into text, Disney took text and turned it into images and songs that achieved iconic status in twentieth-century popular culture; has any lyric ever had a greater impact than "Some Day My Prince Will Come"? If we can learn a good deal about the worlds of Perrault and the Grimms from how they tell their tales, the same can be said of how Disney makes his movies: what he adds, what he leaves out, even how the cartoon format affects the tale itself.

The reaction to the established notion of the significance of fairy tales and their impact began in the 1970s, instigated primarily by feminist writers and scholars who objected to the tales' depiction of gender roles, exemplified in the helpless passivity and dependence of the princess, on the one hand, and the demonization of the powerful older woman, on the other. Likewise, the child psychologist Bruno Bettelheim opened up a new perspective on fairy tales with his influential book *The Uses of Enchantment* (1976),[1] in which he argued that they provided psychological support for children in overcoming the emotional crises that come with growing up. Such controversial theories had the effect of provoking a renewed interest in the tales and a realization that there was much in them that had been overlooked through seeing them simply as "children's stories." Along with the demolition came reconstruction; these same years witnessed some remarkable new approaches to the fairy tale by writers such as Donald Barthelme (*Snow White*, 1967), Robert Coover (*Pricksongs and Descants*, 1969), and Angela Carter (*The Bloody Chamber*, 1979), the precursors of a robust revival—or, to be more precise, adaptation—of what we may term the classic fairy tale.

The modern version of the fairy tale—whether book, comic book, or movie—may well owe allegiance to one or more different genres, such as satiric, horror, psychological, or sexual, and in many instances is intended for the adult or young

---

1 Bruno Bettelheim, *The Uses of Enchantment: The Meaning and Importance of Fairy Tales* (New York: Alfred Knopf, 1976).

adult reader. In a sense, therefore, the folk/fairy tale has come full circle: originally intended for an adult audience, then censored and moralized for the benefit of children, now it is in the process of being returned to the adult reader/viewer, often with as titillating a dose of sex and violence as ever entertained our forebears around the proverbial campfire.[1]

The question is begging to be asked: How can we explain the remarkable explosion of interest in the fairy tale that has taken place over the last decade or so? And again: What have been the most notable *features* of that explosion? One explanation for the popularity of the tale has to do with difficult economic times: when people are struggling with such problems as high unemployment, social discord, and gloomy prognostications about the future, they are the more likely to seek refuge in a fantasy world where issues are more straightforward and resolvable and "the little guy" can, through a combination of courage and audacity, overcome the odds. At the same time, this celebration of the underdog may well be accompanied by the violence and sexuality that were common ingredients of fairy tale when they provided for pre-literate audiences what police procedurals and soap operas provide today. Indeed, after the long years of refinement and censorship that began with Charles Perrault at the end of the seventeenth century, it's not surprising that the constraints have been thrown off with abandon, judging by some recent print and visual productions. There's no getting away from the long-established fact that sex and violence sell!

Another attraction is the incredible versatility of computer-assisted technology when it comes to creating imaginary worlds and characters, to the extent that we in the audience have come to expect the impossible and the breathtaking as a matter of course. In fact, this limitless potential of the new technology to present the impossible on screen has had the effect of blurring a traditional distinction between child and adult. We have long assumed that children's ready and willing suspension of disbelief (to adapt Coleridge's famous phrase) explains much of their delight in fairy tales. Adults, on the other hand, have customarily been more resistant to the appeal of the supernatural. However, the evidence of recent years seems to suggest that filmmakers have the tools to convince young and old equally; the line between real and unreal has simply disappeared.

---

1 It is worth noting that a survey conducted in the United Kingdom in 2012 indicated that parents are rejecting traditional fairy tales because they perceive them as too scary ("... Nearly half of mothers and fathers refuse to read 'Rumpelstiltskin' to their kids as the themes of the story are kidnapping and execution ..."). "Fairytales too scary for modern children, say parents," *Daily Telegraph* (February 12, 2012), <http://www.telegraph.co.uk/news/newstopics>.

There are implications to such developments, however, that are disturbing. We must ask ourselves if, in broader terms, the recent treatments of fairy tale can be seen as evidence of the erosion of the traditional separation between childhood and adulthood—and, if so, is that a good or a bad thing?[1] In an insightful article in *Time* magazine (May 10, 2007), James Poniewozik makes the crucial point that for child and adult alike, it is becoming increasingly unlikely that the reader (or viewer) will be exposed to what he refers to as "old school fairy tales";[2] for most, the exposure begins with Disney. And what exactly does the term "fairy tale" currently mean? Certainly nothing resembling the "classic" versions attributed to the likes of Perrault and the Grimms.[3] As Poniewozik ruefully puts it: "This is the new world of fairy tales: parodied, ironized, meta-fictionalized, politically adjusted and pop culture saturated."[4] If irony is a key feature of the modern fairy tale, then we are confronting a fundamental disconnect, since irony can only be appreciated when the incongruity between old and new is recognized. As we shall see in the chapters that follow, many contemporary fairy-tale treatments deal with that gap by virtually abandoning the old altogether. Thus, we may be drawn to the inescapable conclusion that the fairy tale has been hijacked, hollowed out; nothing remains except those strange magical names that still have the power to evoke visions of a simpler, more colorful world. It is this recent phenomenon in particular that compels us to define what we mean by "retelling" since one obvious feature of all these productions is their distance from the original. Indeed, in some cases, even to use the term "adaptation" is a bit of a stretch—the Grimms would be more than a little startled to see what Snow White and Rumpelstiltskin are up to these days!

---

1 These ideas owe a debt to Neil Postman's influential book *The Disappearance of Childhood* (New York: Random House, 1994).

2 James Poniewozik, "The End of Fairy Tales? How Shrek and Friends Have Changed Children's Stories," *Time* (May 10, 2007). Quoted in Martin Hallett and Barbara Karasek, eds., *Folk & Fairy Tales: Concise Edition* (Peterborough: Broadview, 2009) 157.

3 The bicentennial of the first publication of the Grimms' fairy tales in 1812 passed with little fanfare; Philip Pullman's selection of his 50 favorite Grimm tales, *Fairy Tales from the Brothers Grimm* (New York: Penguin, 2012), was arguably the highest-profile acknowledgement in the English-speaking world.

4 Poniewozik, "The End of Fairy Tales?," 157.

PROSE

THE STATEMENT THAT FAIRY TALES HAVE BEEN AROUND FOR A VERY long time is at the same time true and rather misleading, in the sense that early versions, which can in some instances be traced back hundreds, even thousands of years, may bear little overall resemblance to the tales that we are familiar with today. One remarkable quality of the fairy tale is what might be termed its "evolutionary versatility" (memes in motion?) as common elements of character and plot can be found in sources as disparate as Greek myth ("Cinderella"), medieval romance ("Sleeping Beauty"), and legend ("Bluebeard"). Through time, a story may speak to a variety of social or cultural issues and undergo significant reworking, the better to reflect those interests—and that dynamic process continues in the modern retelling, which reinterprets familiar material such as the nineteenth-century tales collected by the Brothers Grimm (who themselves transformed folktales into children's literature) to arrive at insights, perspectives, and questions that pertain to the contemporary world.

In retrospect, it might be said that the Grimms came along just when the fairy tale needed them. At the beginning of the nineteenth century, the agrarian world was coming under increasing pressure from new industrial towns so that traditional country life was giving way to the demands for labor in factories and mines, where prospects for employment were much brighter. As the oral tale faded away with the rural villages that had nurtured it, its literary successor was born and prospered in the nurseries and libraries of the prosperous middle classes whose children were entranced by these strange little stories that the Grimms had published. Thus, in the Western world at least, the tale's typical audience changed from adult to child, which remained the case until the twentieth century, which saw the development of a radically different attitude toward the juvenile years. Through the spread and prolongation of education, childhood became more clearly defined, which in turn led to the identification of adolescence as a transitional stage of development.

Many critics have pointed out that it is increasingly unlikely that the modern child will have access to classic tales that still resemble their early printed form. That may be because of parental concern about their content (see "The Art of Retelling," p. 20, note 1); we must not forget, after all, that these tales, with rare exceptions, were not originally intended for children. Alternatively, it may have more to do with the assumption that the old versions no longer have what it takes to attract the child that is bombarded on a daily basis by a gang of competing media.[1] As a result, the perceived need has been filled by the publication of what are often termed "fractured fairy tales,"[2] which set out to bring the old tales up to speed through the injection of humor and contemporary values on the one hand and an encouragement to "see all sides" on the other. Yet, one may be forgiven for wondering why, if the fairy tale is so beset with anachronistic attitudes and values, do writers for children—and, for that matter, adults as well—still turn to it for inspiration? Certainly, the "fractured" tale assumes a familiarity with the characters and plot of its "classic" forebear or else much of the point is lost. So perhaps it is a desire for *continuity*, a constant weaving of cultural bonds that take on new patterns to reflect a different reality. The contemporary or unusual settings and the frequent references to popular culture represent a new gloss (in more senses than one!) on an old and treasured toy—one that will stay with the family for some time to come.

Several tales of this kind have been written by Gregory Maguire, who has made a substantial contribution to the evolution of the fairy tale with adult-oriented retellings such as *Confessions of an Ugly Stepsister* (1999) and *Mirror, Mirror* (2003), although he may be better known for the musical adaptation of his Oz-inspired book *Wicked* (1995). Even though "The Three Little Penguins and the Big Bad Walrus" (2004),[3] with its message of tolerance and acceptance, is clearly intended for children, it contains enough incongruous moments to suggest a certain "crossover" appeal: would the young reader appreciate the joke in the youngest

---

1 The purists might well argue that we started down that slippery slope with the introduction of illustrations in fairy-tale books, since the images on the page preempted those in the imagination.

2 The concept of the "fractured fairy tale" is not new; it was developed in the early days of the cartoon. See our discussion in the "Movies" section.

3 The whimsical nature of Maguire's approach can be gauged from other titles in this collection: "Leaping Beauty," "Hamster and Gerbil," "Little Red Robin Hood," "So What and the Seven Giraffes," and so on.

penguin's decision to "make up a new dance called the Collapse of the Housing Industry" or the reference to Isadora Penguin? At the same time, Maguire is keen to pay homage to the tale he's busy fracturing: "You haven't got any hair on your chinny chin chin," said the walrus. "Come to think of it, you haven't got much of a chinny chin chin, either" (33).[1]

While Maguire relies on allusion and word-games for effect, Adam Gidwitz, author of *A Tale Dark and Grimm* (2011), goes even more postmodern by pushing the "oral illusion" as far as it will go. A former second-grade teacher, he readily acknowledges the debt he owes to his student task-masters ("We want a story NOW!") for the pacing, economy, and directness that are features of his writing (and, of course, of the fairy tale).[2] By way of introduction, Gidwitz manages to boil 200 years of fairy-tale history down to less than three pages and still make us feel the urgency of the story, at the same time emphasizing the point that in becoming children's literature, the tale lost much of its juiciness, with the result that "you're so bored you've passed out on the floor." His solution is to restore to "Hansel and Gretel" all those "scary, bloody scenes" that, as we are discovering, are regarded as "awesome" by young and old alike.

The teenage years are perceived as a time of physical and emotional maturation, as the young person prepares for adulthood and its responsibilities. Given the important role of culture in this transition, it should come as no surprise that the last half of the twentieth century witnessed the development of a literature aimed specifically at teenagers, which has proved to be highly successful. "Just last year [2011], the Association of American Publishers ranked Children's/Young Adult books as the single fastest-growing publishing category."[3] Predictably, since the majority of these books concentrate on themes dealing with the challenges of growing up, their authors have turned to the traditional fairy tale for inspiration.[4] As we have seen, these tales, with rare exceptions, were not intended for children, even though most of them deal with precisely the trials and tribulations of entering the adult world.

Contemporary writers, however, have adapted and retold these stories to suit their own sensibilities as well as those of their readers, most notably in terms of reinterpreting the tales from a feminist perspective. The fact that this branch of Young Adult (YA) literature is dominated by women (both writers and readers) is not

---

1 For much the same reason, Roald Dahl quotes the same challenge-and-response in his rhyming version of "The Three Little Pigs"; see p. 83.
2 Gidwitz talks about the birth of his book on <http://www.youtube.com/watch?v=vJ77 QvwRowA>.
3 *Your Favorites: 100 Best Ever Teen Novels*, <http://www.npr.org/2012>.
4 For example, the publishing house Simon and Schuster has a series entitled *Once Upon a Time*, published under one of its imprints, Simon Pulse.

surprising, given the preponderance of female protagonists among the "classic" fairy tales and the rise of feminism in the last half century. Women who grew up with what many consider to be outdated stereotypical female protagonists, especially those found in Disney's early animations, have felt the need to provide today's girls with alternative role models. Some explore the darker side of the fairy tale, manifested in those elements of violence and sexuality that were eliminated as the tales were adapted for younger readers; others subvert the traditional roles and messages (the villain and heroine are not who you'd expect, nor does the princess always marry the prince to live happily ever after); and some set the stories in a particular historical period, in the everyday present, even in the world of science fiction. The stories may be recognizable retellings of traditional tales, free adaptations, or versions that retain no more than hints and motifs of the world of fairy tale. Despite such variety in the *treatment* of the fairy tale, there is also an interesting similarity: almost all these writers have chosen to expand the typical brevity of the oral tale into a full-length novel, since the cumulative presence of print invites detailed exploration of character, event, and motive.

Although their work cannot be satisfactorily represented in an anthology such as this, writers such as Robin McKinley, Donna Jo Napoli, and Gail Carson Levine have produced novel-length retellings of fairy tales, which have in fact become a prolific branch of fairy-tale development, catering primarily to the demand for romantic fantasy.[1] While these books are generally identified as part of the YA market (itself a bright spot in an otherwise moribund publishing industry), it seems that their appeal is widening: "One U.S. study [has] found that 55% of YA buyers were adults purchasing books for themselves" which has in turn "... fuelled a race to uncover the next breakout book series with just the right mix of romance, supernatural and dystopian elements that will win over readers (and movie producers)."[2] With the possible exception of the dystopian aspect that reflects our current pessimistic outlook, these ingredients surely mirror those demanded by the fairy-tale audiences of long ago—and for many of the same reasons. Be that as it may, there can be little argument that fairy tales provide a motherlode of material for this crossover segment of the market.

---

1 Stefanie Meyer's extraordinarily popular *Twilight* series serves as an excellent example of how far adaptation and length have gone. For instance, the series makes use of a number of traditional fairy-tale motifs (the creatures of fantasy, the isolated heroine and hero) and plots ("Little Red Riding Hood," "Beauty and the Beast"). Its popularity among teenage girls (and also their mothers) has ensured an audience for the subsequent movie versions. In fact, the book series, followed by the movie tie-in, has now become an established popular culture duet.

2 Graham F. Scott, "Reads Like Teen Spirit," *Canadian Business* (February 18, 2013): 68.

Our focus here, however, is on a selection of modern retellings that, for the most part, are of comparable length to their originals and that illuminate the ways in which the fairy tale has been adapted to contemporary tastes. The reader cannot fail to note how radically some of these retellings differ from the original—a characteristic that is equally apparent in other media, such as comic books, movies, and television. Is the transformation simply a measure of the extent to which our personal and social lives have changed? How much does the contrast between old and new reveal about who we are and where we are going?

As we suggested earlier, the most popular segment of the fairy-tale market in recent years has been the romance. Protests from feminist and psychological critics notwithstanding, Disney's reassurance that "some day my prince will come" has continued to strike a resonant chord with many female readers. We need to note, however, that this hopeful message has a long and honorable pedigree; it can be argued that from the earliest times one crucial function of the fairy tale was to inject some optimism into an otherwise oppressive existence. Circumstances have changed, to be sure, but the hope for love (and all that it implies) is timeless. In such novels as *Beauty* (1978), *Deerskin* (1993), and *Spindle's End* (2000), Robin McKinley has gone well beyond Disney's dictum in her explorations of love in the fairy tale, not least by giving her heroines a depth of personality that defies stereotype. Her short story "The Princess and the Frog" (1981) shows how effective some character development and plot rationalization can be in adjusting a tale to modern tastes: the cumulative pressure of events transforms the princess from frightened child to decisive young woman,[1] and the addition of two new characters permits McKinley to explain the enchantment of the frog, introduce a rivalry for the princess's hand, and examine the harm that can be done by an unscrupulous and domineering personality. At the same time, she retains many typical fairy-tale characteristics, such as the good vs. evil contrast between the brothers and the quasi-medieval elegance of the royal setting.

A significant development in more recent retellings—particularly those intended for older readers—is the much greater emphasis on the element of horror, an ingredient that was likely a staple of the genre before such rough edges were smoothed away in the process of transforming the spoken to the written word, particularly in light of the perceived need to protect the young reader. It is reasonable to suppose, however, that the *concept* of horror has changed over the years; whereas early

---

1 Her defeat of the villainous younger brother is curiously similar to Dorothy's victory over the Wicked Witch of the West, in *The Wonderful Wizard of Oz* (1900). Both instances clearly mark a coming of age, so might we see the water as having a sort of reverse baptismal significance?

versions relied primarily on explicit descriptions of violence and cruelty, modern tastes have expanded to include an *inner* dimension. Thus, while we too may be entertained by lurid descriptions of blood and gore, we are also drawn to psychological aspects such as motive: Why does Bluebeard want to kill his wives? Why does Rumpelstiltskin want the queen's baby? How do we feel about Snow White sitting by while her stepmother dances herself to death in red-hot shoes? It seems that we see the world rather differently than our ancestors did—but that change in perspective creates great potential for radical reinterpretation of the old tales, as we can see, for example, in Garth Nix's "Hansel's Eyes" (2000).

To bring the traditional tale in tune with the contemporary world, one obvious change is to replace the rural setting with an urban one, which is Nix's approach in his retelling of "Hansel and Gretel." Just as the dark forest customarily represents the hostile unknown in the original, Nix's bleak cityscape is equally disturbing; description is tantalizingly brief, but this appears to be a dystopian urban environment ravaged by fires and rioting, as empty of humanity as the forest itself. The gingerbread house is now a video-game store, the witch's cannibalistic appetites transformed into an involvement in the capture of children in order to harvest their organs.[1] (Nix's choice of this equivalence is apposite, given its current status as an urban legend.) At the very least, this "de-coding" of the fairy tale provides valuable insight into the fears and aberrations against which the tale has always been a means of both escape and defence. It is worth noting that in this compromised world, innocence can only signify vulnerability; thus, hope for the future lies in Gretel's having become "more than half a witch" and Hansel's "strange powers" attributable to his transplanted eye.

Neil Gaiman also adopts the familiar "old wine in new bottles" approach in "Snow, Glass, Apples" (1998), not only by telling the story from a first-person perspective but by choosing for that role the stepmother/Queen, who is here presented in an unusually sympathetic light. Gaiman's tactic is indicative of an important trend in modern retellings: the black-and-white morality of the early tales has been moderated to shades of grey, reflecting our awareness of human complexity and motivation. We commented above on the widespread fascination with the darkness of the aberrant personality that finds abundant raw material in the memorable villains of fairy tale, particularly since as characters they are so *flat*. In addition, it is Gaiman's intention to complicate matters further by turning the familiar inside-out: now Snow White is the villain of the piece, as demonically driven and heartless (quite literally!) as her stepmother ever was, with the addition of sexual depravity for good measure; the dwarves have become "people in the forest" whom Gaiman characterizes as "greedy,

---

1 It is interesting to note that we encounter this modern interpretation of the story again in an episode of the TV series *Grimm*; see "Television," p. 123.

feral, dangerous"—and then there's the prince, with his taste for extreme passivity in women ...[1]

Snow White is also the inspiration for Kim Addonizio's story "Ever After" (2006), which demonstrates very effectively just how fertile and multi-faceted the fairy tale can be in suggesting fresh perspectives to the creative imagination. The indeterminacy of a quasi-medieval palace or the specificity of contemporary Los Angeles: both settings enable the writers to draw new meaning from the old tale. In her version, however, Addonizio has implicitly acknowledged the cultural predominance of Disney's version over that of the Grimms, notwithstanding the fact that her "urbanized" treatment of the tale is a sardonic response to Disney sentimentality; in the mean streets of "la la land," the cute names of the individual dwarves take on a more disturbing meaning. What makes this retelling unusual, though, is the *absence* of Snow White; with varying degrees of conviction, the dwarves believe that she will come because the "Book" says so—and when she comes, they will be saved ("She'll make us six feet if we want to be."). Addonizio's own view is bluntly pessimistic; in an Afterword she comments, "I don't see any difference between worshipping Snow White or the Virgin Mary or Allah, since they're all fantasies."[2] The prospect may be existentially bleak, but these all-too-obvious representatives of the Little Man retain their humanity, if not their illusions. It's a small but significant victory.

The nature of fairy tale is such that it lends itself very easily to parody; the cynical postmodern mind finds easy pickings in the domestic arrangements of Snow White and the seven dwarves or the consequences of a princess kissing a frog. It is a testament to the fairy tale's resilience that such exploitation of its oddities and absurdities generally reflects more on us than on the tale itself. This fact is borne out by the title of James Finn Garner's collection of parodies, *Politically Correct Bedtime Stories: Modern Tales for Our Life & Times* (1994), from which "Jack and the Beanstalk" is taken. Once again, it is the universal familiarity of the fairy tale that is the focus here; Garner's primary intention is to satirize some of the "oddities and absurdities"

---

1 One need look no further than *The Sleeping Beauty Trilogy* (1983-85), by Anne Rice, to appreciate how effectively the sexual element in the fairy tale can be exploited. As is the custom with recent adaptations, Rice's extended erotic narrative, which caters to specialized tastes collectively referred to as BDSM (bondage, discipline, sado-masochism), owes little beyond the name of the central character to any version of the fairy tale. That did not prevent the books from becoming best-sellers;—in fact, in light of the runaway success of the *Fifty Shades Trilogy* (2011), itself born out of fan-fiction response to the *Twilight* series, Rice's books have been reprinted (2012).

2 Kim Addonizio, "Ever After," in *My Mother She Killed Me, My Father He Ate Me*, ed. Kate Bernheimer (New York: Penguin, 2010) 526.

of contemporary life—and what better way to point out the gap between the old-established and the newfangled than by using a fairy tale?

Postscript

One intriguing motif that crops up in several different media is the role of the book—generally, a book of fairy tales. For instance, the early fairy-tale animations made by Walt Disney all open with the tale beginning in the pages of an old volume, perhaps a means of establishing the authenticity and substance of the story to come. We note above Kim Addonizio's inference in "Ever After" that the Book (of Grimm tales) has taken on a quasi-biblical significance for the dwarfs, not least because of its promise of "happily ever after." The book of fairy tales that belongs to Henry, in the ABC series *Once Upon a Time*, has a similar status; the wise child perceives it as guiding and explaining the fates of the enchanted fairy-tale characters of Storyville, Maine. And although the book in the rival NBC series *Grimm* contains a collection of monsters rather than fairy tales, it too represents that source of authority and information to which the humans go for guidance. In short, the message seems to be that while the book is old, by that token it lays claim to a wisdom that we cannot afford to ignore.

THE THREE LITTLE PENGUINS AND THE BIG BAD WALRUS[1]

Gregory Maguire

ONCE THERE WERE THREE LITTLE PENGUINS WHO LIVED IN AN IGLOO with their mother.

The oldest penguin liked to eat fish.

The middle penguin liked to eat fish.

The youngest penguin liked to get dressed up in a ballet costume and put on a show. This was not usual for penguins, and it worried old Mama Penguin a lot. But whenever her baby put on a show, she always applauded the loudest. She clapped so hard that she found herself wheezing and short of breath.

She took herself to the doctor, who was a walrus. He told Mama Penguin that her blood was sluggish. He said she should move to an island in the South Seas.

---

1 From *Leaping Beauty and Other Animal Fairy Tales* (New York: HarperCollins, 2004).

"I do feel a bit under the weather," said old Mama Penguin. "Not up to my usual strength. But what will my penguin children do without me? They haven't got a whole lot of common sense, even for penguins. They wouldn't know enough to come out of the cold unless I called them, and do you think they would floss regularly?"

"They're old enough to take care of themselves," said Doc Walrus.

"Do you really think so?" said Mama Penguin. "A mother worries."

"A mother should learn not to worry so much," said Doc Walrus firmly. "You've done a good job raising your children. It's time to let go and enjoy your happy golden sunset years. You're looking weak and frail. There's an iceberg leaving tonight. Why don't you hop aboard?"

"Perhaps," said Mama Penguin, and sighed.

She didn't intend to follow the doc's advice. But while she was away, the oldest penguin had accidentally left the oven on, and the middle penguin had accidentally left the oven door open, and the youngest penguin was skating around in baubles and bangles and beads, being Cleopatra the Queen of the Nile, not paying much attention. And while this was happening the heat from the oven had melted the igloo right down to the very tundra on which it had been built. By the time that Mama Penguin got home, there wasn't much home left to come to. So old Mama Penguin called her children to her side.

"My dears," she said, "it is time for you to go out into the world and find your own homes. As you can see, there's not much left of mine. So your dear mother is going to go on a cruise to the South Seas and try to build up her health. I'll send postcards. Meanwhile, some good advice. First, floss your teeth every day."

Then she smacked the oldest penguin on the bottom with her walking stick. "And don't leave the oven on!"

She smacked the middle penguin on the bottom, too. "Don't leave the oven door open!"

She kissed the youngest penguin and said, "Dear, a little less lipstick and it will go much better for you in life."

Then she hobbled onto a passing iceberg and soon was lost to view.

The three penguins were very sad. "What shall we do?" said the oldest penguin. "Perhaps we should build ourselves three homes. I will build my home out of straw."

"I will build my home out of twigs," said the middle penguin.

"I will make up a new dance called the Collapse of the Housing Industry," cried the youngest penguin, and began collapsing all over the place.

"Oh please," said the oldest and the middle penguins, and went to find housing materials.

Now who should come along but a seal driving a bobsled. Tied onto the back of it was a huge rick of straw.

"Straw! Straw for sale!" cried the seal.

"I'll have that straw to build myself a house," cried the oldest penguin, and bought the whole lot right there.

"I thought I was selling it for packing fine china in, but you can do what you want with it," said the seal, pocketing the money and driving away.

The oldest penguin built a handsome house. It had a straw veranda, a straw balcony, and a straw tower perched on top. The oldest penguin was quite happy. With a new stove and a nice pot of fish to cook up on it, there was nothing more to want in life.

The middle penguin was wandering around when the seal came driving the bobsled back, this time with a load of twigs in it. "Who'll buy my twigs, fine twigs for sale!" cried the seal.

"I'll have the lot, my good seal," said the middle penguin. "Just dump them right there, if you please. This is as good a place as any to build myself a house."

"Suit yourself," said the seal, "I had thought to sell them for kindling, but you know best." The seal put the money in his wallet and drove his bobsled away.

The middle penguin built a beautiful house out of twigs. It had a twig porch, a twig staircase, and a twig widow's walk on top. The middle penguin bought an oven just right for cooking pots of fish in, and all seemed very cozy indeed.

The youngest penguin invented a new dance called Isadora Penguin. It involved dressing in gauzy colored veils.

Along came the seal on his bobsled once again. "Coal! Lots of coal for sale!" he cried. "A very hot building material these days!"

"Who would build a house out of coal?" asked the youngest penguin. "Wouldn't it burn up?"

"I give folks what they want," said the seal. "You'd be surprised at recent styles. You could call it a warming trend."

"Well, what I would like is a full-length mirror," said the youngest penguin. "I need to see myself dance so I can know if it's beautiful enough."

"I can't sell you a mirror, for I haven't got one," said the seal. "But I can sell you a blowtorch. You can cut a sheet of ice out of the glacier. That'll do for a mirror."

"I suppose you're right," said the youngest penguin. "Here's the money."

"Thanks," said the seal. As he handed over the blowtorch, he added, "Your eyelashes are awfully long and curly for a penguin."

"Is that a compliment?" said the youngest penguin, and practiced using the blowtorch in the seal's direction. The seal and the bobsled sped away very quickly.

Who should come along next but Doc Walrus.

The truth needs to be told. It is bitter and it is ugly, but so was the walrus.

The cunning old doctor wanted to eat all three of the penguin children. That was why he had advised poor Mama Penguin to move to the South Seas. Her blood wasn't really as sluggish as the doctor had said. It was all a fiendish plot to provide him with fresh penguin steaks.

Far away, as her iceberg began to melt in the heat of the tropical seas, old Mama Penguin was wondering if she had made the right decision. But didn't all children need to grow up and leave home sometime?

The walrus waddled up to the house built out of straw. He was exceedingly hungry. He knocked on the front door and said, "Little penguin, little penguin, let me come in."

The oldest penguin looked out the peephole. "Why are you carrying a knife and a fork and a jar of salsa?" he asked.

"I bought them at a garage sale," said the walrus, "I've come to check your pulse. Your mama told me to look in on you from time to time. I need to make sure you're flossing regularly. So let me come in."

"Not by the hair of my chinny chin chin," said the penguin.

"You haven't got any hair on your chinny chin chin," said the walrus.

"That's what I mean," said the penguin, and slammed the peephole shut.

"Then I'll huff and I'll puff and I'll blow your house in," said the walrus.

The walrus couldn't really blow the house in. He wasn't good at huffing and puffing, just bluffing. Besides, the penguin was too busy heating up a pot of fish to pay attention.

Unfortunately, the penguin left the oven on and the door open, and the house of straw went up in flames. The penguin just barely escaped through the back door, and he ran to the house of twigs, which was nearby.

"Save me!" cried the oldest penguin.

"Oh, okay," said the middle penguin. "Would you stir these fish while I go answer the doorbell?"

It was the walrus again. "It's the good old kindly doc who makes house calls," said the walrus through the screen door. "I've come to take your temperature. And I have to check to see if you're flossing as you should. Your mama told me to keep an eye out for your health, and I intend to."

"Then what are you doing with that paring knife and the sack of onions and the sprigs of fresh coriander?" asked the middle penguin.

"I'm on my way to a cooking class over at the community college," said the walrus. "At this rate, I'm going to be late. So little penguin, little penguin, let me come in."

"Not by the hair of my chinny chin chin," said the middle penguin.

"You haven't got any hair on your chinny chin chin," said the walrus, "Come to think of it, you haven't got much of a chinny chin chin, either."

"That about settles it, then," said the middle penguin, and slammed the door.

"Then I'll huff and I'll puff and I'll blow your house in," said the walrus.

"Enough with this huffing and puffing stuff," called the oldest penguin. But meanwhile, the middle penguin had left the oven on and the door open. The house of twigs caught fire and burned to the ground. The two penguins barely escaped with their lives.

They raced next door.

The youngest penguin had been having fun with the blowtorch. It was easy to use it to slice blocks of glacial ice into huge cubes. The youngest penguin had built a dance studio with a full wall of mirrors and a café and a lounge, complete with a jukebox all made of ice. The youngest penguin was busy perfecting an ensemble piece to go in the ballet about Cleopatra the Queen of the Nile. This number was called the Dance of the Sugarplum Pharaohs.

"Let us in!" cried the oldest penguin and the middle penguin.

"Did you come to see the show?" asked the youngest penguin. "It's not finished yet, but I can show you what I have so far."

"There's a hungry walrus outside," cried the other penguins. "Whatever you do, don't answer the door!"

Just then there was a knock. "Who is it?" called the youngest penguin, looking through the French doors.

"It's me, old Doc Walrus," said the walrus. "I've come to give you an examination."

"I'm fine," said the youngest penguin. "Go away. I'm busy flossing my teeth."

"You look as if you have a fever. Your cheeks are cherry red."

"It's a little blush. Arctic Evenings. Use a flesh-colored foundation and blend well. You should try some."

"Let me in and I will."

"But why are you carrying a meat cleaver and a hibachi?"

"I'm delivering them to my granny, who is sick in bed. She's fading fast. Little penguin, little penguin, let me come in."

"Not by the hair of my chinny chin chin."

"You haven't got any hair on your chinny chin chin," said the walrus.

"Let me check the prop department and I'll get back to you," said the penguin. But by now the walrus had had enough. He was very hungry indeed. He found the blowtorch that the littlest penguin carelessly had left lying around outside. Then Doc Walrus aimed it at the dance studio made of carved ice.

"I'll have penguin patties before the night is out!" he cried, and turned on the blowtorch.

Meanwhile, old Mama Penguin's bad feeling about this whole business had only gotten stronger. She had turned around. She arrived at the front door of the dance studio just in time to see the walrus start to attack the building with fire.

"Oh no, you don't," she yelled, and launched herself through the air.

The walrus never knew what hit him. He was out cold, with little *X*'s in his eyes and birdies tweeting over his head, just as in the cartoons.

"My babies!" cried old Mama Penguin, calling them to her side.

"Mama!" they said, clapping their flippers. They came sliding over the ice to her. "How did you ever knock out that old walrus?"

"My blood isn't as sluggish as all *that*," she said. "Besides, as the iceberg began to melt, I had to paddle it all the way home against the current. I built up my upper body muscles. A little exercise does wonders, my dears. But enough about me. Tell me this, my children. Has anyone left the oven on and burned up any houses lately?"

The oldest penguin and the middle penguin hung their heads in shame. The youngest penguin said, "Look, Ma, I can do a split now," and showed her how.

"My baby," said Mama Penguin fondly. "I guess I'll have to move back in and do the cooking. Nobody touches the oven or I'll spank you on your bottoms. Understood?"

"Yes, Mama," they said.

They tied up the walrus with dental floss. When the seal with the bobsled came along, they piled the walrus on top and told the seal to take him away to the county jail. Then old Mama Penguin made some fish soup for dinner, and the oldest penguin and middle penguin told her how beautiful their houses had been.

The youngest penguin worked on a new dance, called the Ice of Spring. It was intended to be danced, daringly, in the nude, but since penguins don't usually wear clothes, nobody especially noticed the difference.

INTRODUCTION[1]

Adam Gidwitz

ONCE UPON A TIME, FAIRY TALES WERE AWESOME.

I know, I know. You don't believe me. I don't blame you. A little while ago, I wouldn't have believed it myself. Little girls in red caps skipping around the forest? Awesome? I don't think so.

But then I started to read them. The real, Grimm ones. Very few little girls in red caps in those.

Well, there's one. But she gets eaten.

"Okay," you're probably saying, "if fairy tales are awesome, why are all the ones I've heard so unbelievably, mind-numbingly boring?" You know how it is with stories. Someone tells a story. Then somebody repeats it and it changes. Someone else repeats it, and it changes again. Then someone's telling it to their kid and taking out all the scary, bloody scenes—in other words, the awesome parts—and the next thing you know the story's about an adorable little girl in a red cap, skipping through the forest to take cookies to her granny. And you're so bored you've passed out on the floor.

The real Grimm stories are not like that.

Take *Hansel and Gretel*, for example. Two greedy little children try to eat a witch's house, so she decides to cook and eat them instead—which is fair, it seems to me. But before she can follow through on her (perfectly reasonable) plan, they lock her in an oven and bake her to death.

Which is pretty cool, you have to admit.

But maybe it's not awesome.

Except—and here's the thing—that's not the real story of Hansel and Gretel.

You see, there is another story in Grimm's *Fairy Tales*. A story that winds all throughout that moldy, mysterious tome—like a trail of bread crumbs winding through a forest. It appears in tales you may never have heard, like *Faithful Johannes* and *Brother and Sister*. And in some that you have—*Hansel and Gretel*, for instance.

It is the story of two children—a girl named Gretel and a boy named Hansel—traveling through a magical and terrifying world. It is the story of two children striving, and failing, and then not failing. It is the story of two children finding out the meanings of things.

---

1   From *A Tale Dark and Grimm* (New York: Puffin, 2011).

Before I go on, a word of warning: Grimm's stories—the ones that weren't changed for little kids—are violent and bloody. And what you're going to hear now, the one true tale in *The Tales of Grimm*, is as violent and bloody as you can imagine.

Really.

So if such things bother you, we should probably stop right now.

You see, the land of Grimm can be a harrowing place. But it is worth exploring. For, in life, it is in the darkest zones one finds the brightest beauty and the most luminous wisdom.

And, of course, the most blood.

THE PRINCESS AND THE FROG[1]

Robin McKinley

Part One

SHE HELD THE PALE NECKLACE IN HER HAND AND STARED AT IT AS she walked. Her feet evidently knew where they were going, for they did not stumble although her eyes gave them no guidance. Her eyes remained fixed on the glowing round stones in her hand.

These stones were as smooth as pearls, and their color, at first sight, seemed as pure. But they were much larger than any pearls she had ever seen, as large as the dark sweet cherries she plucked in the palace gardens. And their pale creamy color did not lie quiet and reflect the sunlight, but shimmered and shifted, and seemed to offer her glimpses of something mysterious in their hearts, something she waited to see, almost with dread, which was always at the last minute hidden from her. And they seemed to have a heat of their own that owed nothing to her hand as she held them, rather they burned against her cold fingers. Her hand trembled, and their cloudy swirling seemed to shiver in response; the swiftness of their ebb and flow seemed to mock the pounding of her heart.

Prince Aliyander had just given her the necklace, with one of the dark-eyed smiles she had learned to fear so much, for while he had done nothing to her yet—but then, he had *done* nothing to any of them—she knew that her own brother was under his invisible spell. This spell he called "friendship" with his flashing smile and another look from his black eyes; and her own father, the King, was afraid of him. She

---

1 From *The Door in the Hedge* (New York: HarperCollins, 1981).

also knew he meant to marry her, and knew her strength could not hold out against him long, once he set himself to win her. His "friendship" had already subdued the Crown Prince, only a few months ago a merry and mischievous lad, into a dog to follow at his heels and go where he was told.

This morning, as they stood together in the Great Hall, herself, and her father, and Prince Aliyander, with the young Crown Prince a half-step behind Aliyander's right shoulder, and their courtiers around them, Aliyander had reached into a pocket and brought out the necklace. It gleamed and seemed to shiver with life as he held it up, and all the courtiers murmured with awe. "For you, Lady Princess," said Aliyander, with a graceful bow and his smile, and he moved to fasten it around her neck: "a small gift, to tell you of just the smallest portion of my esteem for Your Highness."

She started back with a suddenness that surprised even her; and her heart flew up in her throat and beat there wildly as the great jewels danced before her eyes. And she felt rather than saw the flicker in Aliyander's eyes when she moved away from him.

"Forgive me," she stammered, "they are so lovely, you must let me look at them a little first." Her voice felt thick; it was hard to speak. "I shan't be able to admire them as they deserve, when they lie beneath my chin."

"Of course," said Aliyander, but she could not look at his smile. "All pretty ladies love to look at pretty things," and the edge in his voice was such that only she felt it; and she had to look away from the Crown Prince, whose eyes were shining with the delight of his friend's generosity.

"May I—may I take your—gracious gift outside, and look at it in the sunlight?" she faltered. The high vaulted ceiling and mullioned windows seemed suddenly narrow and stifling, with the great glowing stones only inches from her face. The touch of sunlight would be healing. She reached out blindly, and tried not to wince as Aliyander laid the necklace across her hand.

"I hope you will return wearing my poor gift," he said, with the same edge to his words, "so that it may flatter itself in the light of Your Highness's beauty, and bring joy to the heart of your unworthy admirer."

"Yes—yes, I will," she said, and turned, and only her Princess's training prevented her from fleeing, picking up her skirts with her free hand and running the long length of the Hall to the arched doors, and outside to the gardens. Or perhaps it was the imponderable weight in her hand that held her down.

But outside, at least the sky did not shut down on her as the walls and groined ceiling of the Hall had, and the sun seemed to lie gently and sympathetically across her shoulders even if it could not help itself against Aliyander's jewels, and dripped and ran across them until her eyes were dazzled.

Her feet stopped at last, and she blinked and looked up. Near the edge of the garden, near the great outer wall of the palace, was a quiet pool with a few trees close around it, so that much of the water stood in shadow wherever the sun stood in the sky. There was a small white marble bench under one of the trees, pushed close enough that a sitter might lean comfortably against the broad bole behind him. Aside from the bench there was no other ornament; as the palace gardens went, it was almost wild, for the grass was allowed to grow a little shaggy before it was cut back, and wildflowers grew here occasionally, and were undisturbed. The Princess had discovered this spot—for no one else seemed to come here but the occasional gardener and his clippers—about a year ago; a little before Prince Aliyander had ridden into their lives. Since that riding, their lives had changed, and she had come here more and more often, to be quiet and alone, if only for a little time.

Now she stood at the brink of the pond, the strange necklace clutched in her unwilling fingers, and closed her eyes. She took a few long breaths, hoping that the cool peacefulness of this place would somehow help even this trouble. She did not want to wear this necklace, to place it around her throat; she felt that the strange jewels would strangle her, stop her breath till she breathed in the same rhythm as Aliyander, and as her poor brother.

Her trembling stopped, the hand with the necklace dropped a few inches. She felt better. But as soon as she opened her eyes, she would see those terrible cloudy stones again. She raised her chin. At least the first thing she would see was the quiet water. She began to open her eyes, and then a great *croak* bellowed from, it seemed, a place just beside her feet; and her overtaxed nerves broke out in a sharp "Oh," and she leaped away from the sound. As she leaped, her fingers opened, and the necklace dropped with the softest splash, a lingering and caressing sound, and disappeared under the water.

Her first thought was relief that the stones no longer held and threatened her; and then she remembered Aliyander, and her heart shrank within her. She remembered his look when she had refused his gift; and the sound of his voice when he hoped she would wear it upon her return to the Hall—where he was even now awaiting her. She dared not face him without it round her neck; and he would never believe in this accident. And, indeed, if she had cared for the thing, she would have pulled it to her instead of losing it in her alarm.

She knelt at the edge of the pool and looked in, but while the water seemed clear, and the sunlight penetrated a long way, still she could not see the bottom, but only a misty greyness that drowned at last to utter black. "Oh dear," she whispered. "I *must* get it back. But how?"

"Well," said a voice diffidently, "I think I could probably fetch it for you."

She had forgotten the noise that had startled her. The voice came from very low down, she was kneeling with her hands so near the pool's edge that her fingertips were lightly brushed by the water's smallest ripples. She turned her head and looked down still farther; and sitting on the bank at her side she saw one of the largest frogs she had ever seen. She did not even think to be startled. "It was rather my fault anyway," added the frog.

"Oh—could you?" she said. She hardly thought of the phenomenon of a frog that talked; her mind was taken up with wishing to have the necklace back, and reluctance to see and touch it again. Here was one part of her problem solved, the medium of the solution did not matter to her.

The frog said no more, but dived into the water with scarcely more noise than the necklace had made in falling; in what seemed only a moment its green head emerged again, with two of the round stones in its wide mouth. It clambered back onto the bank, getting entangled in the trailing necklace as it did so. A frog is a silly creature, and this one looked absurd, with a king's ransom of smooth heavy jewels twisted round its squat figure; but she did not think of this. She reached out to help, and it wasn't till she had Aliyander's gift in her hands again that she noticed the change.

The stones were as large and round and perfect as they had been before; but the weird creamy light of them was gone. They lay dim and grey and quiet against her palm, as cool as the water of the pond, and strengthless.

Such was her relief and pleasure that she sprang to her feet, spreading the necklace to its fullest extent and turning it this way and that in the sunlight, to be certain of what she saw; and she forgot even to thank the frog, still sitting patiently on the bank where she had rescued it from the binding necklace.

"Excuse me," it said at last, and then she remembered it, and looked down and said, "Oh, thank you," with such a bright and glowing look that it might move even a frog's cold heart.

"You're quite welcome, I'm sure," said the frog mechanically. "But I wonder if I might ask you a favor."

"Certainly. Anything." Even facing Aliyander seemed less dreadful, now the necklace was quenched: she felt that perhaps he could be resisted. Her joy made her silly; it was the first time anything of Aliyander's making had missed its mark, and for a moment she had no thoughts for the struggle ahead, but only for the present victory. Perhaps even the Crown Prince could be saved.

"Would you let me live with you at the palace for a little time?"

Her wild thoughts halted for a moment, and she looked down bewildered at the frog. What would a frog want with a palace? For that matter—as if she had only just noticed it—why did this frog talk?

"I find this pool rather dull," said the frog fastidiously, as if this were an explanation.

She hesitated, dropping her hands again, but this time the stones hung limply, hiding in a fold of her wide skirts. She had told the frog, "Certainly, anything"; and her father had brought her up to understand that she must always keep her word, the more so because as Princess there was no one who could force her to. "Very well," she said at last. "If you wish it." And she realized after she spoke that part of her hesitation was reluctance that anything, even a frog, should see her palace, her family, now; it would hurt her. But she had given her word, and there could be no harm in a frog.

"Thank you," said the frog gravely, and with surprising dignity for a small green thing with long thin flipper-footed legs and popping eyes.

There was a pause, and then she said, "I—er—I think I should go back now. Will you be along later or—?"

"I'll be along later," replied the frog at once, as if he recognized her embarrassment; as if he were a poor relation who yet had a sense of his own worth.

She hesitated a moment longer, wondering to how many people she would have to explain her talking frog, and added, "I dine alone with my father at eight." Prince Inthur never took his meals with his father and sister any more; he ate with Aliyander or alone, miserably, in his room, if Aliyander chose to overlook him. Then she raised the grey necklace to clasp it round her throat, and remembered that it was, after all, her talking frog's pool that had put out the ill light of Aliyander's work. She smiled once more at the frog, a little guiltily, for she believed one should be kind to one's poor relations; and she said, "You'll be my talisman."

She turned and walked quickly away, back toward the palace, and the Hall, and Aliyander.

Part Two

But she made a serious mistake, for she walked swiftly back to the Hall, and blithely through the door, with her head up and her eyes sparkling with happiness and release; she met Aliyander's black eyes too quickly, and smiled without thinking. It was only then she realized what her thoughtlessness had done, when she saw his eyes move swiftly from her face to the jewels at her throat, and then as he saw her smile his own face twisted with a rage so intense it seemed for a moment that his sallow skin would turn black with it. And even her little brother, the Crown Prince, looked at his hero a little strangely, and said, "Is anything wrong?"

Aliyander did not answer. He turned on his heel and left, going toward the door opposite that which the Princess had entered, the door that led into the rest of the palace. Everyone seemed to be holding his or her breath while the quiet footfalls retreated, for there was no other noise; even the air had stopped moving through the windows. Then there was the sound of the heavy door opening, and closing, and Aliyander was gone.

The courtiers blinked and looked at one another. The Crown Prince looked as if he might cry: his master had left him behind. The King turned to his daughter with .

the closing of that far door, and he saw first her white frightened face; and then his gaze dropped to the round stones of her necklace, and there, for several moments, it remained.

No one of the courtiers looked at her directly; but when she caught their sidelong looks, there was blankness in their eyes, not understanding. None addressed a word to her, although all had seen that she, somehow, was the cause of Aliyander's anger. But then, for months now it had been considered bad luck to discuss anything that Aliyander did.

Inthur, the Crown Prince, still loved his father and sister in spite of the cloud that Aliyander had cast over his mind, and little did he know how awkward Aliyander found that simple and indestructible love. But now Inthur saw his sister standing alone in the doorway to the garden, her face as white as her dress, and as a little gust of wind blew her skirts around her, and her fair hair across her face, she gasped and gave a shudder, and one hand touched her necklace. With Aliyander absent, even the cloud on Inthur lifted a little, although he himself did not know this, for he never thought about himself. Instead he ran the several steps to where his sister stood, and threw his arms around her; he looked up into her face and said, "Don't worry, Rana dear, he's never angry long." His boy's gaze passed over the necklace without a pause.

She nodded down at him and tried to smile, but her eyes filled with tears; and with a little brother's horror of tears, particularly sister's tears, he let go of her at once and said quickly, with the air of one who changes the subject from one proved dangerous, "What did you do?"

She blinked back her tears, recognizing the dismay on Inthur's face; he would not know that it was his hug that had brought them, and the look on his face when he tried to comfort her: just as he had used to look before Aliyander came. Now he rarely glanced at either his father or his sister except vaguely, as if half asleep, or with his thoughts far away. "I don't know," she said, with a fair attempt at calmness, "but perhaps it is not important."

He patted her hand as if he were her uncle, and said, "That's all right. You just apologize to him when you see him next, and it'll be over."

She smiled wanly as she remembered that her own brother belonged to Aliyander now and she could not trust him. Then the King came up beside them, and when her eyes met his she read knowledge in them, of what Aliyander had seen, in her face and round her neck; and a reflection of her own fear. He said nothing to her.

The rest of the day passed slowly, for while they did not see Aliyander again, the weight of his absence was almost as great as his presence would have been. The Crown Prince grew cross and fretful, and glowered at everyone; the courtiers seemed nervous, and whispered among themselves, looking often over their shoulders as if for the ghosts of their great-grandmothers. Even those who came from the city, or the far-flung towns beyond, to kneel before the King and crave a favor seemed more to crouch and plead, as if for mercy; and their faces were never happy when they went away, whatever the King had granted them.

Rana felt as grey as Aliyander's jewels.

The sun set at last, and its final rays touched the faces in the Hall with the first color most of them had had all day; and as servants came in to light the candles everyone looked paler and more uncomfortable than ever.

One of Aliyander's personal servants approached the throne soon after the candles were lit; the King sat with his children in smaller chairs at his feet. The man offered the Crown Prince a folded slip of paper; his obeisance to the King first was a gesture so cursory as to be insulting, but the King made no move to reprimand him. The Hall was as still as it had been that morning when Aliyander had left it; and the sound of Inthur's impatient opening of the note crackled loudly. He leaped to his feet and said joyfully, "I'm to dine with him!" and with a dreadful look of triumph round the Hall, and then at his father and sister—Rana closed her eyes—he ran off, the servant following with the dignity of a nobleman.

It seemed a sign. The King stood up wearily and clapped his hands once; and the courtiers made their bows and began to drift away, to quarters in the palace, or to grand houses outside in the city. Rana followed her father to the door that led to the rest of the palace, where the Crown Prince had just disappeared, and there the King turned and said, "I will see you at eight, my child?" And Rana's eyes again filled with tears at the question in his voice, behind his words. She only nodded, afraid to speak, and he turned away. "We dine alone," he said, and left her.

She spent two long and bitter hours staring at nothing, sitting alone in her room; in spite of the gold-and-white hangings, and the bright blue coverlet on her bed, it refused to look cheerful for her tonight. She removed her necklace and stuffed it into an empty jar and put the lid on quickly, as if it were a snake that might escape, although she knew that it itself had no further power to harm her.

She joined her father with a heavy heart; in place of Aliyander's jewels she wore a golden pendant that her mother had given her. The two of them ate in a little room with a small round table, where her family had always gathered when there was no formal banquet. When she was very small, and Inthur only a baby, she had sat here with both her parents; then her pretty, fragile mother had died, and she and Inthur and their father had faced each other around this table alone. Now it was just the King and herself. There had been few banquets in the last months. As she looked at her father now, she was suddenly frightened at how old and weak he looked. Aliyander could gain no hold over him, for his mind and his will were too pure for Aliyander's nets; but his presence aged him quickly, too quickly. And the next King would be Inthur, who followed Aliyander everywhere, a pace behind his right shoulder. And Inthur would be delighted at his best friend's marrying his sister.

The dining-room was round like the table within it; it was the first floor of a tower that stood at one of the many corners of the Palace. It had windows on two sides, and a door through which the servants brought the covered dishes and the wine, and another door that led down a flight of stone steps to the garden.

Neither she nor her father ate much, nor spoke at all, and the room was very quiet. So it was that when an odd muffled thump struck the garden door, they both looked up at once. Whatever it was, after a moment it struck again. They stared at each other, puzzled, and because since Aliyander had come all things unknown were dreaded, their looks were also fearful. When the third thump came, Rana stood up and went over to the door and flung it open.

There sat her frog.

"Oh!" she exclaimed. "It's you."

If a frog could turn its foolish mouth to a smile, this one did. "Good evening," it replied.

"Who is it?" said the King, standing up; for he could see nothing, yet he heard the strange deep voice.

"It's a frog," Rana said, somewhat embarrassed. "I dropped that necklace in a pool today, and he fetched it out for me. He asked a favor in return, that he might live with me in the palace."

"If you made a promise, child, you must keep it," said the King; and for a moment he looked as he had before Aliyander came. "Invite him in." And his eyes rested on his daughter thoughtfully, remembering the change in those jewels that he had seen.

The Princess stood aside, and the frog hopped in. The King and Princess stood, feeling silly, looking down, while the frog looked up; then Rana shook herself, and shut the door, and returned to the table. "Would you—er—like some dinner? There's plenty."

She took the frog back to her own room in her pocket. Her father had said nothing to her about their odd visitor, but she knew from the look on his face when he bade her good night that he would mention it to no one. The frog said gravely that her room was a very handsome one; then it leaped up onto a sofa and settled itself among the cushions. Rana blew the lights out and undressed and climbed into bed, and lay, staring up, thinking.

"I will go with you to the Hall tomorrow, if I may," said the frog's voice from the darkness, breaking in on her dark thoughts.

"Certainly," she said, as she had said once before. "You're my talisman," she added, with a catch in her voice.

"All is not well here," said the frog gently; and the deep sympathetic voice might have been anyone, not a frog, but her old nurse, perhaps, when she was a baby and needed comforting because of a scratched knee; or the best friend she had never had, because she was a Princess, the only Princess of the greatest realm in all the lands from the western to the eastern seas; and to her horror, she burst into tears and found herself between gulps telling that voice everything. How Aliyander had ridden up one day, without warning, ridden in from the north, where his father still ruled as king over a country bordering her father's. How Aliyander was now declared the heir apparent, for his elder brother, Lian, had disappeared over a year before; and while this sad loss continued mysteriously, still it was necessary for the peace of the country to secure the succession. Aliyander's first official performance as heir apparent was this visit to his kingdom's nearest neighbor to the south, for he knew that it was his father's dearest wish that the friendship between their two lands continue close and loyal.

And for the first time they saw Aliyander smile. The Crown Prince had turned away, for he was then free and innocent; the King stiffened and grew pale; and Rana did not guess how she might have looked.

"I had known Lian when we were children," Rana continued; she no longer cared who was listening, or if anything was. "He was kind and patient with Inthur, who was only a baby; I—I thought him wonderful," she whispered. "I heard my parents discussing him one night, him and me."

Aliyander's visit had lengthened—a fortnight, a month, two months; it had been almost a year since he rode through their gates. Messengers passed between him and his father—he said; but here he stayed, and entrapped the Crown Prince; and next he would have the Princess.

"I don't know what to do," she said at last, wearily. "There is nothing I can do."

"I'm sorry," said the voice, and it was sad, and wistful, and kind.

And human. Her mind wavered from the single thought of *Aliyander, Aliyander,* and she remembered to whom—or what—she spoke; and the sympathy in the creature's voice puzzled her even more than the fact that the voice could use human speech.

"You cannot be a frog," she said stupidly. "You must be—under a spell." And she found she could spare a little pity from her own family's plight to give to this spellbound creature who spoke like a human being.

"Of course," snapped the frog. "Frogs don't talk."

She was silent, sorry that her own pain had made her thoughtless, made her wound another's feelings.

"I'm sorry," said the frog for the second time, and in the same gentle tone. "You see, one never quite grows accustomed."

She answered after a moment: "Yes. I think I do understand, a little."

"Thank you," said the frog.

"Yes," she said again. "Good night."

"Good night."

But just before she fell asleep, she heard the voice once more: "I have one more favor to ask. That you do not mention, when you take me to the Hall tomorrow, that I talk."

"Very well," she said drowsily.

Part Three

There was a ripple of nervous laughter when the Princess Rana appeared in the Great Hall on the next morning, carrying a large frog. She held her right arm bent at the elbow and curled lightly against her side; and the frog rode quietly on her forearm. She was wearing a dress of pale blue, with lace at her neck, and her fair hair hung loose over her shoulders, and a silver circlet was around her brow; the big green frog showed brilliantly and absurdly against her pale loveliness. She sat on her low chair before her father's throne; the frog climbed, or slithered, or leaped, to her lap, and lay, blinking foolishly at the noblemen in their rich dresses, and the palace servants in their handsome livery; but it was perhaps too stupid to be frightened, for it made no other motion.

She had seen Aliyander standing with the Crown Prince when she entered, but she avoided his eyes; at last he came to stand before her, legs apart, staring down at her bent head with a heat from his black eyes that scorched her skin.

"You dare to mock me," he said, his voice almost a hiss, thick with a venomous hatred she could not mistake.

She looked up in terror, and he gestured at the frog. "Ah, no, I meant no—" she pleaded, and then her voice died, but the heat of Aliyander's look ebbed a little as he read the fear in her face.

"A frog, Princess?" he said, his voice still hurt her, but now it was heavy with scorn, and pitched so that many in the Hall would hear him. "I thought Princesses preferred kittens, or greyhounds."

"I—" She paused, and licked her dry lips. "I found it in the garden." She dropped her eyes again; she could think of nothing else to say. If only he would turn away from her—just for a minute, a minute to gather her wits; but he would not leave her, and her wits would only scatter again when next he addressed her.

He made now a gesture of disgust; and then straightened up, as if he would turn away from her at last, and she clenched her hands on the arms of her chair—and at that moment the frog gave its great bellow, the noise that had startled her yesterday into dropping the necklace into the pool. And Aliyander was startled, he jerked

[46]

visibly—and the courtiers laughed.

It was only the barest titter, and strangled instantly; but Aliyander heard it, and he turned, his face black with rage as if it had been yesterday when Rana had returned wearing a cold grey necklace; and he seized the frog by the leg and hurled it against the heavy stone wall opposite the thrones, which stood halfway down the long length of the Hall and faced across the narrow width to tall windows that looked out upon the courtyard.

Rana was frozen with horror for the moment it took Aliyander to fling the creature; and then as it struck the wall, there was a dreadful sound, and the skin of the frog seemed to—burst—and she closed her eyes.

The sudden gasp of all those around her made her eyes open against her will. And she in her turn gasped.

For the frog that Aliyander had hurled against the wall was there no longer; as it struck and fell, it became a tall young man, who stood there now, his ruddy hair falling past his broad shoulders, his blue eyes blazing as he stared at his attacker.

"Aliyander," he said, and his voice fell like a stone in the silence. Aliyander stood as if his name on those lips had turned him to stone indeed.

"Aliyander. My little brother."

No one moved but Rana, her hands stirred of their own accord. They crept across the spot on her lap where the frog had lain only a minute ago; and they seized each other.

Aliyander laughed—a terrible, ugly sound. "I defeated you once, big brother. I will defeat you again. You are weaker than I. You always will be."

The blue eyes never wavered. "Yes, I am weaker," Lian replied, "as you have proven already. I do not choose your sort of power."

Aliyander's face twisted as Rana had seen it before. She stood up suddenly, but he paid no attention to her; the heat of his gaze was now reserved for his brother, who stood calmly enough, staring back at Aliyander's distorted face.

"You made the wrong choice," Aliyander said, in a voice as black as his look; "and I will prove it to you. You will have no chance to return and inconvenience me a second time."

It was as if no one else could move; the eyes of all were riveted on the two antagonists; even the Crown Prince did not move to be closer to his hero.

The Princess turned and ran. She paused on the threshold of the door to the garden, and picked up a tall flagon that had held wine and was now sitting forgotten on a deep windowsill. Then she ran out, down the white paths; she had no eyes for the trees and the flowers, or the smooth sand of the courtyard to her right; she felt as numb as she had the day before with her handful of round and glowing jewels; but today her eyes watched where her feet led her, and her mind said *hurry, hurry, hurry.*

She ran to the pond where she had found the frog, or where the frog had found her. She knelt quickly on the bank, and rinsed the sour wine dregs from the bottom of the flagon she carried, emptying the tainted water on the grass behind her, where it would not run back into the pool. Then she dipped the jug full, and carried it, brimming, back to the Great Hall.

She had to walk slowly this time, for the flagon was full and very heavy, and she did not wish to spill even a drop of it. Her feet seemed to sink ankle-deep in the ground with every step, although in fact the white pebbles held no footprint as she passed, and only bruised her small feet in their thin-soled slippers.

She paused on the Hall's threshold again, this time for her eyes to adjust to the dimmer light. No one had moved; and no one looked at her.

She saw Aliyander raise his hand and bring it like a back-handed slap against the air before him, and though Lian stood across the room from him, she saw his head jerk as if from the force of a blow; and a thin line formed on his cheek, and after a moment blood welled and dripped from it.

Aliyander waved his hand so the sharp stone of his ring glittered, and he laughed.

Rana started forward again, step by step, as slowly as she had paced the garden, although only a few steps more were needed. Her arms had begun to shiver with the weight of her burden. Still Aliyander did not look at her; for while his might be the greater strength at last, still he could not tear his eyes away from the calm clear gaze of his brother's; his brother yet held him.

Rana walked up the narrow way till she was so close to Aliyander that she might have touched his sleeve if she had not needed both hands to hold the flagon. Then, at last, Aliyander broke away to look at her; and as he did she lifted the great jug, and with a strength she thought was not hers alone, hurled the contents full upon the man before her.

He gave a strangled cry, and brushed desperately with his hands as if he could sweep the water away; but he was drenched with it, his hair plastered to his head and his clothes to his body. He looked suddenly small, wizened and old. He still looked at her, but she met his gaze fearlessly, and he did not seem to recognize her.

His face turned as grey as his jewels. His eyes, she thought, were as opaque as the eyes of marble statues; and then he fell down full-length upon the floor, heavily, without sound, with no attempt to catch himself. He moved no more.

Inthur leaped up then with a cry, and ran to his fallen friend, and Rana saw the quick tears on his cheeks; but when he looked up he looked straight at her, and his eyes were clear. "He was my friend," he said simply; but there was no memory in him of what that friendship had been.

The King stood down stiffly from his throne, and the courtiers moved, and shook themselves as if from sleep, and stared without sorrow at the still body of Aliyander, and with curiosity and awe and a little hesitant but hopeful joy at Lian.

"I welcome you," said the King, with the pride of the master of his own hall, and of a king of a long line of kings. "I welcome you, Prince Lian, to my country, and to my people." And his gaze flickered only briefly to the thing on the floor; at his gesture, a servant stepped forward and threw a dark cloth over it.

"Thank you," said Lian gravely; and the Princess realized that he had come up silently and was standing at her side. She glanced up and saw him looking down at her; and the knowledge of what they had done together, and what neither could have done alone, passed between them; and with it an understanding that they would never discuss it. She said aloud "I—I welcome you, Prince Lian."

"Thank you," he said again, but she heard the change of tone in his voice; and from the corner of her eye she saw her father smile. She offered Lian her hand, and he took it, and raised it slowly to his lips.

HANSEL'S EYES[1]

Garth Nix

HANSEL WAS TEN AND HIS SISTER, GRETEL, WAS ELEVEN WHEN THEIR stepmother decided to get rid of them. They didn't catch on at first, because the Hagmom (their secret name for her) had always hated them. So leaving them behind at the supermarket or forgetting to pick them up after school was no big deal.

It was only when their father got in on the "disappearing the kids" act that they realized it was serious. Although he was a weak man, they thought he might still love them enough to stand up to the Hagmom.

They realized he didn't the day he took them out into the woods. Hansel wanted to do the whole Boy Scout thing and take a water bottle and a pile of other stuff, but their dad said they wouldn't need it. It'd only be a short walk.

Then he dumped them. They'd just gotten out of the car when he took off. They didn't try to chase him. They knew the signs. The Hagmom had hypnotized him again or whatever she did to make him do things.

"Guess she's going to get a nasty surprise when we get back," said Hansel, taking out the map he'd stuffed down the front of his shirt. Gretel silently handed him the compass she'd tucked into her sock.

---

1 Originally published in *A Wolf at the Door: And Other Retold Fairy Tales*, ed. Ellen Datlow and Terry Windling (New York: Simon and Schuster, 2000). Reprinted by permission of the author.

It took them three hours to get home, first walking, then in a highway patrol cruiser, and finally in their dad's car. They were almost back when the Hagmom called on the cell phone. Hansel and Gretel could hear her screaming. But when they finally got home, she smiled and kissed the air near their cheeks.

"She's planning something," said Gretel. "Something bad."

Hansel agreed, and they both slept in their clothes, with some maps, the compass, and candy bars stuffed down their shirts.

Gretel dreamed a terrible dream. She saw the Hagmom creep into their room, quiet as a cat in her velvet slippers. She had a big yellow sponge in her hand, a sponge that smelled sweet, but too sweet to be anything but awful. She went to Hansel's bunk and pushed the sponge against his nose and face. His arms and legs thrashed for a second, then he fell back like he was dead.

Gretel tried and tried to wake from the dream, but when she finally opened her eyes, there was the yellow sponge and the Hagmom's smiling face and then the dream was gone and there was nothing but total, absolute darkness.

When Gretel did wake up, she wasn't at home. She was lying in an alley. Her head hurt, and she could hardly open her eyes because the sun seemed too bright.

"Chloroform," whispered Hansel. "The Hagmom drugged us and got Dad to dump us."

"I feel sick," said Gretel. She forced herself to stand and noticed that there was nothing tucked into her shirt, or Hansel's, either. The maps, candy bars, and compass were gone.

"This looks bad," said Hansel, shielding his eyes with his hand and taking in the piles of trash, the broken windows, and the lingering charcoal smell of past fires. "We're in the old part of the city that got fenced off after the riots."

"She must hope someone will kill us," said Gretel. She scowled and picked up a jagged piece of glass, winding an old rag around it so she could use it like a knife.

"Probably," agreed Hansel, who wasn't fooled. He knew Gretel was scared, and so was he.

"Let's look around," Gretel said. Doing something would be better than just standing still, letting the fear grow inside them.

They walked in silence, much closer together than usual, their elbows almost bumping. The alley opened into a wide street that wasn't any better. The only sign of life was a flock of pigeons.

But around the next corner, Hansel backed up so suddenly that Gretel's glass knife almost went into his side. She was so upset, she threw it away. The sound of shattering glass echoed through the empty streets and sent the pigeons flying.

"I almost stabbed you, you moron!" exclaimed Gretel. "Why did you stop?"

"There's a shop," said Hansel, "A brand-new one."

Kind of reminds me of home alone.

"Let me see," said Gretel. She looked around the corner for a long time, till Hansel got impatient and tugged at her collar, cutting off her breath.

"It is a shop," she said. "A Sony PlayStation shop. That's what's in the windows. Lots of games."

"Weird," said Hansel, "I mean, there's nothing here. No one to buy anything."

Gretel frowned. Somehow the shop frightened her, but the more she tried not to think of that, the more scared she got.

"Maybe it got left by accident," added Hansel. "You know, when they just fenced the whole area off after the fires."

"Maybe …" said Gretel.

"Let's check it out," said Hansel. He could sense Gretel's uneasiness, but to him the shop seemed like a good sign.

"I don't want to," said Gretel, shaking her head.

"Well, I'm going," said Hansel. After he'd gone six or seven steps, Gretel caught up with him.

Hansel smiled to himself.

Gretel could never stay behind.

The shop was strange. The windows were so clear that you could see all the way inside to the rows of PlayStations all set up ready to go, connected to really big television screens. There was even a Coke machine and a snack machine at the back.

Hansel touched the door with one finger, a bit hesitantly. Half of him wanted it to be locked, and half of him wanted it to give a little under his hand. But it did more than that. It slid open automatically, and a cool breeze of air-conditioned air blew across his face.

He stepped inside. Gretel reluctantly followed. The door shut behind them, and instantly all the screens came on and were running games. Then the Coke machine clunked out a couple of cans of Coke, and the snack machine whirred and hummed and a whole bunch of candy bars and chocolate piled up outside the slot.

"Excellent!" exclaimed Hansel happily, and he went over and picked up a Coke. Gretel put out her hand to stop him, but it was too late.

"Hansel, I don't like this," said Gretel, moving back to the door. There was something strange about all this—the flicker of the television screens reaching out to her beckoning her to play, trying to draw them both in …

Hansel ignored her, as if she had ceased to exist. He swigged from the can and started playing a game. Gretel ran over and tugged at his arm, but his eyes never left the screen.

"Hansel!" Gretel screamed. "We have to get out of here!"

"Why?" asked a soft voice.

Gretel shivered. The voice sounded human enough, but it instantly gave her the mental picture of a spider, welcoming flies. Flies it meant to suck dry and hang like trophies in its web.

She turned around slowly, telling herself it couldn't really be a spider, trying to blank out the image of a hideous eight-legged, fat-bellied, fanged monstrosity.

When she saw it was only a woman, she didn't feel any better. A woman in her mid-forties, maybe, in a plain black dress, showing her bare arms. Long, sinewy arms that ended in narrow hands and long, grasping fingers. Gretel couldn't look directly at her face, just glimpsing bright-red lipstick, a hungry mouth, and the darkest of sunglasses.

"So you don't want to play the games like your brother, Hansel," said the woman. "But you can feel their power, can't you, Gretel?"

Gretel couldn't move. Her whole body was filled up with fear, because this woman was a spider, Gretel thought, a hunting spider in human shape, and she and Hansel were well and truly caught. Without thinking, she blurted out, "Spider!"

"A spider?" laughed the woman, her red mouth spreading wide, lips peeling back to reveal nicotine-stained teeth. "I'm not a spider, Gretel. I'm a shadow against the moon, a dark shape in the night doorway, a catch-as-catch-can … witch!"

"A witch," whispered Gretel. "What are you going to do with us?"

"I'm going to give you a choice that I have never given before," whispered the witch. "You have some smattering of power, Gretel. You dream true and strong enough that my machines cannot catch you in their dreaming. The seed of a witch lies in your heart, and I will tend it and make it grow. You will be my apprentice and learn the secrets of my power, the secrets of the night and the moon, of the twilight and the dawn. Magic, Gretel, magic! Power and freedom and dominion over beasts and men!

"Or you can take the other path," she continued, leaning in close till her breath washed into Gretel's nose, foul breath that smelled of cigarettes and whiskey. "The path that ends in the end of Gretel. Pulled apart for your heart and lungs and liver and kidneys. Transplant organs are so in demand, particularly for sick little children with very rich parents! Strange—they never ask me where the organs come from."

"And Hansel?" whispered Gretel, without thinking of her own danger, or the seed in her heart that begged to be made a witch, "What about Hansel?"

"Ah, Hansel," cried the witch. She clicked her fingers, and Hansel walked over to them like a zombie, his fingers still twitching from the game.

"I have a particular plan for Hansel," crooned the witch. "Hansel with the beautiful, beautiful blue eyes."

She tilted Hansel's head back so his eyes caught the light, glimmering blue. Then she took off her sunglasses, and Gretel saw that the witch's own eyes were shriveled like raisins and thick with fat white lines like webs.

"Hansel's eyes go to a very special customer," whispered the witch. "And the rest of him? That depends on Gretel. If she's a good apprentice, the boy shall live. Better blind than dead, don't you think?" She snapped out her arm on the last word and grabbed Gretel, stopping her movement toward the door.

"You can't go without my leave, Gretel," said the witch, "Not when there's so much still for you to see. Ah, to see again, all crisp and clean, with eyes so blue and bright. Lazarus!"

An animal padded out from the rear of the shop and came up to the witch's hand. It was a cat, of sorts. It stood almost to the witch's waist, and it was multicolored, and terribly scarred, lines of bare skin running between patches of different-colored fur like a horrible jigsaw. Even its ears were different colors, and its tail seemed to be made of seven quite distinct rings of fur. Gretel felt sick as she realized it was a patchwork beast, sewn together from many different cats and given life by the witch's magic.

Then Gretel noticed that whenever the witch turned her head, so did Lazarus. If she looked up, the cat looked up. If she turned her head left, it turned left. Clearly, the witch saw the world through the cat's eyes.

With the cat at her side, the witch pushed Gretel ahead of her and whistled for Hansel to follow. They went through the back of the shop, then down a long stairway, deep into the earth. At the bottom, the witch unlocked the door with a key of polished bone.

Beyond the door was a huge cave, ill lit by seven soot-darkened lanterns. One side of the cave was lined with empty cages, each just big enough to house a standing child.

There was also an industrial cold room—a shed-size refrigerator that had a row of toothy icicles hanging from the gutters of its sloping roof—that dominated the other side of the cave. Next to the cold room was a slab of marble that served as a table. Behind it, hanging from hooks in the damp stone of the cave wall, were a dozen knives and cruel-looking instruments of steel.

"Into the cage, young Hansel," commanded the witch, and Hansel did as he was told, without a word. The patchwork cat slunk after him and shot the bolt home with a slap of its paw.

"Now, Gretel," said the witch. "Will you become a witch or be broken into bits?"

Gretel looked at Hansel in his cage, and then at the marble slab and the knives. There seemed to be no choice. At least if she chose the path of witchery Hansel would only … only … lose his eyes. And perhaps they would get a chance to escape. "I will learn to be a witch," she said finally. "If you promise to take no more of Hansel than his eyes."

The witch laughed and took Gretel's hands in a bony grip, ignoring the girl's shudder. Then she started to dance, swinging Gretel around and around, with Lazarus leaping and screeching between them.

As she danced, the witch sang:

"Gretel's chosen the witch's way. And Hansel will be the one to pay. Sister sees more and brother less—Hansel and Gretel, what a mess!"

Then she suddenly stopped and let go. Gretel spun across the cave and crashed into the door of one of the cages.

"You'll live down here," said the witch. "There's food in the cold room, and a bathroom in the last cage. I will instruct you on your duties each morning. If you try to escape, you will be punished."

Gretel nodded, but she couldn't help looking across at the knives sparkling on the wall. The witch and Lazarus looked, too, and the witch laughed again. "No steel can cut me, or rod mark my back," she said. "But if you wish to test that, it is Hansel I will punish."

Then the witch left, with Lazarus padding alongside her.

Gretel immediately went to Hansel, but he was still in the grip of the PlayStation spell, eyes and fingers locked in some phantom game.

Next she tried the door, but sparks flew up and burned her when she stuck a knife in the lock.

The door to the cold room opened easily enough, though, frosted air and bright fluorescent light spilling out. It was much colder inside than a normal refrigerator. One side of the room was stacked high with chiller boxes, each labeled with a red cross and a bright sticker that said URGENT: HUMAN TRANSPLANT. Gretel tried not to look at them, or think about what they contained. The other side was stacked with all kinds of frozen food. Gretel took some spinach. She hated it, but spinach was the most opposite food to meat she could imagine. She didn't even want to think about eating meat.

The next day marked the first of many in the cave. The witch gave Gretel chores to do, mostly cleaning or packing up boxes from the cold room in special messenger bags the witch brought down. Then the witch would teach Gretel magic, such as the spell that would keep herself and Hansel warm.

Always, Gretel lived with the fear that the witch would choose that day to bring down another child to be cut up on the marble slab, or to take Hansel's eyes. But the witch always came alone, and merely looked at Hansel through Lazarus's eyes and muttered, "Not ready."

So Gretel worked and learned, fed Hansel and whispered to him. She constantly told him not to get better, to pretend that he was still under the spell. Either Hansel listened and pretended, even to her, or he really was still entranced.

Days went by, then weeks, and Gretel realized that she enjoyed learning magic too much.

She looked forward to her lessons, and sometimes she would forget about Hansel for hours, forget that he would soon lose his eyes.

When she realized that she might forget Hansel altogether, Gretel decided that she had to kill the witch. She told Hansel that night, whispering her fears to him and trying to think of a plan. But nothing came to her, for now Gretel had learned enough to know the witch really couldn't be cut by metal or struck down by a blow.

The next morning, Hansel spoke in his sleep while the witch was in the cave. Gretel cried out from where she was scrubbing the floor, to try and cover it up, but it was too late. The witch came over and glared through the bars.

"So you've been shamming," she said. "But now I shall take your left eye, for the spell to graft it to my own socket must be fueled by your fear. And your sister will help me."

"No, I won't!" cried Gretel. But the witch just laughed and blew on Gretel's chest. The breath sank into her heart, and the ember of witchcraft that was there blazed up and grew, spreading through her body. Higher and higher it rose, till Gretel grew small inside her own head and could feel herself move around only at the witch's whim.

Then the witch took Hansel from the cage and bound him with red rope. She laid him on the marble slab, and Lazarus jumped up so she could see. Gretel brought her herbs, and the wand of ivory, the wand of jet, and the wand of horn. Finally, the witch chanted her spell. Gretel's mind went away completely then. When she came back to herself, Hansel was in his cage, one eye bandaged with a thick pad of cobwebs. He looked at Gretel through his other, tear-filled eye.

"She's going to take the other one tomorrow," he whispered.

"No," said Gretel, sobbing. "No."

"I know it isn't really you helping her," said Hansel. "But what can you do?"

"I don't know," said Gretel. "We have to kill her—but she'll punish you if we try and we fail."

"I wish it was a dream," said Hansel. "Dreams end, and you wake up. But I'm not asleep, am I? It's too cold, and my eye … it hurts."

Gretel opened the cage to hug him and cast the spell that would warm them. But she was thinking about cold—and the witch. "If we could trap the witch and Lazarus in the cold room somehow, they might freeze to death," she said slowly. "But we'd have to make it much colder so she wouldn't have time to cast a spell."

They went to look at the cold room and found that it was set as cold as it would go. But Hansel found a barrel of liquid nitrogen at the back, and that gave him an idea.

An hour later, they'd rigged their instant witch-freezing trap. Using one of the knives Hansel unscrewed the inside handle of the door so there was no way to get out. Then they balanced the barrel on top of a pile of boxes just past the door. Finally, they poured water everywhere to completely ice up the floor.

Then they took turns sleeping till Gretel heard the click of the witch's key in the door. She sprang up and went to the cold room. Leaving the door ajar, she carefully stood on the ice and took the lid off the liquid nitrogen. Then she stepped back outside, pinching her nose and gasping. "Something's wrong, Mistress!" she exclaimed. "Everything's gone rotten."

"What!" cried the witch, dashing across the cave, her one blue eye glittering. Lazarus ran at her heels from habit, though she no longer needed his sight.

Gretel stood aside as she ran past, then gave her a hefty push. The witch skidded on the ice, crashed into the boxes, and fell flat on her back just as the barrel toppled over. An instant later, her final scream was smothered in a cloud of freezing vapor.

But Lazarus, quicker than any normal cat, did a backflip in midair, even as Gretel slammed the door. Ancient stitches gave way, and the cat started coming apart accompanied by an explosion of the magic silver dust that filled it and gave it life.

Gretel relaxed for an instant as the dust obscured the beast, then screamed as the front part of Lazarus jumped out at her, teeth snapping. She kicked at it, but the cat was too swift, its great jaws meeting around her ankle. Gretel screamed again, and then Hansel was there, shaking the strange dust out of the broken body as if he were emptying a vacuum cleaner. In a few seconds there was nothing left of Lazarus but its head and an empty skin. Even then it wouldn't let go, till Hansel forced its mouth open with a broomstick and pushed the snarling remnant across the floor and into one of the cages.

Gretel hopped across and watched it biting the bars, its green eyes still filled with magical life and hatred. "Hansel," she said, "your own eye is frozen with the witch. But I think I can remember the spell—and there is an eye for the taking here."

So it was that when they entered the cold room later to take the key of bone from the frozen, twisted body of the witch, Hansel saw the world through one eye of blue and one of green.

Later, when they found their way home, it was the sight of that green eye that gave the Hagmom a heart attack and made her die. But their father was still a weak man, and within a year he thought to marry another woman who had no love for his children. Only this time the new Hagmom faced a Gretel who was more than half a witch, and a Hansel who had gained strange powers from his magic cat's eye.

But that is all another story ...

SNOW, GLASS, APPLES[1]

Neil Gaiman

I DO NOT KNOW WHAT MANNER OF THING SHE IS. NONE OF US ᴅᴏ. SHE killed her mother in the birthing, but that's never enough to account for it.

They call me wise, but I am far from wise, for all that I foresaw fragments of it, frozen moments caught in pools of water or in the cold glass of my mirror. If I were wise I would not have tried to change what I saw. If I were wise I would have killed myself before ever I encountered her, before ever I caught him.

Wise, and a witch, or so they said, and I'd seen his face in my dreams and in reflections for all my life: sixteen years of dreaming of him before he reined his horse by the bridge that morning and asked my name. He helped me onto his high horse and we rode together to my little cottage, my face buried in the gold of his hair. He asked for the best of what I had; a king's right, it was.

His beard was red-bronze in the morning light, and I knew him, not as a king, for I knew nothing of kings then, but as my love. He took all he wanted from me, the right of kings, but he returned to me on the following day and on the night after that: his beard so red, his hair so gold, his eyes the blue of a summer sky, his skin tanned the gentle brown of ripe wheat.

His daughter was only a child: no more than five years of age when I came to the palace. A portrait of her dead mother hung in the princess's tower room: a tall woman, hair the color of dark wood, eyes nut-brown. She was of a different blood to her pale daughter.

The girl would not eat with us.

I do not know where in the palace she ate.

I had my own chambers. My husband the king, he had his own rooms also. When he wanted me he would send for me, and I would go to him, and pleasure him, and take my pleasure with him.

One night, several months after I was brought to the palace, she came to my rooms. She was six. I was embroidering by lamplight, squinting my eyes against the lamp's smoke and fitful illumination. When I looked up, she was there.

"Princess?"

She said nothing. Her eyes were black as coal, black as her hair; her lips were redder than blood. She looked up at me and smiled. Her teeth seemed sharp, even then, in the lamplight.

"What are you doing away from your room?"

---

[1] From *Smoke and Mirrors* (New York: Avon Books, 1998.)

"I'm hungry," she said, like any child.

It was winter, when fresh food is a dream of warmth and sunlight; but I had strings of whole apples, cored and dried, hanging from the beams of my chamber, and I pulled an apple down for her.

"Here."

Autumn is the time of drying, of preserving, a time of picking apples, of rendering the goose fat. Winter is the time of hunger, of snow, and of death; and it is the time of the midwinter feast, when we rub the goose fat into the skin of a whole pig, stuffed with that autumn's apples; then we roast it or spit it, and we prepare to feast upon the crackling.

She took the dried apple from me and began to chew it with her sharp yellow teeth.

"Is it good?"

She nodded. I had always been scared of the little princess, but at that moment I warmed to her and, with my fingers, gently, I stroked her cheek. She looked at me and smiled—she smiled but rarely—then she sank her teeth into the base of my thumb, the Mound of Venus, and she drew blood.

I began to shriek, from pain and from surprise, but she looked at me and I fell silent.

The little princess fastened her mouth to my hand and licked and sucked and drank. When she was finished, she left my chamber. Beneath my gaze the cut that she had made began to close, to scab, and to heal. The next day it was an old scar: I might have cut my hand with a pocketknife in my childhood.

I had been frozen by her, owned and dominated. That scared me, more than the blood she had fed on. After that night I locked my chamber door at dusk, barring it with an oaken pole, and I had the smith forge iron bars, which he placed across my windows.

My husband, my love, my king, sent for me less and less, and when I came to him he was dizzy, listless, confused. He could no longer make love as a man makes love, and he would not permit me to pleasure him with my mouth: the one time I tried, he started violently, and began to weep. I pulled my mouth away and held him tightly until the sobbing had stopped, and he slept, like a child.

I ran my fingers across his skin as he slept. It was covered in a multitude of ancient scars. But I could recall no scars from the days of our courtship, save one, on his side, where a boar had gored him when he was a youth.

Soon he was a shadow of the man I had met and loved by the bridge. His bones showed, blue and white, beneath his skin. I was with him at the last: his hands were cold as stone, his eyes milky blue, his hair and beard faded and lustreless and limp. He died unshriven, his skin nipped and pocked from head to toe with tiny, old scars.

He weighed near to nothing. The ground was frozen hard, and we could dig no grave for him, so we made a cairn of rocks and stones above his body, as a memorial only, for there was little enough of him left to protect from the hunger of the beasts and the birds.

So I was queen.

And I was foolish, and young—eighteen summers had come and gone since first I saw daylight—and I did not do what I would do, now.

If it were today, I would have her heart cut out, true. But then I would have her head and arms and legs cut off. I would have them disembowel her. And then I would watch in the town square as the hangman heated the fire to white-heat with bellows, watch unblinking as he consigned each part of her to the fire. I would have archers around the square, who would shoot any bird or animal that came close to the flames, any raven or dog or hawk or rat. And I would not close my eyes until the princess was ash, and a gentle wind could scatter her like snow.

I did not do this thing, and we pay for our mistakes.

They say I was fooled; that it was not her heart. That it was the heart of an animal—a stag, perhaps, or a boar. They say that, and they are wrong.

And some say (but it is *her* lie, not mine) that I was given the heart, and that I ate it. Lies and half-truths fall like snow, covering the things that I remember, the things I saw. A landscape, unrecognizable after a snowfall; that is what she has made of my life.

There were scars on my love, her father's thighs, and on his ballock-pouch, and on his male member, when he died.

I did not go with them. They took her in the day, while she slept, and was at her weakest. They took her to the heart of the forest, and there they opened her blouse, and they cut out her heart, and they left her dead, in a gully, for the forest to swallow.

The forest is a dark place, the border to many kingdoms; no one would be foolish enough to claim jurisdiction over it. Outlaws live in the forest. Robbers live in the forest, and so do wolves. You can ride through the forest for a dozen days and never see a soul; but there are eyes upon you the entire time.

They brought me her heart. I know it was hers—no sow's heart or doe's would have continued to beat and pulse after it had been cut out, as that one did.

I took it to my chamber.

I did not eat it: I hung it from the beams above my bed, placed it on a length of twine that I strung with rowan berries, orange-red as a robin's breast, and with bulbs of garlic.

Outside the snow fell, covering the footprints of my huntsmen, covering her tiny body in the forest where it lay.

I had the smith remove the iron bars from my windows, and I would spend some time in my room each afternoon through the short winter days, gazing out over the forest, until darkness fell.

There were, as I have already stated, people in the forest. They would come out, some of them, for the Spring Fair: a greedy, feral, dangerous people; some were stunted—dwarfs and midgets and hunchbacks; others had the huge teeth and vacant gazes of idiots; some had fingers like flippers or crab claws. They would creep out of the forest each year for the Spring Fair, held when the snows had melted.

As a young lass I had worked at the fair, and they had scared me then, the forest folk. I told fortunes for the fairgoers, scrying in a pool of still water; and later, when I was older, in a disk of polished glass, its back all silvered—a gift from a merchant whose straying horse I had seen in a pool of ink.

The stallholders at the fair were afraid of the forest folk; they would nail their wares to the bare boards of their stalls—slabs of gingerbread or leather belts were nailed with great iron nails to the wood. If their wares were not nailed, they said, the forest folk would take them and run away, chewing on the stolen gingerbread, flailing about them with the belts.

The forest folk had money, though: a coin here, another there, sometimes stained green by time or the earth, the face on the coin unknown to even the oldest of us. Also they had things to trade, and thus the fair continued, serving the outcasts and the dwarfs, serving the robbers (if they were circumspect) who preyed on the rare travelers from lands beyond the forest, or on gypsies, or on the deer. (This was robbery in the eyes of the law. The deer were the queen's.)

The years passed by slowly, and my people claimed that I ruled them with wisdom. The heart still hung above my bed, pulsing gently in the night. If there were any who mourned the child, I saw no evidence: she was a thing of terror, back then, and they believed themselves well rid of her.

Spring Fair followed Spring Fair: five of them, each sadder, poorer, shoddier than the one before. Fewer of the forest folk came out of the forest to buy. Those who did seemed subdued and listless. The stallholders stopped nailing their wares to the boards of their stalls. And by the fifth year but a handful of folk came from the forest—a fearful huddle of little hairy men, and no one else.

The Lord of the Fair, and his page, came to me when the fair was done. I had known him slightly, before I was queen.

"I do not come to you as my queen," he said.

I said nothing. I listened.

"I come to you because you are wise," he continued. "When you were a child you found a strayed foal by staring into a pool of ink; when you were a maiden you found a lost infant who had wandered far from her mother, by staring into that mirror of yours. You know secrets and you can seek out things hidden. My queen," he asked, "what is taking the forest folk? Next year there will be no Spring Fair. The travelers from other kingdoms have grown scarce and few, the folk of the forest are almost gone. Another year like the last, and we shall all starve."

I commanded my maidservant to bring me my looking glass. It was a simple thing, a silver-backed glass disk, which I kept wrapped in a doeskin, in a chest, in my chamber.

They brought it to me then, and I gazed into it:

She was twelve and she was no longer a little child. Her skin was still pale, her eyes and hair coal-black, her lips blood-red. She wore the clothes she had worn when she left the castle for the last time—the blouse, the skirt—although they were much let-out, much mended. Over them she wore a leather cloak, and instead of boots she had leather bags, tied with thongs, over her tiny feet.

She was standing in the forest, beside a tree.

As I watched, in the eye of my mind, I saw her edge and step and flitter and pad from tree to tree, like an animal: a bat or a wolf. She was following someone.

He was a monk. He wore sackcloth, and his feet were bare and scabbed and hard. His beard and tonsure were of a length, overgrown, unshaven.

She watched him from behind the trees. Eventually he paused for the night and began to make a fire, laying twigs down, breaking up a robin's nest as kindling. He had a tinderbox in his robe, and he knocked the flint against the steel until the sparks caught the tinder and the fire flamed. There had been two eggs in the nest he had found, and these he ate raw. They cannot have been much of a meal for so big a man.

He sat there in the firelight, and she came out from her hiding place. She crouched down on the other side of the fire, and stared at him. He grinned, as if it were a long time since he had seen another human, and beckoned her over to him.

She stood up and walked around the fire, and waited, an arm's length away. He pulled in his robe until he found a coin—a tiny copper penny—and tossed it to her. She caught it, and nodded, and went to him. He pulled at the rope around his waist, and his robe swung open. His body was as hairy as a bear's. She pushed him back onto the moss. One hand crept, spiderlike, through the tangle of hair, until it closed on his manhood; the other hand traced a circle on his left nipple. He closed his eyes and fumbled one huge hand under her skirt. She lowered her mouth to the nipple she had been teasing, her smooth skin white on the furry brown body of him.

She sank her teeth deep into his breast. His eyes opened, then they closed again, and she drank.

She straddled him, and she fed. As she did so, a thin blackish liquid began to dribble from between her legs …

"Do you know what is keeping the travelers from our town? What is happening to the forest people?" asked the Lord of the Fair.

I covered the mirror in doeskin, and told him that I would personally take it upon myself to make the forest safe once more.

I had to, although she terrified me. I was the queen.

A foolish woman would have gone then into the forest and tried to capture the creature; but I had been foolish once and had no wish to be so a second time.

I spent time with old books. I spent time with the gypsy women (who passed through our country across the mountains to the south, rather than cross the forest to the north and the west).

I prepared myself and obtained those things I would need, and when the first snows began to fall, I was ready.

Naked, I was, and alone in the highest tower of the palace, a place open to the sky. The winds chilled my body; goose pimples crept across my arms and thighs and breasts. I carried a silver basin, and a basket in which I had placed a silver knife, a silver pin, some tongs, a gray robe, and three green apples.

I put them down and stood there, unclothed, on the tower, humble before the night sky and the wind. Had any man seen me standing there, I would have had his eyes; but there was no one to spy. Clouds scudded across the sky, hiding and uncovering the waning moon.

I took the silver knife and slashed my left arm—once, twice, three times. The blood dripped into the basin, scarlet seeming black in the moonlight.

I added the powder from the vial that hung around my neck. It was a brown dust, made of dried herbs and the skin of a particular toad, and from certain other things. It thickened the blood, while preventing it from clotting.

I took the three apples, one by one, and pricked their skins gently with my silver pin. Then I placed the apples in the silver bowl and let them sit there while the first tiny flakes of snow of the year fell slowly onto my skin, and onto the apples, and onto the blood.

When dawn began to brighten the sky I covered myself with the gray cloak, and took the red apples from the silver bowl, one by one, lifting each into my basket with silver tongs, taking care not to touch it. There was nothing left of my blood or of the brown powder in the silver bowl, nothing save a black residue, like a verdigris, on the inside.

I buried the bowl in the earth. Then I cast a glamour on the apples (as once, years before, by a bridge, I had cast a glamour on myself), that they were, beyond any doubt, the most wonderful apples in the world, and the crimson blush of their skins was the warm color of fresh blood.

I pulled the hood of my cloak low over my face, and I took ribbons and pretty hair ornaments with me, placed them above the apples in the reed basket, and I walked alone into the forest until I came to her dwelling: a high sandstone cliff, laced with deep caves going back a way into the rock wall.

There were trees and boulders around the cliff face, and I walked quietly and gently from tree to tree without disturbing a twig or a fallen leaf. Eventually I found my place to hide, and I waited, and I watched.

After some hours, a clutch of dwarfs crawled out of the hole in the cave front—ugly, misshapen, hairy little men, the old inhabitants of this country. You saw them seldom now.

They vanished into the wood, and none of them espied me, though one of them stopped to piss against the rock I hid behind.

I waited. No more came out.

I went to the cave entrance and hallooed into it, in a cracked old voice.

The scar on my Mound of Venus throbbed and pulsed as she came toward me, out of the darkness, naked and alone.

She was thirteen years of age, my stepdaughter, and nothing marred the perfect whiteness of her skin, save for the livid scar on her left breast, where her heart had been cut from her long since.

The insides of her thighs were stained with wet black filth.

She peered at me, hidden, as I was, in my cloak. She looked at me hungrily. "Ribbons, goodwife," I croaked. "Pretty ribbons for your hair …"

She smiled and beckoned to me. A tug; the scar on my hand was pulling me toward her. I did what I had planned to do, but I did it more readily than I had planned: I dropped my basket and screeched like the bloodless old peddler woman I was pretending to be, and I ran.

My gray cloak was the color of the forest, and I was fast; she did not catch me.

I made my way back to the palace.

I did not see it. Let us imagine, though, the girl returning, frustrated and hungry, to her cave, and finding my fallen basket on the ground.

What did she do?

I like to think she played first with the ribbons, twined them into her raven hair, looped them around her pale neck or her tiny waist.

And then, curious, she moved the cloth to see what else was in the basket, and she saw the red, red apples.

They smelled like fresh apples, of course; and they also smelled of blood. And she was hungry. I imagine her picking up an apple, pressing it against her cheek, feeling the cold smoothness of it against her skin.

And she opened her mouth and bit deep into it …

By the time I reached my chambers, the heart that hung from the roof beam, with the apples and hams and the dried sausages, had ceased to beat. It hung there, quietly, without motion or life, and I felt safe once more.

That winter the snows were high and deep, and were late melting. We were all hungry come the spring.

The Spring Fair was slightly improved that year. The forest folk were few, but they were there, and there were travelers from the lands beyond the forest.

I saw the little hairy men of the forest cave buying and bargaining for pieces of glass, and lumps of crystal and of quartz rock. They paid for the glass with silver coins—the spoils of my stepdaughter's depredations, I had no doubt. When it got about what they were buying, townsfolk rushed back to their homes and came back with their lucky crystals, and, in a few cases, with whole sheets of glass.

I thought briefly about having the little men killed, but I did not. As long as the heart hung, silent and immobile and cold, from the beam of my chamber, I was safe, and so were the folk of the forest, and, thus, eventually, the folk of the town.

My twenty-fifth year came, and my stepdaughter had eaten the poisoned fruit two winters back, when the prince came to my palace. He was tall, very tall, with cold green eyes and the swarthy skin of those from beyond the mountains.

He rode with a small retinue: large enough to defend him, small enough that another monarch—myself, for instance—would not view him as a potential threat.

I was practical: I thought of the alliance of our lands, thought of the kingdom running from the forests all the way south to the sea; I thought of my golden-haired bearded love, dead these eight years; and, in the night, I went to the prince's room.

I am no innocent, although my late husband, who was once my king, was truly my first lover, no matter what they say.

At first the prince seemed excited. He bade me remove my shift, and made me stand in front of the opened window, far from the fire, until my skin was chilled stone-cold. Then he asked me to lie upon my back, with my hands folded across my breasts, my eyes wide open—but staring only at the beams above. He told me not to move, and to breathe as little as possible. He implored me to say nothing. He spread my legs apart.

It was then that he entered me.

As he began to thrust inside me, I felt my hips raise, felt myself begin to match him, grind for grind, push for push. I moaned. I could not help myself.

His manhood slid out of me. I reached out and touched it, a tiny, slippery thing.

"Please," he said softly. "You must neither move nor speak. Just lie there on the stones, so cold and so fair."

I tried, but he had lost whatever force it was that had made him virile; and, some short while later, I left the prince's room, his curses and tears still resounding in my ears.

He left early the next morning, with all his men, and they rode off into the forest.

I imagine his loins, now, as he rode, a knot of frustration at the base of his manhood. I imagine his pale lips pressed so tightly together. Then I imagine his little troupe riding through the forest, finally coming upon the glass-and-crystal cairn of my stepdaughter. So pale. So cold. Naked beneath the glass, and little more than a girl, and dead.

In my fancy, I can almost feel the sudden hardness of his manhood inside his britches, envision the lust that took him then, the prayers he muttered beneath his breath in thanks for his good fortune. I imagine him negotiating with the little hairy men—offering them gold and spices for the lovely corpse under the crystal mound.

Did they take his gold willingly? Or did they look up to see his men on their horses, with their sharp swords and their spears, and realize they had no alternative?

I do not know. I was not there; I was not scrying. I can only imagine …

Hands, pulling off the lumps of glass and quartz from her cold body. Hands, gently caressing her cold cheek, moving her cold arm, rejoicing to find the corpse still fresh and pliable.

Did he take her there, in front of them all? Or did he have her carried to a secluded nook before he mounted her?

I cannot say.

Did he shake the apple from her throat? Or did her eyes slowly open as he pounded into her cold body; did her mouth open, those red lips part, those sharp yellow teeth close on his swarthy neck, as the blood, which is the life, trickled down her throat, washing down and away the lump of apple, my own, my poison?

I imagine; I do not know.

This I do know: I was woken in the night by her heart pulsing and beating once more. Salt blood dripped onto my face from above. I sat up. My hand burned and pounded as if I had hit the base of my thumb with a rock.

There was a hammering on the door. I felt afraid, but I am a queen, and I would not show fear. I opened the door.

First his men walked into my chamber and stood around me, with their sharp swords, and their long spears.

Then he came in; and he spat in my face.

Finally, she walked into my chamber, as she had when I was first a queen and she was a child of six. She had not changed. Not really.

She pulled down the twine on which her heart was hanging. She pulled off the rowan berries, one by one; pulled off the garlic bulb—now a dried thing, after all these years; then she took up her own, her pumping heart—a small thing, no larger than that of a nanny goat or a she-bear—as it brimmed and pumped its blood into her hand.

Her fingernails must have been as sharp as glass: she opened her breast with them, running them over the purple scar. Her chest gaped, suddenly, open and bloodless. She licked her heart, once, as the blood ran over her hands, and she pushed the heart deep into her breast.

I saw her do it. I saw her close the flesh of her breast once more. I saw the purple scar begin to fade.

Her prince looked briefly concerned, but he put his arm around her nonetheless, and they stood, side by side, and they waited.

And she stayed cold, and the bloom of death remained on her lips, and his lust was not diminished in any way.

They told me they would marry, and the kingdoms would indeed be joined. They told me that I would be with them on their wedding day.

It is starting to get hot in here.

They have told the people bad things about me; a little truth to add savor to the dish, but mixed with many lies.

I was bound and kept in a tiny stone cell beneath the palace, and I remained there through the autumn. Today they fetched me out of the cell; they stripped the rags from me, and washed the filth from me, and then they shaved my head and my loins, and they rubbed my skin with goose-grease.

The snow was falling as they carried me—two men at each hand, two men at each leg—utterly exposed, and spread-eagled and cold, through the midwinter crowds, and brought me to this kiln.

My stepdaughter stood there with her prince. She watched me, in my indignity, but she said nothing.

As they thrust me inside, jeering and chaffing as they did so, I saw one snowflake land upon her white cheek, and remain there without melting.

They closed the kiln door behind me. It is getting hotter in here, and outside they are singing and cheering and banging on the sides of the kiln.

She was not laughing, or jeering, or talking. She did not sneer at me or turn away. She looked at me, though; and for a moment I saw myself reflected in her eyes.

I will not scream. I will not give them that satisfaction. They will have my body, but my soul and my story are my own, and will die with me.

The goose-grease begins to melt and glisten upon my skin. I shall make no sound at all. I shall think no more on this.

I shall think instead of the snowflake on her cheek.

I think of her hair as black as coal, her lips, redder than blood, her skin, snow-white.

EVER AFTER[1]

Kim Addonizio

THE LOFT WHERE THE DWARVES LIVED HAD A VIEW OF THE CITY AND hardwood floors and skylights, but it was overpriced, and too small now that there were seven of them. It was a fifth-floor walkup, one soaring, track-lighted room. At the far end was the platform where Doc, Sneezy, Sleepy, and Bashful slept side by side on futons. Beneath them, Happy and Dopey shared a double bed. Grumpy, who pretty much stayed to himself, kept his nylon sleeping bag in a corner during the day and unrolled it at night on the floor between the couch and the coffee table. The kitchen was two facing zinc counters, a built-in range and microwave, and a steel refrigerator, all hidden behind a long bamboo partition that Doc had bought and Sneezy had painted a color called Cherry Jubilee. The kitchen and bathroom were the only places any sort of privacy was possible. To make the rent they all pooled their money from their jobs at the restaurant, except for Dopey, who didn't have a job unless you counted selling drugs when he wasn't running them up his arm; and Grumpy, who panhandled every day for spare change and never came up with more than a few wrinkled dollar bills when the first of the month rolled around. Sometimes the rest of them talked about kicking out Dopey and Grumpy, but no one quite had the heart. Besides, the Book said there were seven when she arrived, seven disciples of the goddess who would come with the sacred apple and transform them. How, exactly, they would be transformed was a mystery that would be revealed when she got there. In the meantime, it was their job to wait.

"When she comes, she'll make us big," said Sneezy. He had the comics section of the Sunday paper, and an egg of Silly Putty, and was flattening a doughy oval onto a panel of Calvin and Hobbes.

"Oh, bullshit," said Grumpy. "It's about *inner* transformation, man. That's the whole point. Materialism is a trap. Identifying with your body is a trap. All this shit"—Grumpy swept his arm to indicate not just their loft but the tall downtown buildings beyond the windows, and maybe more—"is an illusion. Maya. Samsara." He shook out the last Marlboro from a pack, crumpled the pack, and tried a hook shot into a wicker wastebasket by the window, but missed. He looked around. "Matches? Lighter? Who's going for more cigs?"

"She will," insisted Sneezy. "She'll make us six feet if we want to be."

"She can't change genetics, you dope," Grumpy said.

---

1 First appeared in *Fairy Tale Review: The Blue Issue*, 2006. Copyright Kim Addonizio, 2006. Reprinted by permission of the author.

At the word *dope*, Dopey's head jerked up for an instant. He was nodding on the couch at the opposite end from Grumpy, a lit cigarette ready to fall from his hand. The couch had a few burn holes already. One of these days, Doc thought, he's going to set the fucking place on fire, and then where will we be? How will she ever find us? He got up from the floor, where he'd been doing yoga stretches, and slid the cigarette from Dopey's stained fingers. He ground it out in an ashtray on the table, in the blue ceramic water of a moat that circled a ceramic castle. From the castle's tiny windows, a little incense smoke—sandalwood—drifted out.

"She's not an alien from outer space who's going to perform weird experiments," Doc said. He hunted through the newspaper for the Food section.

"Where is she from, then?" Sneezy said. Sneezy was a sixteen-year-old runaway, the youngest of them. From the sweet credulousness of his expression, you'd never know what terrible things he had endured. He'd been beaten, scarred between his shoulder blades with boiling water, forced into sex with his mother by his own father. Sneezy liked to ask the obvious questions for the sake of receiving the familiar, predictable answers.

"She's from the castle," Doc said. "She's the fairest in the land. She will come with the sacred apple and all will be changed." This much the Book said. *Once upon a time*, it said. But when was that, exactly? Doc wondered. They'd been here for more than six years already. Or he had, anyway. Ever since he'd found the Book in a Dumpster—the covers ripped away, most of its pages stained and torn—where he'd been looking for food a nearby restaurant always threw out. He'd been on the streets, addicted to cheap wine, not giving a shit about anything or anyone. He'd slept on cardboard in doorways, with a Buck knife under the rolled poncho he used for a pillow, had stolen children's shoes from outside the Moon Bounce at the park. He had humiliated himself performing drunken jigs in the bank plaza for change tossed into a baseball cap. The Book had changed all that. It had shown him there was a purpose to his life. To gather the others, to come to this place and make it ready. He had quit drinking and found a job, at the very restaurant whose Dumpster he used to scrounge through. He had gathered his brethren, one by one, as they drifted into the city from other places, broke and down on their luck, headed for the streets and shelters. They had become his staff—two dishwashers, a busboy, and a fry cook. The restaurant's name was Oz, and the owner had been willing to hire dwarf after dwarf and present them as ersatz munchkins. There had been a feature article in the *Weekly*, and write-ups in some food magazines, which had drawn a lot of business. The dwarves were mentioned in the guidebooks, so there were often tourists from Canada and Denmark and Japan, who brought their cameras to record the enchanting moment the dwarves trooped from the kitchen with a candle-lit torte to stand around a table and sing happy birthday. They used fake high voices, as though they'd been sucking on helium.

"Why is the apple sacred?" Sneezy said dreamily. He had abandoned the comics and now had a few Magic cards spread out on the floor and was picking them up one by one, studying them.

"Because she will die of the apple and be resurrected," Doc said. He glanced at one of Sneezy's cards: *Capashen Unicorn.* An armored unicorn raced through a glittery field, a white-robed rider on its back. Underneath, Doc read, *Capashen riders were stern and humorless even before their ancestral home was reduced to rubble.*

"Why do you collect that crap?" Doc said. "And those comic books you've always got your nose buried in. Read the Book again. Every time I read it, I discover something new. The Book is all you need. You have to focus on the Book."

"Check her out." Sneezy held up another card, of an anorectic-looking woman with green skin in a gold ballerina outfit. One long-nailed thumb and forefinger were raised in the air in some kind of salute. In her other hand she held aloft a green and white flag. A couple of men in armor rode behind her and behind them rose broccoli-like trees, being erased by mist rising out of the ground. Doc read: *Llanowar Vanguard. Creature—Dryad. Llanowar rallied around Eladamri's banner and united in his name.*

"Will *she* look like that?" Sneezy asked.

"Give it a rest," Grumpy said, and nudged Dopey with his foot, "Hey, man," he said. "We're out of cigs."

Sneezy will outgrow it, Doc thought. Dryads and unicorns. Made-up creatures and clans and battles. "I don't know what she'll look like, exactly," he sighed. He stood up and began tidying the coffee table. Empty semicrushed cans of Bud Light that Grumpy and Dopey had drunk the night before. A half-eaten bag of tortilla chips. A plastic tub of salsa had spilled on the naked body of a Penthouse Pet. The magazine lay open to her spread legs, her long slender fingers teasingly positioned above her pink slit; it glistened, as though it had been basted. What would *she* look like? Maybe she would look like this, would come and drag her fingers through the graying hair on his chest and position her sweet eager hips above him. Maybe she would whisper to Doc that he was the one she came for, the only one; they could leave all the others behind, now that she was there. They would leave the city and move to an Airstream in the woods, overlooking a little river, where he could catch bass and bluegills. She would stand in front of their stove in cutoffs and a white blouse, sliding a spatula under a fish sputtering in a pan. When the moon rose, the two of them would go down to the river and float together, naked. Their heads would be the same height above the water. Doc closed the magazine. He gathered up the beer cans, carried them into the kitchen, and threw them on top of the pile of trash overflowing from the can.

The next afternoon he left a note on the refrigerator, securing it with a magnet Bashful had bought, of the Virgin Mary's stroller with the baby Jesus riding in it. The magnet set included Mary in a nightgown, her hands raised in prayer, with several changes of clothes and accessories including a skateboard, a waitress uniform, flowered pants and a hippie shirt, a plaid skirt, and roller skates. Right now Mary had on just the nightgown, and was riding the skateboard. Another magnet, of a small Magic 8 Ball, had been stuck over her face. HOUSE MEETING 7 P.M., Doc had written. IMPORTANT!!! PLEASE EVERYONE. I'LL BUY THE BEER. He knew that would ensure that Grumpy and Dopey showed.

Dopey didn't arrive until 7:30, strolling in with a bag of peanut M&M's. But at least they were all there, with a couple of six-packs and cigarettes and Nacho Cheese Doritos in a bowl on the table. Doc was drinking his usual, caffeine-free Diet Coke. Bashful passed around a large order of McDonald's fries and unwrapped a Big Mac. Crap, Doc thought, watching him eat, but it smelled pretty good, and he couldn't resist a couple of the fries.

"Why do we need a house meeting?" Grumpy said. "I got things to do." He hadn't shaved in a while, and his black beard stubble went halfway down his neck. Not so long ago, Doc remembered, Grumpy used to shave every day, no matter what.

"Oh, I love house meetings," Happy said. Happy loved nearly everything. He loved communal living, and being a bus boy at Oz. He loved being one of the Chosen who had been selected to wait. He loved the Book and would defend it when anyone criticized it, which seemed to be more and more often lately. Just a couple of days ago, Sleepy, who was taking a community college class, had come home talking nonsense. "It's like the Bible," he said. "It's, like, a metaphor or something. You know the cross? Jesus on the cross? The professor said the cross is really like a pagan fertility symbol." Sleepy had no idea what a metaphor was, though. When pressed, he couldn't define *symbol*, either. "You don't know what you're saying," Happy had concluded, and Doc explained to Sleepy that the Book was nothing like the Bible. The Bible was meant for normals, Doc said, but the Book was for dwarves.

"I called the meeting," Doc said, "because I'm sick of picking up after all of you. Sleepy cleaned the bathroom and left soap streaks all over the mirror. I can barely see myself in it. And you, Grumpy, you and Dopey—all you do is strew beer cans and cigarette butts and fast-food trash from one end of this place to the other. And this morning Bashful put the dishes from the dishwasher back in the cupboards when they hadn't even been washed yet."

"Sorry," Bashful muttered.

"I have to do everything around here," Doc said.

"Don't be such a goddamned martyr," Grumpy said, popping his second bottle of Red Hook.

"You should try pulling your own weight for once," Doc said. "Don't think we're going to carry you forever."

"Oh, but we love you, Grumpy," Happy said. He put his hand on Grumpy's shoulder. "You're the bomb," Happy said, using an expression he'd picked up from Sneezy.

"Get your paw off me," Grumpy said, "Freak."

"Look who's talking." Happy had an edge in his voice now. The one thing Happy didn't love was being a dwarf. At four foot ten, Happy was the closest to normal-sized, and Doc often wondered if Happy stayed not only because of his dedication to the Book but because this was the only place he got to be bigger than everyone else.

"I don't need you freaks," Grumpy said, giving Happy a shove. They were sitting on the floor, and the shove sent Happy into the coffee table. He banged his head on the corner.

"Look what you did," Happy said, holding his temple. "I'm bleeding."

"He's bleeding," everyone concurred, in unison. All except Grumpy, who glared defiantly at the circle of dwarves, his arms crossed in front of him.

"Violence can't be tolerated," Doc said sternly.

"Oh, yeah? What are you gonna do about it?" Grumpy said. "You and your stupid Book. Nobody believes in that shit but you. They're all just humoring you, man."

"You're lying," Doc said. He looked around at the others. "He's lying, right?"

"Yeah, right," Sneezy said. "We believe."

"We believe," the others said. But it sounded wrong. Doc could hear the doubt in their voices, could see it in the way they shifted their eyes to the floor, hunching their shoulders. Bashful picked up his Big Mac in both hands and chewed, his head down.

"I absolutely, positively, believe," Sneezy said.

But Sneezy was a kid, Doc thought, who believed in dryads and unicorns, wizards and fairies, in Spiderman and Wolverine and other bullshit superheroes. Sneezy sat rapt in front of the Saturday morning cartoons, saying "Rad" and "Awesome." Sneezy's belief was not hard-won.

"Whatever gets you through," Dopey said, surprising everyone. Dopey never talked at house meetings. "It's cool," Dopey said. "She'll come, dudes." He lay back against the armrest of the couch and closed his eyes.

"It's just—" Bashful said.

"Just what," Doc said, his voice flat.

"We're kind of in a rut, I think. Maybe. Or something." Bashful stared at the hamburger in his hands. A little dribble of pink sauce was falling right onto the table Doc had cleaned.

"You have doubts," Doc said. "That's okay, that's perfectly natural."

But didn't Doc have his doubts, too? Didn't he lie awake at night, listening to the snores of the others, wondering if maybe she wasn't coming after all; didn't he try to bury those thoughts, to tell himself to be patient, to withstand the test of these long years? Some nights, when he couldn't sleep, he would get up and take the Book from the wooden lectern Bashful had built for it, and he would go into the bathroom and sit on the toilet lid and read it again. *Once upon a time. She ate the apple, she fell.* The dwarves were there, in the story—they took care of her. The Book was a mess of half-pages, missing pages, the story erratic, interrupted. But some things were clear. A few powerful words shone forth, in large letters. There were faded illustrations that had once been bright: a man with an ax. A hand holding a huge, shining red apple. The stepmother and her mirror. But the page that might reveal *her*, that page was only a scrap, and all it showed was a short puffy white sleeve, and an inch of a pale arm, against which lay a heartbreaking curl of long, blue-black hair. So many mysteries, so many things they might never know. But in the end, on the very last page of the Book, the promise, the words that had given him such hope the first time he read them: *They lived happily ever after.* She and the dwarves, Doc thought, all of them together. She would come, and see that he had made things ready. She would take the pain that had always been with him, the great ache of loneliness at the center of his life, into her hands, like a trembling bird; she would sing to it, and caress it, and then with one gesture fling it into the sky. A flutter of wings and it would rise away from him forever.

"They don't buy any of your religious mumbo-jumbo," Grumpy said. "They're just too chickenshit to tell you. Well, I'm done, buddy boy. *Basta.*" He lifted his chin and scratched his stubble, glaring at Doc.

"Grumpy," Sleepy said. "Don't go."

"And my name isn't Grumpy," Grumpy said. "It's Carlos. I'm a Puerto Rican—" he paused "—*little person,*" he said. "I'm sick of all of you with your fake names and voodoo loser fantasies about some chick who ain't coming. She ain't coming, man. Get it through your fat heads."

No one looked at him. Grumpy stood up.

"All right then," he said. He went to the corner where he kept his sleeping bag, and picked it up. "Adios, you chumps. See you around."

Doc listened to his boots on the stairs. It doesn't matter, he told himself. It doesn't matter. She'll still come.

"A dwarf by any other name—" Happy said.

"Would still be an asshole," Sleepy said.

"My name used to be Steven," Sneezy said, and Sleepy told him to shut his fucking piehole.

It was a Friday afternoon in November, full of wind and rain, and everyone who came into Oz shook out their umbrellas and dripped water onto the yellow brick tiles in the foyer, and asked for one of the tables close to the big stone fireplace.

Doc was short-staffed. A waiter was out with the flu, and Bashful had left town on Tuesday to attend an aunt's funeral. On Thursday, he had called to say he might not be coming back, except to pick up a few of his things.

"Of course you're coming back," Doc had said.

"She left me some money," Bashful said. "Nobody thought she had any, she lived in this crummy little studio apartment and never bought a thing. Turns out she had stocks from my grandfather, and she left it all to me and her cat. I'm the trustee for the cat."

"You can't just take off."

"I want to live here for a while. See how things go. I'm sorry, Doc. This just seems like the right thing for me now."

A couple of men came into the restaurant, dressed in matching red parkas, their arms around each other. The first man's hair was blond and combed back off a perfectly proportioned face; the other man had a square jaw, outlined by a thin black beard, and when he shucked his parka Doc saw his chest and biceps outlined in a tight thermal shirt.

"Nasty weather out there," Doc said. He stepped down from his stool behind the podium to lead them to a table near the fireplace. He heard one man whisper something to the other, and the second's "Shh, he'll hear you." He was used to comments. On the street, teenagers yelled to him from passing cars. People stared, or else tried not to, averting their eyes and then casting furtive glances in his direction. Children walked right up to him, fascinated that he was their size, but different. He'd learned to block it out. But when the men were seated he walked away from them feeling a sudden, overwhelming rage.

Things were falling apart at home. At night he would sit on the couch, the Book on his lap, and read a few sentences aloud. In the old days, everyone would gather around, relaxing with cigarettes and beers, and maybe some dessert they'd brought back from the restaurant. But now they drifted away. To the kitchen, or up to the loft to turn on the TV and watch some inane show he could hear as he tried to focus on the words in the Book, the all-important words that were going to change their lives. That had changed Doc's life, given him hope. But now that hope was being drained away. One by one they were going to leave him. And she would never come, not to a lone dwarf. An old, balding dwarf whose feet and back hurt him every night so that he had to soak in a hot bath for some relief. She wouldn't take his gnarled, aching feet in her hands and massage them. In the black nights when he lay awake and empty, she wouldn't lay her long white body, smelling of apples, on top of his.

As the evening went on he forced himself to greet customers pleasantly, not to yell at Sleepy when he dropped a bus tray, or at Happy when he mixed up orders— Happy was usually a dishwasher, but he was filling in tonight for the absent waiter. Doc focused on keeping everything running smoothly, not letting it get chaotic. He let a German woman pull him onto her lap so her friends could take a picture with their cell phone, beaming the image to other friends in Stuttgart. He sang "Happy Birthday" with the other dwarves and handed a giant lollipop to a girl with a magenta buzz-cut and several facial piercings while her parents sat there with strained smiles on their faces, obviously uncomfortable that they found themselves with such a weird-looking daughter and were now confronted with several pseudo-munchkins in striped tights. By closing time he wanted to hit something. He took his time totaling up the evening's receipts, to give everyone time to finish up in the kitchen and leave him alone. Finally Sleepy, Happy, and Sneezy were finished and hovering around the office door.

"Just go," Doc said.

"What's the matter?" Happy said. "Is it me? I did my best. It's hard being a waiter. I never realized it was so hard, keeping everything straight."

"You did fine," Doc said.

"Do you really think so?" Happy looked thrilled.

"We'll wait for you," Sleepy said. "We can all share a cab."

"You guys go," Doc said.

"Cool, a cab," Sneezy said. "Here's something weird," he said. "Whenever I get in somebody's car, I make sure to buckle up. But in a cab, I never put on a seat belt. Isn't that weird?"

"You should," Doc said. He wanted to slap them. "Go," he said. "Just get the fuck out of here and leave me alone."

Sneezy and Happy stared. Sleepy pulled them each by a jacket sleeve. "Sure, man," Sleepy said. "No problem. You want to be alone, we'll leave you alone."

Finally they were gone. "Over the Rainbow" was playing softly on the stereo. Judy Garland's voice usually soothed him, but now Doc felt mocked by the promise in the song, the sappy land where dreams came true, the bluebirds and the bright colors everywhere, troubles melting away.

He locked the zippered bag of credit card slips and money into the safe. He switched off the stereo and straightened the stack of CDs beside it, then turned off the last of the lights. The alarm code had to be set by punching numbers into a keypad by the door that led from the kitchen to the alley; he was about to set it, but stopped. He walked back through the dark kitchen, out the swinging doors into the restaurant, and behind the bar, and took a bottle of Johnny Walker and a rocks glass.

At four A.M. the streets in this part of the city looked like a movie set about to be struck. The storefront businesses had mostly failed. Lights shone in the tall office buildings, where janitors were emptying wastebaskets and running vacuum cleaners. Doc knew what that was like; he'd done it, years ago, a flask in his back pocket that he'd drink from through the night, working under the fluorescent glare while everyone else slept. At dawn he'd be ready to pass out, and would reel off to find a hospitable bench or doorway. He'd forgotten the feeling of drunkenness, the happy, buzzy glow, how the world shifted pleasantly out of focus and retreated to a manageable distance. He staggered in the direction of the loft, clutching the bottle to his coat, hardly feeling the rain that was still falling, though not with its earlier force. Now it was soft, almost a mist, cold kisses on the top of his bare head, a damp chill coming up through his shoes.

He sang "Brown Eyed Girl" and "Swanee River." He stopped in the middle of the street and looked around to see if anyone had heard him, but there was no one. A cat slid away, around the corner of a building, pale against the dark bricks. He was breathing kind of hard, he realized. He stopped to rest in a small park, a square of grass with a single wrought-iron bench, a narrow border of dirt—mud, now—where there were white flowers in spring. He remembered the flowers, and looked sadly at the wet soil. No flowers. There would never be flowers again. It was never going to stop raining. The rain would wash away the soil, and the park, and himself; he would float down the river of rain, endlessly, until he sank beneath the surface of the water, down to the bottom like a rock, dead and inert, and finally at peace. He looked for his glass, to pour himself more liquor, but he had lost it somewhere. He had a vague memory of seeing it smash against bricks, the pieces, glittering like the rain, lying under a streetlight. He took a pull from the bottle and slumped against the freezing iron of the bench.

His dreams were confused: having his picture taken with tourists at the restaurant, only the restaurant was really an office building and their meals were being served on desks, and water was seeping through the carpet and he was down on his knees trying to find where it was coming from. When he woke he was lying on the wet grass, under a dripping tree. The rain had let up. It was getting light; the air was slate-colored. He was still slightly drunk, and could feel underneath the cushion of alcohol the hard, unyielding bedrock of a massive hangover. He got up and walked over to the bench, where the bottle was lying tucked under a newspaper like a tiny version of a homeless man. He picked up both and laid them gently in the wire trash receptacle next to the bench.

On the way home he passed a few actual homeless people, still asleep in doorways. He peered at each of them, but none of them was Grumpy. It had been nearly a month since he'd left, and no one had seen him. There was one dog, black and scrawny, that raised its head as Doc passed and then settled, sighing, next to its master.

He let himself into the building and trudged upstairs, stopping on each landing to catch his breath and stop the grinding in his head. He opened the door to the loft quietly, in case anyone was up. But it was too early. He could hear the steady snores of Happy and Sleepy, and Sneezy's asthmatic breathing. Dopey slept alone in the double bed, angled across it, one arm dangling out from the covers. Beside the bed were an overflowing ashtray, a box of wooden matches, and a litter of pistachio shells. Doc knelt down and scooped up the shells and threw them away in the kitchen. He went back and got the ashtray and matches, emptied the ashtray, put the box of matches on the shelf where they belonged. He rinsed a few dishes that were in the sink and set them in the dishwasher, then tidied up the counter—someone had apparently consumed a late-night snack of cereal and pretzels.

Someone had also brought home flowers. There were irises in a vase—a vase stolen from the restaurant, Doc noted—set on a cleared section of the counter. Around the main room were stalks of star lilies in quart beer bottles. On the coffee table, which had been cleaned off, was a Pyrex bowl of fruit—oranges and grapefruits and apples and a bunch of bananas—flanked by two candles that had burned down to stumps. Also on the table was a homemade card, featuring a drawing that looked like Sneezy's work. It was a pretty good likeness of Doc, and on the inside, in Happy's loopy script, *We Love You Doc* was written in blue across the yellow construction paper.

Doc took an apple and went to the row of windows. A few cars crawled by below, the first trickle of morning commuters, their headlights still on. Clouds hung over the city, gray and pearl smudges above gray buildings. There wasn't any glorious shaft of sunlight breaking through to set the thousands of windows glittering, or any rainbow arcing over the dense trees of the park at the far end of the city. There was no black-haired goddess, eyes dark and full of love, floating toward him. He polished the apple on his shirt. His was a small life. His head was barely higher than the windowsill, but he could see that out there, in the big world, there was nothing anymore to wish for.

JACK AND THE BEANSTALK[1]

James Finn Garner

ONCE UPON A TIME, ON A LITTLE FARM, THERE LIVED A BOY NAMED Jack. He lived on the farm with his mother, and they were very excluded from the normal circles of economic activity. This cruel reality kept them in straits of direness,

---

1 From *Politically Correct Bedtime Stories* (New York: MacMillan, 1994).

until one day Jack's mother told him to take the family cow into town and sell it for as much as he could.

Never mind the thousands of gallons of milk they had stolen from her! Never mind the hours of pleasure their bovine animal companion had provided! And forget about the manure they had appropriated for their garden! She was now just another piece of property to them. Jack, who didn't realize that nonhuman animals have as many rights as human animals—perhaps even more—did as his mother asked.

On his way to town, Jack met an old magic vegetarian, who warned Jack of the dangers of eating beef and dairy products.

"Oh, I'm not going to eat this cow," said Jack. "I'm going to take her into town and sell her."

"But by doing that, you'll just perpetuate the cultural mythos of beef, ignoring the negative impact of the cattle industry on our ecology and the health and social problems that arise from meat consumption. But you look too simple to be able to make these connections, my boy. I'll tell you what I'll do: I'll offer a trade of your cow for these three magic beans, which have as much protein as that entire cow but none of the fat or sodium."

Jack made the trade gladly and took the beans home to his mother. When he told her about the deal he had made, she grew very upset. She used to think her son was merely a conceptual rather than a linear thinker, but now she was sure that he was downright differently abled. She grabbed the three magic beans and threw them out the window in disgust. Later that day, she attended her first support-group meeting with Mothers of Storybook Children.

The next morning, Jack stuck his head out the window to see if the sun had risen in the east again (he was beginning to see a pattern in this). But outside the window, the beans had grown into a huge stalk that reached through the clouds. Because he no longer had a cow to milk in the morning, Jack climbed the beanstalk into the sky.

At the top, above the clouds, he found a huge castle. It was not only big, but it was built to larger-than-average scale, as if it were the home of someone who just happened to be a giant. Jack entered the castle and heard beautiful music wafting through the air. He followed this sound until he found its source: a golden harp that played music without being touched. Next to this self-actualized harp was a hen sitting on a pile of golden eggs.

Now, the prospect of easy wealth and mindless entertainment appealed to Jack's bourgeois sensibilities, so he picked up both the harp and the hen and started to run for the front door. Then he heard thundering footsteps and a booming voice that said:

"FEE, FIE, FOE, FUM,
"I smell the blood of an English person!
"I'd like to learn about his culture and views on life!
"And share my own perspectives in an open and generous way!"

Unfortunately Jack was too crazed with greed to accept the giant's offer of a cultural interchange. "It's only a trick," thought Jack. "Besides, what's a giant doing with such fine, delicate things? He must have stolen them from somewhere else, so I have every right to take them." His frantic justifications—remarkable for someone with his overtaxed mental resources—revealed a terrible callousness to the giant's personal rights. Jack apparently was a complete sizeist, who thought that all giants were clumsy, knowledge-impaired, and exploitable.

When the giant saw Jack with the magic harp and the hen, he asked, "Why are you taking what belongs to me?"

Jack knew he couldn't outrun the giant, so he had to think fast. He blurted out, "I'm not taking them, my friend. I am merely placing them in my stewardship so that they can be properly managed and brought to their fullest potential. Pardon my bluntness, but you giants are too simple in the head and don't know how to manage your resources properly. I'm just looking out for your interests. You'll thank me for this later."

Jack held his breath to see if the bluff would save his skin. The giant sighed heavily and said, "Yes, you are right. We giants do use our resources foolishly. Why, we can't even discover a new beanstalk before we get so excited and pick away at it so much that we pull the poor thing right out of the ground!"

Jack's heart sank. He turned and looked out the front door of the castle. Sure enough, the giant had destroyed his beanstalk. Jack grew frightened and cried, "Now I'm trapped here in the clouds with you forever!"

The giant said, "Don't worry, my little friend. We are strict vegetarians up here, and there are always plenty of beans to eat. And besides, you won't be alone. Thirteen other men of your size have already climbed up beanstalks to visit us and stayed."

So Jack resigned himself to his fate as a member of the giant's cloud commune. He didn't miss his mother or their farm much, because up in the sky there was less work to do and more than enough to eat. And he gradually learned not to judge people based on their size ever again, except for those shorter than he.

POETRY AND LYRICS

THE FAIRY TALE IS FIRST AND FOREMOST A SHORT STORY AND THERE-
fore a prose form. It is true that the tale has on occasion been versified, generally
with the notion of making it more suitable for children—although whether lines
such as

> Bags of gold and silver Jack took
> home, but still his mind did lean
> Towards another prize and journey
> up the lucky stalk of bean ... [1]

really engage the young imagination is up for debate. In fact, there have been very
few successful attempts to transpose the classic fairy tales into poetic form. Creative
energy has been much more directed at *responding to* the tale and its world, as the
poet reaps a harvest of meaning and memory bound up in our experience of fairy
tale, whether it is from childhood or recent rediscovery.

It follows that a retrospective view such as this would generally be directed at
the older reader, but we cannot deny that the young reader also is well-served by
the work of Roald Dahl, whose exuberant wit in *Revolting Rhymes* (1982) reminds
us that a clever parody is funny at any age—and is often better poetry than the
original. The book is unquestionably written for children, but Dahl is too good
a writer to make that an excuse for compromise; there is a crispness and verve

---

1   Walter Crane, *Jack and the Beanstalk* (London: George Routledge and Sons, 1875).

to his language that pleases at any age, and in "The Three Little Pigs" he seizes the opportunity to flex his intertextual muscles by having the third little pig put a call into the battle-hardened Little Red Riding Hood for help in solving his wolf-related problems. In the Dahlian universe, however, things tend not to work out as one expects: this young lady has developed an eye for fashion as well as a means for acquiring it. The mood is simultaneously jolly and bloodthirsty, a combination that most children find irresistible.

Another writer whose appeal defies easy categorization is Shel Silverstein, whose book *The Giving Tree* (1964) achieved iconic status among those who came of age in the Sixties, exemplified in the "hippie generation." In reaction to what was seen as a belligerent and materialistic Establishment, many young people were drawn to the escapist appeal of other "worlds," whether geographical, religious, or perceptual. As a result, the concept of the child and, by extension, the fairy tale attained a whole new level of popularity; to embrace fantasy, in whatever form, was to reject a society obsessed with the acquisition of wealth and power. In this context, Silverstein's characteristic combination of whimsy and hipness in "Mirror, Mirror" (1996) is incisive; beneath its deceptive simplicity, his purpose is to suggest the ruthlessness that goes hand-in-hand with narcissism. Magic though he may be, the mirror doesn't stand a chance.

In general, however, fairy-tale poetry is characteristically ironic in tone as befits a contemporary form that is based on stories stemming from a very different time. The nature of that irony has itself evolved along with our view of the fairy tale, as we have brought ourselves to confront the moral ambiguity and cruelty that is obviously inappropriate in children's literature. One favored approach is to arbitrarily place a familiar tale or character in a modern cultural context, which is what Tim Seibles does in "What Bugs Bunny Said to Red Riding Hood" (1999).[1] At first glance, one might assume that such a meeting between these popular icons would be exclusively for the amusement of the child-reader (although this is a poem designed to be *heard*!), but that is not the case. Seibles uses the slangy street smarts that we so readily associate with Bugs Bunny to point out the foolish naiveté of Red Riding Hood's journey through the forest ("You want friendly you better / try Detroit"). The tone is sassy but also ambiguous; we are reminded that as a member of the Ancient Brotherhood of Tricksters, Bugs Bunny may well represent the fire after the frying-pan ...

There is a collision of worlds in Katharyn Howd Machan's "Hazel Tells Laverne" (1981) as well, but to very different effect. In Seibles's poem, one fantasy-figure meets

---

1 Seibles is surely exploiting popular culture's propensity for self-reference in that Bugs Bunny is no stranger to the tale, having starred in the *Merrie Melodies* cartoon "Little Red Riding Rabbit" (Warner Bros, 1944).

another, whereas in "Hazel tells Laverne" the creative spark is generated by friction between fantasy and reality. Machan confronts this credibility gap and exploits its comic absurdity in order to show just how un-fairy-tale-like the real world can be. Like Seibles, Machan works hard to give her narrator a distinctive voice; who Hazel is plays an important part in what the poem has to say. The well in a palace garden is indeed a far cry from the toilet in a Howard Johnson's ladies' room—and Hazel is under no illusions about kissing a frog or becoming a princess.

It is fair to say that in English-speaking culture at least, poetry has long been an interest of the few rather than the many, but the opposite is true in the case of the popular song, particularly since options for its dissemination have grown so exponentially. Like poetry, the song lyric and its cousin, the ballad, have been around for a long time, often claiming oral origins similar to the traditional folktale. As the form more attuned to narrative, the ballad contains frequent references to fairies, doubtless because they are magical beings and the human experience of mysteries such as love, fate, and the unknown has often been expressed in terms of magic and enchantment. It is intriguing to note that in modern usage the term "ballad" has come to signify "a popular song especially of a romantic or sentimental nature,"[1] again suggesting threads of continuity in popular culture that reach back several hundred years.

The presence of fairies in song, however, does not mean the presence of fairy *tales*. That is a much more recent phenomenon that derives in large part from Disney's adaptations of the last century. As we have already noted, some of the lyrics that were written for these movies have left a lasting impression on generations of children—and perhaps adults, too. This is partly due to Disney's marketing acumen: the music to *Snow White* was the first time a movie soundtrack was issued commercially, which ensured its widespread popularity. The theme songs from this first wave of fairy-tale animations[2]—*Snow White* (1937), *Pinocchio* (1940), *Cinderella* (1950), and *Sleeping Beauty* (1959)—established the characteristic Disney association of dreams with wishes. The rest, as they say, is history. It would be another 30 years, however, before the second wave, sometimes referred to as the Disney Renaissance, re-established the studio's hold on the fairy-tale melody. Songs from *The Little Mermaid* (1989) and *Beauty and the Beast* (1991), by Alan Menkin (composer) and Howard Ashman (lyrics), were even more successful, winning many Golden

---

1 *The American Heritage Dictionary of the English Language,* 4th ed. (New York: Houghton Mifflin, 2000; updated in 2009), <http://www.thefreedictionary.com>.

2 While *Pinocchio* is not in the strict sense a fairy tale, it certainly belongs to that select group of literary fantasies (including such works as *The Wonderful Wizard of Oz* and *Peter Pan*) that aspire to that status.

Globe, Grammy, and Academy awards. Their performance by well-known artists[1] at the globally televised Grammy and Oscar presentations further ensured that "A Tale as Old as Time" was heard and remembered by millions around the globe.

Implicit evidence of the impact of what we may term the Disney vision is to be found in the lyrics to Anita Baker's song "Fairy Tales" (1990). It is worth noting that Baker, an award-winning rhythm and blues/soul/jazz singer and songwriter, was born in 1958, which would mean that she grew up at a time when Disney's influence was at its height. The experience of a mother's fantasy-filled promises of a "happily ever after" life for her daughter being shattered by events in the real world has surely been common to many girls growing up during the past 80 years. By contrast, the disillusionment that fills Sara Bareilles's pop-song "Fairytale" (2004) can be seen as a measure of the feminist rejection of any role based on passivity and subservience. Like many modern adapters of fairy tale, Bareilles[2] emphasizes character over story, although of all the renowned females mentioned, only Cinderella and her problem with alcohol is completely outside her original context. Whereas Baker's lyrics focus on the shock of discovering the discrepancy between fantasy and reality, Bareilles, as a younger woman (b. 1979), is ready to seek a solution: "the story needs some mending and a better happy ending ..."

While *extent* of reference varies widely, sometimes being little more than use of the term "fairytale," as in "fairytale wedding," the fact remains that a number of pop stars including Taylor Swift ("Today Was a Fairytale"), Justin Bieber ("Fairytale"), Toni Braxton ("Fairy Tale"), and Tori Amos ("A Sorta Fairytale") have chosen to record songs that for the most part draw on that resilient romantic aspect that Baker dismisses; in a very different vein is "A Gangsta's Fairytale" (1990), by the rapper Ice Cube, whose lyrics satirize fairy-tale characters in a savage portrait of inner-city life. Finally, to underline the fairy tale's international popularity, we must add that in 2009 a Norwegian by the name of Alexander Rybak won the venerable Eurovision Song Contest with the highest point tally in the history of the contest with a song entitled "Fairytale."

---

1 Celine Dion's rendition (with Peabo Bryson) of the theme song from *Beauty and the Beast* is regarded by many in the music industry as having established her career.

2 Bareilles came to prominence in 2007 with her hit single "Love Song"; she has since been nominated three times for a Grammy award.

THE THREE LITTLE PIGS[1]

Roald Dahl

The animal I really dig
Above all others is the pig.
Pigs are noble. Pigs are clever,
Pigs are courteous. However,
Now and then, to break this rule,
One meets a pig who is a fool.
What, for example, would you say
If strolling through the woods one day,
Right there in front of you you saw
A pig who'd built his house of STRAW?
The Wolf who saw it licked his lips,
And said, "That pig has had his chips."

"Little pig, little pig, let me come in!"
"No, no, by the hairs on my chinny-chin-chin!"
"Then I'll huff and I'll puff and I'll blow your house in!"

The little pig began to pray,
But Wolfie blew his house away.
He shouted, "Bacon, pork and ham!
"Oh, what a lucky Wolf I am!"
And though he ate the pig quite fast,
He carefully kept the tail till last.
Wolf wandered on, a trifle bloated.
Surprise, surprise, for soon he noted
Another little house for pigs,
And this one had been built of TWIGS!

"Little pig, little pig, let me come in!"
"No, no, by the hairs of my chinny-chin-chin!"
"Then I'll huff and I'll puff and I'll blow your house in!"

---

1 From *Revolting Rhymes* (New York: Puffin, 1995).

The Wolf said, "Okay, here we go!"
He then began to blow and blow.
The little pig began to squeal.
He cried, "Oh Wolf, you've had *one* meal!
"Why can't we talk and make a deal?"
The Wolf replied, "Not on your nelly!"
And soon the pig was in his belly.
"Two juicy little pigs!" Wolf cried,
"But still I am not satisfied!
"I know full well my Tummy's bulging,
"But oh, how I adore indulging."

So creeping quietly as a mouse,
The Wolf approached another house,
A house which also had inside
A little piggy trying to hide.
But this one, Piggy Number Three,
Was bright and brainy as could be.
No straw for him, no twigs or sticks.
This pig had built his house of BRICKS.
"You'll not get *me*!" the Piggy cried.
"I'll blow you down!" the Wolf replied.
"You'll need," Pig said, "a lot of puff,
"And I don't think you've got enough."
Wolf huffed and puffed and blew and blew.
The house stayed up as good as new.
"If I can't blow it *down*," Wolf said,
"I'll have to blow it *up* instead.
"I'll come back in the dead of night
"And blow it up with dynamite!"
Pig cried, "You brute! I might have known!"
Then, picking up the telephone,
He dialled as quickly as he could
The number of Red Riding Hood.

"Hello," she said. "Who's speaking? *Who?*
"Oh, hello Piggy, how d'you do?"
Pig cried, "I need your help, Miss Hood!
"Oh help me, please! D'you think you could?"

"I'll try, of course," Miss Hood replied.
"What's on your mind?" … "*A Wolf!*" Pig cried.
"I know you've dealt with wolves before,
"And now I've got one at my door!"
"My darling Pig," she said, "my sweet,
"That's something *really* up my street.
"I've just begun to wash my hair.
"But when it's dry, I'll be right there."
A short while later, through the wood,
Came striding brave Miss Riding Hood.
The Wolf stood there, his eyes ablaze
And yellowish, like mayonnaise.
His teeth were sharp, his gums were raw,
And spit was dripping from his jaw.

Once more the maiden's eyelid flickers.
She draws the pistol from her knickers.
Once more, she hits the vital spot,
And kills him with a single shot.
Pig, peeping through the window, stood
And yelled, "Well done, Miss Riding Hood!"

Ah, Piglet, you must never trust
Young ladies from the upper crust.
For now, Miss Riding Hood, one notes,
Not only has *two* wolfskin coats,
But when she goes from place to place,
She has a PIGSKIN TRAVELLING CASE.

MIRROR, MIRROR[1]

Shel Silverstein

QUEEN:
Mirror, mirror on the wall.
Who is the fairest of them all?

MIRROR:
Snow White, Snow White, Snow White—
I've told you a million times tonight.

QUEEN:
Mirror, mirror on the wall,
What would happen if I let you fall?
You'd shatter to bits with a clang and a crash,
Your glass would be splintered—swept out with the trash,
Your frame would be bent, lying here on the floor—

MIRROR:
Hey ... go ahead, ask me just once more.

QUEEN:
Mirror, mirror on the wall.
Who is the fairest of them all?

MIRROR:
You—you—It's true
The fairest of all is you—you—you.
(Whew!)

---

1 From *Falling Up* (New York: HarperCollins, 1996).

WHAT BUGS BUNNY SAID TO RED RIDING HOOD[1]

Tim Seibles

Say, good lookin, what brings you out thisaway
amongst the fanged and the fluffy?
Grandma, huh?
Some ol bag too lazy to pick up a pot, too feeble
to flip a flapjack—
and you all dolled up like a fire engine
to cruise these woods?

This was your **mother's** idea?
She been livin in a *CrackerJack* box or somethin?
This is a tough neighborhood, mutton chops—
you gotchur badgers, your wild boar, your
hardcore grizzlies   and lately,
this one wolf's been actin pretty big and bad.

I mean, what's up, doc?
Didn anybody ever tell you it ain't smart
to stick out in wild places?
Friendly? You want friendly you better
try Detroit. I mean
you're safe wit me, sweetcakes,
but I ain't a meat-eater.

You heard about Goldie Locks, didn'cha? Well,
didn'cha? Yeah, well, little Miss Sunshine—
little Miss *I'm-so-much-cuter-than-thee*—
got caught on one of her sneaky porridge runs
and the Three Bears weren't in the mood:
so last week the game warden nabs baby bear
passin out her fingers to his pals.

That's right. Maybe your motha should
turn off her soaps, take a peek at a newspaper,

---

1 First appeared in *Hammerlock* (Cleveland, OH: Cleveland State UP, 1999), © 1999 by
Tim Seibles, reprinted by permission of the author.

turn on some cartoons, for Pete's sake:
this woyld is about teeth, bubble buns—who's bitin
and who's gettin bit. The noyve a'that broad
sendin you out here lookin like a ripe tomata.
Why don't she just hang a sign aroun your neck:
Get over here and bite my legs off!
Cover me wit mustid—call me a hotdawg!

Alright, alright, I'll stop.
Listen, Red, I'd hate for somethin unpleasant
to find you out here all alone. Grandma-shmandma—let'er call *Domino's*.
They're paid to deliver. Besides, toots,
it's already later than you think—
get a load a'that chubby moon up there.

Ya can't count on Casper tanight either.
They ran that potata-head outta town two months ago—
tryin to make friends all the time—
he makes you sick after awhile.
Look, Cinderella, I got some candles and some
cold uncola back at my place—whaddaya say?

Got any artichokies in that basket?

HAZEL TELLS LAVERNE[1]

Katharyn Howd Machan

last night
im cleanin out my
howard johnsons ladies room
when all of a sudden
up pops this frog
musta come from the sewer
swimmin aroun an tryin ta
climb up the sida the bowl
so i goes ta flushm down
but sohelpmegod he starts talkin
bout a golden ball
an how i can be a princess
me a princess
well my mouth drops
all the way to the floor
an he says
kiss me just kiss me
once on the nose
well i screams
ya little green pervert
an I hitsm with my mop
an has ta flush
the toilet down three times
me
a princess

---

1 First appeared in *Rapscallion's Dream*, Vol. 1 (November 1981), © 1977 by Kathryn Howd Machan, reprinted by permission of the author.

FAIRY TALES[1]

Anita Baker

I can remember stories, those things my mother said
She told me fairy tales before I went to bed
She spoke of happy endings then tucked me in real tight
She turned my night light on and kissed my face good night

My mind would fill with visions of perfect paradise
She told me everything, she said he'd be so nice
He'd ride up on his horse and take me away one night
I'd be so happy with him, we'd ride clean out of sight
She never said that we would curse, cry and scream and lie
She never said that maybe, someday he'd say goodbye

The story ends, as stories do
Reality steps into view
No longer living life in paradise
Of fairy tales, no

She spoke about happy endings, of stories not like this
She said he'd slay all dragons, defeat the evil prince
She said he'd come to save me, swim through the stormy seas
I'd understand the story, it would be good for me
You never came to save me, you let me stand alone
Out in the wilderness, alone in the cold

My story ends, as stories do
Reality steps into view
No longer living life in paradise
No fairy tales, yes

I don't look for pie up in the sky, baby
Need reality, now, said I
Don't feel the need to be pacified, don't cha try

---

1   Anita Baker, Vernon Fails, James McBride, and Michael Powell, "Fairy Tales," Elektra
    Records, 1990.

Honey, I know you lied

You never came to save me, you let me stand alone
Out in the wilderness, alone in the cold
I found no magic potion, no horse with wings to fly
I found the poison apple, my destiny to die
No royal kiss could save me, no magic spell to spin
My fantasy is over, my life must now begin

My story end, as stories do
Reality steps into view
No longer living life in paradise
No fairy tales, hey, hey
Oh, Lord

FAIRYTALE[1]

Sara Bareilles

Cinderella's on her bedroom floor
She's got a
Crush on the guy at the liquor store
'cause Mr. Charming don't come home anymore
And she forgets why she came here
Sleeping Beauty's in a foul mood
For shame she says
None for you dear prince, I'm tired today
I'd rather sleep my whole life away than have you keep me from dreaming

[*Chorus:*]
'cause I don't care for your fairytales
You're so worried about the maiden though you know
She's only waiting on the next best thing

Snow White is doing dishes again cause
What else can you do
With seven itty-bitty men?
Sends them to bed and calls up a friend
Says will you meet me at midnight?
The tall blonde lets out a cry of despair says
Would have cut it myself if I knew men could climb hair
I'll have to find another tower somewhere and keep away from the windows

[*Chorus*]

Once upon a time in a faraway kingdom
Man made up a story said that I should believe him
Go and tell your white knight that he's handsome in hindsight
But I don't want the next best thing
So I sing and hold my head down and I break these walls round me
Can't take no more of your fairytale love

---

1   Sara Bareilles, "Fairytale," Tiny Bear Music, Sony/ATV Tunes LLC, 2004.

[*Chorus*]

I don't care
I don't care
Worry bout the maiden though you know
She's only waiting spent the whole life being graded on the sanctity of patience and
   a dumb
Appreciation
But the story needs some mending and a better happy ending
Cause I don't want the next best thing
No no I don't want the next best thing

THE COMIC BOOK AND THE GRAPHIC NOVEL

"Comic books are the Grimms' fairy tales of the popular culture."[1]

—Harlan Ellison

IF WE WERE TO SEEK OUT THE EARLIEST EXAMPLES OF THE FAIRY tale appearing in a style comparable to the comic book, we would look not in the illustrated versions that quickly followed the publication of the texts themselves but in what are termed "chapbooks" after the chapmen or traveling peddlers who sold these cheap booklets at country fairs and alehouses as far back as the seventeenth century. The chapbook was in fact an important part of the popular culture of the time, providing amusement for an increasingly literate rural population that would have been already familiar with these tales in their *oral* form; now they were available in print, accompanied by crude woodcuts that assisted the novice reader. This use of image to support the act of reading surely indicates a similarity to the modern comic book, regardless of the fact that the most popular comic books based on fairy tale are intended for adults. There is undeniably an element of *class* involved here; just as the chapbook was literature for the folk, the comic book was originally conceived as popular rather than literary art, although the new century

---

1   Harlan Ellison, *The Masters of Comic Book Art* (VHS video recording), Los Angeles: Rhino/WEA, 1987.

has seen it attain the status of an art form in its own right. It has certainly conquered the world; as David M. Kunzle points out, "The newspaper strip and comic book have become arguably the largest and most influential iconographic field in history."[1]

The appeal of the fairy tale to comic book artists (and, for that matter, to all who work in the visual media) is obvious: its world is external, in the sense that appearance is generally a clear indication of reality. Thus, beauty denotes goodness, ugliness signifies wickedness, and "thinks" is a verb rarely encountered. Then there is the memorable imagery at the heart of so many tales: Rapunzel's hair tumbling from her tower window, the candy-covered house in "Hansel and Gretel," and the fairy godmother's magical exploits in "Cinderella" provide unique challenges for the illustrator's mind's eye.

One of the most remarkable recent events in the evolution of the fairy tale is the renewed interest on the part of the adult reader. From the early years of the nineteenth century, when the Grimm brothers inadvertently became pioneers of a major branch of children's literature, the fairy tale has been perceived as the exclusive property of childhood. It's not easy to identify when and why the shift began, but one might point to the rebellious Sixties as a possibility: these were the years when no self-respecting student was without a copy of Tolkien's *Ring* trilogy, or C.S. Lewis's *Narnia Chronicles*, or an Arthur Rackham poster. Fantasy was respectable again—and in the last 50 years has become a tidal wave.

The adult reappropriation of the fairy tale is very visible in the comic book and graphic novel. Compare, for example, the simplicity of Will Eisner's approach in his version (Figure 1, 1999) of the Grimms' "The Frog King" with the darker, much more allusive world of Bill Willingham's *Fables*[2] (Figure 2, 2002). Eisner[3] stays relatively close to the original story, although he adds a prequel explaining how the prince was transformed into a frog in the first place. The mood of his retelling is bright and lively, emphasized by cheerful colors and a vivacious airhead of a princess—characteristics that lead one to conclude that Eisner is aiming squarely at the younger reader. Willingham's approach is in complete contrast. His stories are set in the real world—now New York, now the Cascade Mountains—but the central group of characters are a "who's who" of the fairy-tale world: Snow White,

---

1   David M. Kunzle, *Comic Strip: The Comics Industry*, <http://www.britannica.com>.

2   Bill Willingham's *Fables* (2002-present) is one of the longest running comic book series in the history of the medium and has won 14 Eisner Awards.

3   Will Eisner (1917-2005) is revered as a major figure in the coming of age of the comic book, both as a writer and theorist. He is credited with popularizing the term "graphic novel" since much of his later work was in this extended form, most famously *A Contract with God, and Other Tenement Stories* (1978).

Figure 1: *The Princess and the Frog* (1999), Will Eisner

Figure 3: *Grimm Fairy Tales: Hansel and Gretel* (2005), Joe Tyler and Ralph Tedesco

Figure 4: *The Big Book of Grimm: The Stubborn Child* (1999), Jonathan Vankin and Adam DeKraker

Figure 5: *Hansel and Gretel: The Graphic Novel* (2008), Donald Lemke and Sean Dietrich

Figure 6: *Rapunzel's Revenge* (2008), Shannon and Dean Hale, and Nathan Hale

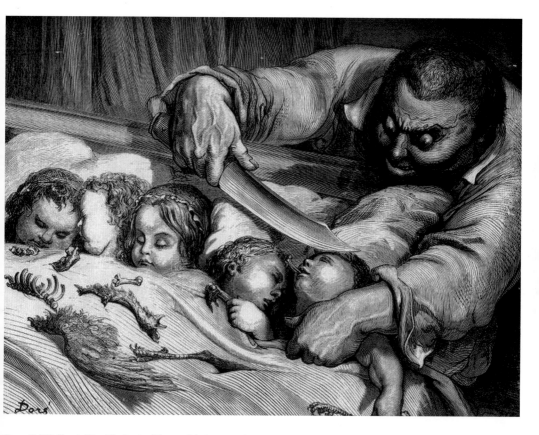

Figure 7: Little Thumb: "He cut the throats of his seven little daughters" (1867), Gustave Doré

Figure 8: The Frog King (1909), Arthur Rackham

Figure 9: Sleeping Beauty (1978), Michael Foreman

Figure 10: Little Red Riding Hood (1983), Sarah Moon

GIANT STORY

THE END

of the evil Stepmother

said "I'll HUFF and SNUFF and

give you three wishes."

The beast changed into

SEVEN DWARVES

HAPPILY EVER AFTER

for a spell had been cast by a Wicked Witch

Once upon a time

"That's your story?" said Jack.
"You've got to be kidding. That's not a
Fairly Stupid Tale. That's an Incredibly Stupid Tale.
That's an Unbelievably Stupid Tale. That is
the Most Stupid Tale I Ever— *awwwk!*"
The Giant grabbed Jack and dragged him to the next page.

Figure 11: The Stinky Cheese Man: Giant Story (1992), Jon Scieszka and Lane Smith

"How did you get to our house?"

ASKED THE DWARFS.

Snow White told them how her stepmother had tried to kill her and how the huntsman had spared her life. She had run all day long until she had arrived at their cottage.

Figure 12: Snow White (2012), Camille Rose Garcia

Figure 13: Born (2002), Kiki Smith

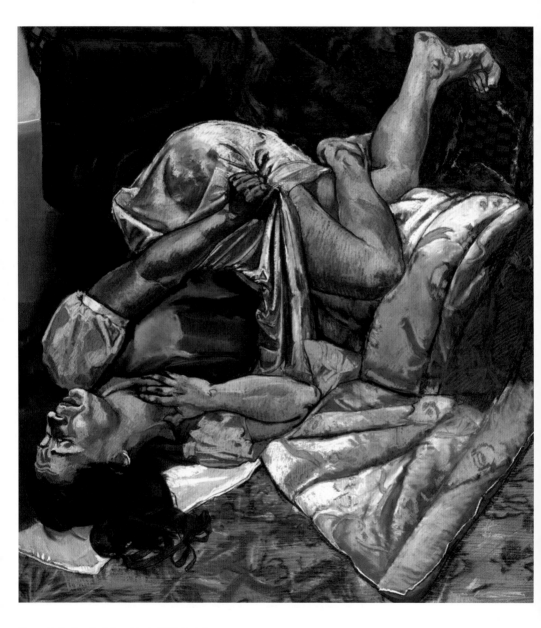

Figure 14: Swallows the Poisoned Apple (1995), Paula Rego

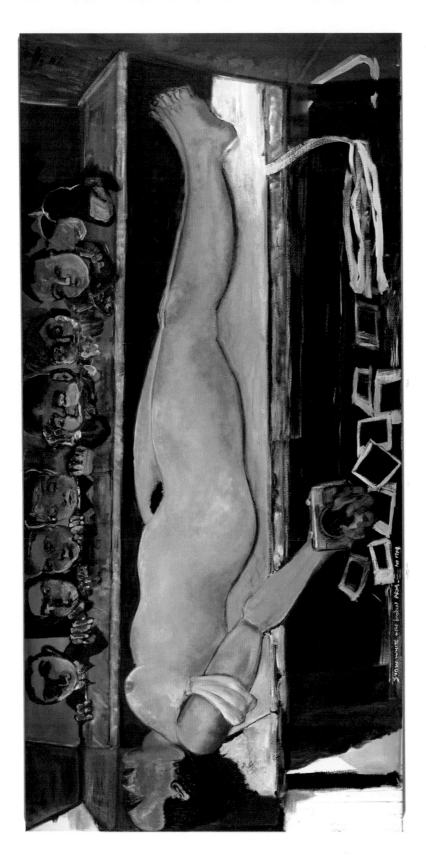

Figure 15: Snow White and the Broken Arm (1988), Marlene Dumas

Figure 16: Little Red Tender (2009), Unitas/RNL

Figure 17: Snow White: Anthropologie Catalogue Cover (2012), Diego Uchitel

Figure 18: Snow White: An Early Pregnancy Is No Fairy Tale (2010), Fuel

Figure 19: Rapunzel: Melissa Bedtime Stories (2007), BorghiErh

PANTENE ANTI-BREAKAGE SHAMPOO:

To demonstrate Pantene's claim of "Really Strong Hair" three Rapunzel-style stunts were staged in downtown Toronto - where live male climbers climbed three different oversized ponytails. On the ground, samples of Pantene Anti-Breakage Shampoo were handed out to curious onlookers. The stunt was performed over two days in Toronto, Canada.

Figure 20: Pantene Anti-Breakage Shampoo Promotional Event (2008), Grey Canada, Full Serve Productions

Figure 21: Cinderella Math Equations (2011), Revolve

Figure 22: Little Red Riding Hood: It's Another Story (2007), Miami Ad School/ESPM

Cinderella, Goldilocks, Bluebeard, Prince Charming—and Bigby Wolf (as in Big Bad Wolf), arguably Willingham's most intriguing character, who is surely based on the mythology surrounding the actor Humphrey Bogart, particularly in his role as Dashiel Hammett's chain-smoking private eye, Sam Spade. Willingham has also solved the problem of the relative obscurity of male "stars" in the Western fairy-tale canon by exploiting the Everyman versatility of the name "Jack" in the English language—from "jack of all trades" to "jack be nimble," from "Jack and Jill" to "Jack the Giant-Killer." In naming his character "Jack of Fables," Willingham is elevating him to quasi-mythic status as a Trickster—thereby uncovering a rich vein of stories for a new spinoff series.

Willingham's choice and expansion of the term "fable" as opposed to "fairy tale" is arguably to draw from a larger frame of reference. While fairy-tale characters remain the core of the adventures, many of the supporting cast are drawn from other classic works of fantasy, such as *Alice's Adventures in Wonderland*, *Pinocchio*, and even *Animal Farm*, not to mention personifications of Nature (North Wind, Jack Frost) and nursery-rhyme characters (Mary Mary Quite Contrary, Little Boy Blue). It is quickly apparent, however, that the female characters in particular bear little resemblance to their originals—or, more accurately, to their depiction in the nineteenth-century texts that we tend to regard as original—and even less to the Disney versions that were so influential in the last century. The innocent damsels-in-distress of yesteryear have been transformed into sophisticated and sensual women who are as ambitious and often as devious as their male counterparts: Snow White is now an unusually glamorous municipal administrator, while Goldilocks has been transformed into a voluptuous psychopath! The frame-story whereby Willingham binds these elements together is both ambitious and ingenious: the fairy-tale world is threatened by the forces of the mysterious Adversary, which is in essence a version of the age-old struggle between Reason and Imagination. Despite the vigor and inventiveness of the narrative, however, we may feel that the connection with the world of fairy tale is often tenuous. By simply adopting the names of classic fairy-tale characters, Willingham is investing his own creations with a power and mystique that they have not earned, although the ongoing popularity of *Fables* suggests that he has re-energized them in their radically different *milieu*. His views on fairy tales and their adaptation are revealing:

> The thing that moved me toward fairy-tale stories: One, it's a group of characters and stories that we all own. Every single person in the world owns all of these characters and stories outright. We're all born with an inheritance that we can take advantage of. I think those of us who are doing fairy-tale-based stories are the ones who are sort of cashing in on our inheritance … You do

not have to get anyone's permission to do a new version of *Snow White*, for example. And we're social people. We get ideas from each other.[1]

The characterization, the diction (sometimes complex, often salty), and the explicit sexuality in Willingham's *Fables* make it clear that these comic books are intended for an adult readership. The Zenescope tales, written by Joe Tyler and Ralph Tedesco (Figure 3, 2005), offer similar ingredients but lack the elaborate frame-story structure of the *Fables* series and rely on a stronger dose of spectacular bosoms and lurid violence to achieve their moral ends. Here, too, the contemporary world exists side-by-side with the fairy-tale world, in this instance presided over by the glamorous and mysterious professor Dr. Sela Mathers, who lectures on topics such as "Fairy Tales, Reality behind the Fantasies?" and provides guidance to her students in a manner that is part psychologist and part Mother Goose, thus giving a clear hint as to one of the ways in which these versions have been "modernized." We are told on the back cover that the volume "… explores a much darker side of the infamous fables you heard as a child as these classic tales are retold and re-imagined with a terrifying twist you'll simply love as an adult." Startling though the blurb and the images may be, what we actually encounter here are tales that have been adapted to deal directly with issues such as sex or the demands of personal relationships; while Charles Perrault might not appreciate the analogy, there is a similarity of intent to the Morals that he appended to his tales back in the seventeenth century. In both cases, there is a desire to underline the *relevance* of these tales in helping us deal with the problems of our own lives.

It is intriguing that three new comic book series all focus on female characters. Two, *Cinderella*[2] and *Fairest*,[3] are spinoffs from the highly successful *Fables* series, the latter describing itself as "Balancing horror, humor and adventure, *Fairest* … explores the secret histories of Sleeping Beauty, Rapunzel, Cinderella, The Snow Queen, Thumbelina, Snow White, Rose Red, and many other characters from *Fables*." *Damsels* introduces itself in strikingly similar fashion: "Cinderella, Sleeping Beauty, The Little Mermaid, and Snow White come together with other damsels in a new adventure filled with danger and intrigue. In *Damsels*, the alluring princesses of classic fairy tales take up arms to save their kingdoms from war …"[4] It is difficult

---

1   "Fable Master: Bill Willingham Modernized Fairy Tales before Modernizing Fairy Tales Was Cool," *Willamette Week* (April 24, 2013), <http://www.wweek.com/portland/article-20556-fable_master.html>.

2   Chris Robertson and Shawn McManus, *Cinderella: Fables Are Forever* (New York: DC Comics, 2012-present).

3   Bill Willingham and Phil Jimenez, *Fairest* (New York: Vertigo, 2012-present).

4   Leah Moore and John Reppion (writers), Aneke and J. Scott Campbell (artists), *Damsels* (Dynamite Entertainment, 2012-present).

to resist the conclusion that the comic book is just discovering the exploitability of militant feminism, although it's quickly apparent that these characters owe much more to *Victoria's Secret* than to the Brothers Grimm.

Unlike the *Fables* or the Zenescope series, *The Big Book of Grimm* (Figure 4, 1999) contains generally accurate retellings of Grimm tales (52 in all), albeit in a more contemporary idiom. There are, however, several features that make it an interesting volume. The principle governing the choice of tales is made clear on the front cover: "Truly scary fairy tales to frighten the whole family!" While popular classics such as "Cinderella" and "Sleeping Beauty" are included (not that even these are lacking their scary moments), the selection includes many less familiar tales that reveal the dark side of the Grimms' collection; while the brothers may have been concerned to censor the sexual content of their tales, the evidence suggests they were less bothered by the violence and *grotesquerie*. The sections into which the book is divided are themselves revealing; titles such as "Family Hell," "Prisoners of Childhood," or "Nuptial Nightmares" suggest a view of life at some distance from that deemed suitable for the child. This emphasis on violence is of course exploited by the fact that it is made *visual*; the reader must deal simultaneously with unexpected content and disturbing image—which brings us to the second intriguing aspect of this collection: the fact that each tale is illustrated by a different artist. This variety is surely comparable to the individual "voices" of different storytellers, each of whom has an idiosyncratic vision of the world. Thus, as readers move from tale to tale, they must adjust to the style of narration, subconsciously assessing how effectively the images illuminate the story.

Oddly enough, fairy-tale comic books for younger readers are not thick on the ground; in the glory days of comic book development,[1] the subject matter was limited to superheroes and humor. While it must be acknowledged that Will Eisner's *The Princess and the Frog* is the only fairy tale in his body of work, Pulitzer Prize winner[2] Art Spiegelman has actively espoused the comic book's potential for encouraging children to read. With his wife, Françoise Mouly, he has produced *Little Lit: Folklore and Fairy Tale Funnies*[3] (2000), which he clearly wanted to be different from adult fairy-tale comics; the book's back cover proclaims "Comics—they're not just for grown-ups any more!" Elsewhere, he comments, "We didn't give [the artists] a vocabulary list, but we did say the stories shouldn't make references to

---

1 From the late 1930s to the early 1970s.

2 Awarded in 1992 for his graphic novel *Maus*, based on his father's experiences as a Holocaust survivor.

3 Art Spiegelman and Françoise Mouly (eds.), *Little Lit: Folklore and Fairy Tale Funnies* (New York: HarperCollins/Joanna Cotler Books, 2000). Spiegelman and Mouly later released a larger edition, *Big Fat Little Lit* (New York: Puffin, 2006).

passing fads and fancies in the media, and we asked them not to go into any mode that's ironic or cynical."[1] At this stage, such instructions seem positively quixotic, given the current predominance of the "fractured" (if not wholly reconstructed) fairy tale.

Comparable to Spiegelman's efforts is the series of "graphic novels" published by Stone Arch Books in which the tales are monitored both by a Librarian Reviewer and a Reading Consultant. Although "Hansel and Gretel" is a relatively familiar re-telling of the story, we can detect unmistakable evidence of the Japanese manga style in the graphic novel artwork (Figure 5, 2008) of Sean Dietrich. While the innocence and anxious state of the children provide some psychological justification, the exaggerated eye size (not to mention the unexpected hair color) has more to do with imposing the characteristics of an innovative and popular illustrative style on the world of fairy tale. This excerpt demonstrates how readily the tale can be adapted to the comic book format: the simple morality, the flatness of character, and the emphasis on sensational incident supply the graphic artist/writer with elements remarkably similar to those of the comic book. The merits of uniting text and image for the purpose of instruction as well as amusement are, of course, long-established; it is curious that in the case of the comic book, the recognition has been slower in coming. The fact is that these "easy reading" fairy-tale versions are for many children their first literary exposure to the world of fairy tales.

Although it is apparent that Shannon and Dean Hale intend their graphic novel-length *Rapunzel's Revenge* (Figure 6, 2008) and *Calamity Jack* (2010) for younger readers, they make use of techniques that are also to be found in similar material for older readers, such as Bill Willingham's *Fables*. For instance, the stories are freely adapted from the original (it would be more accurate to say they are *extensions* of the original) and provide a vivid example of intertextuality in the partnership of Rapunzel and Jack, both of whom have been reconceived as all-American characters: the manner in which Rapunzel uses her braids as whip or lasso surely puts an American reader in mind of Annie Oakley (1860-1926),[2] the legendary sharpshooter who toured with the equally legendary Buffalo Bill's

---

1 Christopher Monte Smith, Interview with Art Spiegelman, <http://www.indiebound. org/author-interviews/spiegelmanart>.

2 In the course of the story, we learn that Rapunzel's mother named her Annie in the first place. At the same time, the feisty and resourceful nature of our heroine can be traced as far back as Giambattista Basile's version of this story in *The Pentamerone* (1634-36)—providing a useful reminder that such dynamic qualities are by no means limited to male characters or to recent retellings.

Wild West Show. For his part, Jack[1] is identified as American Indian. Both tales have distinctly socio-political overtones; Rapunzel's tyrannical witch-mother is ruler of a military-industrial empire that she intends to bequeath to her suitably prepared "daughter," while Jack's giant adversary is now a ruthless robber baron living above it all at the top of a skyscraper.

That both characters are thus associated with the mythology of the Wild West is an indication that in many respects this is the quintessential American fairy-tale setting (Sergio Leone's classic movie *Once Upon a Time in the West* [1968] leaves no doubt about the connection). There is the same moral clarity about the forces of good and evil, the same tendency to correlate virtue and vice with physical appearance, even a similar attitude toward gender stereotyping, which the Hales work hard to avoid. The American flavor of these retellings is even to be found in the contrast between aridity and verdancy in *Rapunzel's Revenge*, which surely owes a debt both to John Ruskin's didactic fairy tale *The King of the Golden River* (1841) and L. Frank Baum's *The Wonderful Wizard of Oz* (1900). In each case, the harsh dryness of the landscape indicates the exploitative greed of the capitalist system that can only be remedied (made green and fruitful) by a more humanistic, compassionate vision. In both books, the Hales retain just enough elements of the original story to draw on the fairy-tale mystique, but—as with the *Fables* series—the characters have little connection with their predecessors beyond their names.

Postscript

In a synergy between creator and consumer that is surely the essence of popular culture, the Zenescope producers launched an appeal (in Spring 2012) encouraging their followers to contribute to the funds necessary to make a pilot for an animated series based on the *Grimm Fairy Tales* series. Over a period of six weeks, 1,174 people pledged a total of $188,970 (inspiring the company to raise their goal to $225,000).[2] We should also note a more conventional instance of the fairy tale being taken transmedia in the announcement of plans to turn the *Fables* series into a movie.[3]

---

1 If the title of the sequel is anything to go by, it seems that the Hales are particularly keen to establish their gender-equality credentials; Calamity Jane (1852-1903) was virtually a contemporary of Annie Oakley and, like her, something of a celebrity by virtue of her "manly" exploits.

2 <http://www.kickstarter.com/projects/212378023/grimm-fairy-tales-animated-series>.

3 <http://www.ign.com/2013/06/04/fables-movie-in-the-works-from-the-team-behind-harry-potter>.

ILLUSTRATION AND ART

AN ILLUSTRATOR IS AN ARTIST, BUT AN ARTIST IS NOT NECESSARILY
an illustrator. This is a conundrum we cannot avoid in a chapter that examines the
still (as opposed to the moving) image depiction of the fairy tale, since we will find
that the intent of the two types of artist is often quite different. In the case of the illustrator, it is reasonable to say that the tale is paramount; it is the illustrator's task to
depict key moments in the story with the purpose of enhancing the pleasure and understanding of the reader. This may not always occur, of course, since no two imaginations are alike, but even in disagreement, a richer conceptualization of the story
may well be achieved. By contrast, the artist's commitment is first and foremost to a
personal vision expressed through reference to a fairy-tale character or episode. In
effect, the artist annexes the popularity of the tale to suggest a connection between
the personal and the universal.

One of the most significant developments in the evolution of the fairy tale has
been the inclusion of illustrations. As we have seen, in its original form the fairy
tale was oral, which accounts for its unique qualities: the emphasis on action, the
absence of physical detail, and the quick movement from one event to the next, all
reflecting the priorities of not only the storyteller but also the illustrator (not to
mention the comic book artist or filmmaker). Although without a teller there is no
story, it can reasonably be argued that without pictures, the text alone is unlikely to
produce the vividness and specificity that can be found in an apposite image. However, given this "stripped-down" nature of the tale, both teller and illustrator have
ample opportunity to inject something of their own world as a means of bringing
new life to an old story.

We might in fact take the argument a step further by suggesting that as our culture has become so visually oriented, the illustration has come to dominate the word to the extent that certain climactic episodes in the classic fairy tales have achieved instant recognizability, not least because the stories are characteristically distilled into one or two key images. A red cloak or a beanstalk become emblematic of an entire tale, so embedded is it in the popular mind, and thus the part replaces the whole. As Sarah Bonner observes in an insightful article (see p. 161) "The text and image are intimately related, yet ... the image contains qualities that release interpretation from the strictures of tradition, making them more relevant and immediate in contemporary society."[1] Thus, an additional ingredient has been added to this dynamic mix in that the contemporary artist is often responding not only to the text but to the iconic image as well.

The earliest classic fairy-tale illustrations date back to the middle of the nineteenth century and are often of a nature that many modern parents would deem unsuitable for innocent eyes, which goes to show that at least one important question has been around for a long time: who are these pictures for anyway? The obvious answer is that they're for children, just like the fairy tales themselves—but that's where the complications begin. As we pointed out in the Introduction, these tales were not originally told to children; in these earlier times, children were not regarded as sufficiently distinct to warrant tales of their own. It could be said that the Brothers Grimm were simply in the right place at the right time; their scholarly interest in fairy tales just happened to coincide with a major shift in social attitudes toward childhood. Once they realized that the popularity of their tales was attributable to a brand new segment of the reading public, they edited them accordingly, in effect identifying the fairy tale as "children's literature." Much the same process took place with the illustrations. The early illustrators, unrestrained by any modern preconceptions about the child's impressionable mind, went about their task with vim and vigor; since such pictures were nevertheless intended for children's eyes, we must conclude that violence was regarded as a normal part of life, even for middle-class children. In other words, the illustrations reveal more than just the story; through the choices made by the artist, they provide a glimpse into the attitudes and preconceptions of their times. Compare, for example, the brutality of Doré's image (Figure 7, 1862) with the elegance and style typical of illustrations by artists such as Arthur Rackham (Figure 8, 1909) or Edmund Dulac, published some 50 years later.[2] In this

---

1 Sarah Bonner, "Visualizing Little Red Riding Hood," *Moveable Type* 2 (2006).

2 Because of the characteristic beauty of color and elegance of design in their work, artists such as Rackham, Dulac, and Kay Nielsen are associated with what is termed the Golden Age of Illustration (1880s to 1920s). One consequence of the rapid improvements in

respect, illustrators are no different from the storytellers or the fairy-tale compilers of the past who kept a careful eye on their audience, making sure that their material was suitably in tune with the times. As a result, the pictures that accompany fairy tales are often as much a mirror of their times as the tales themselves.

For contemporary illustrators, it is as if we have come full circle; the darker side of fairy tales is again being depicted after the benign neglect of most of the twentieth century. This time, however, the illustrators cannot claim ignorance of the probable effect of their images on the child-reader, so how is this new lack of constraint justified? In part, it has to do with society's ever-changing perception of childhood, but more important is the growing popularity of the belief that fairy tales are as much for adults as for children, and, consequently, illustrators need not censor or curtail their work accordingly. Some artists have been ingenious enough to find their own way around the problem by adapting the old adage "What you don't know can't hurt you." For instance, Michael Foreman's sly envisioning of the prince's assault on the hedge of thorns surrounding Sleeping Beauty's castle (Figure 9, 1978) would be far less effective (for the older reader, at least) if certain psycho-sexual theories of Sigmund Freud had not permeated our cultural consciousness!

Other illustrators, however, have produced pictures that would be more difficult to describe as suitable for children. In the case of Sarah Moon, for instance, the issue is straightforward; in choosing to see "Little Red Riding Hood" as dealing with issues such as sexual assault and death, it follows that her illustrations (Figure 10, 1983) would be correspondingly dark and threatening.[1] Locating the tale in a modern urban context and using the popular medium of photojournalism to illustrate the story momentarily frustrate the reader's expectations, but once the associative leap is made, the story's impact is irresistible, so striking and apposite is Moon's imagery. The city street as deep, dark forest; the cold inhumanity of the predator's car as wolf; the caught-in-the-headlights alarm of the little girl: these images are disturbing enough to send a shiver up the spine of an older reader since they capture so unerringly every parent's worst nightmare.

While Moon subverts the conventional reassurance of the fairy-tale format ("once upon a time" leading inevitably to "they all lived happily ever after") by radically relocating a classic tale, the challenge in Jon Szieszka and Lane Smith's *The*

---

color reproduction was to draw attention to the artists who were exploiting these innovations—and thereby making the case for illustrations to be judged as works of art in their own right. The image—often highly stylized and elaborate—took on a life of its own, as the artist indulged his aesthetic vision in a colorful escape from a black-and-white world.

1 Moon's decision to use Perrault's "Little Red Riding Hood" was surely deliberate; it is an oft-forgotten fact that his tale ends tragically, with the death of both the grandmother and Little Red Riding Hood.

Stinky Cheese Man (Figure 11, 1992) is of a totally different nature. A postmodern children's book that is a veritable deconstructor's guide, it cheerfully makes mince-meat of various classic fairy tales (e.g., "Little Red Running Shorts") while revealing the magic tricks involved in creating an imaginary world. ("Could you please stop talking in uppercase letters? It really messes up the page.") Nothing is sacred; narra-tor argues with character,[1] typeface takes on a life of its own, and the illustrations are a blend of collage and surrealism. Although he was referring primarily to fairy-tale movies, the culture critic James Poniewozik offered in 2007 an incisive judgement of the trend that *The Stinky Cheese Man* so clearly indicates: "This is the new world of fairy tales: parodied, ironized, meta-fictionalized, politically adjusted and pop-culture saturated."[2]

The integration of text and illustration is carried yet further by Camille Rose Garcia, bringing us, in a sense, a step closer to full circle, in that her text provides a visual equivalent to the teller's verbal emphasis. In her version of "Snow White" (Figure 12, 2012), overall design, in terms of aspects such as choice of font and size and color of letter, becomes as important to the narrative as the illustrations. Un-like Szieszka and Smith, Garcia has no interest in manipulating the text in order to amuse; on the contrary, her goal is to take the abstraction of the printed text and, through color, shape, and size, infuse it with the energy that its *meaning* contains. At the same time, her illustrations, which interweave a retro, post-Disney jingle with a disturbing, nightmarish jangle, can be seen as reflecting the markedly different ap-proaches to this tale.

The extensive illustration of the fairy tale, together with its wide dissemination through print and visual media, has not only ensured its survival as a staple of popu-lar culture but also attracted the attention of artists who, unencumbered by the text, are free to challenge the tale's prescribed meanings; as Bonner observes, "Fairy tales are re-used for their didactic value to illustrate and record shifts in cultural at-titudes."[3] It's worth noting that the three artists discussed here are all successful and committed—in their different ways—to a feminist perspective in their work. It may, of course, be objected that our selection was made to favor our argument, but as evi-dence in other sections of this book indicates, there can be little doubt that feminism

---

1 Drawing attention to the act of storytelling is a comic ploy also favored by the cartoonist Tex Avery, as in "Swing Shift Cinderella" (1945), where the characters halt the action to inform the "narrator" that they are bored with the same old story and want something new ... (see p. 115).

2 James Poniewozik, "The End of Fairy Tales? How Shrek and Friends Have Changed Children's Stories," *Time* (May 10, 2007) 44.

3 Bonner, "Visualizing Little Red Riding Hood."

has been the most creative force in the evolution of the fairy tale over the last 50 years, with psychology not far behind.

Kiki Smith is clearly attracted to popular images of religion and fairy tale, particularly from the perspective—at least in many of those tales that have established themselves as canonical within the Western tradition—of growing up female. At first glance, her lithograph *Born* (Figure 13, 2002) is immediately recognizable as a famous scene from *Little Red Cap* (the Grimms' more optimistic version of *Little Red Riding Hood*). On closer examination, however, it's clear that Smith is taking the familiar and reimagining it. The moment is apparently that of Little Red Cap's release from the belly of the wolf, but our attention is caught by the fact that there are *two* red-cloaked figures. Is the woman the mother or the grandmother—and why is she too wearing a hood and in a pose reminiscent of the Madonna? Where is the hunter who rescued them? What do we make of the expressions and gestures of child and (grand)mother, which show no hint of the mixture of horror and relief that we might expect, given the violence implied by the blood-stained cloaks and wolf? Smith has observed that, removed from the context of the fairy tale, the composition of the vertical figures of the women being born out of the stomach of the horizontal wolf reminded her of Botticelli's *Birth of Venus* and images of the Virgin Mary standing on a crescent moon.[1] That she chooses to depict the faces of both women as self-portraits further demonstrates the capacity of the fairy tale to convey layers of meaning, both personal and universal.

Paula Rego's art is also a continuing exploration of the female role: sexual, familial, social. Her perspective has surely been influenced by the cultural dissonance between a Portuguese upbringing and an English marriage and home. It should not surprise us, therefore, that her depiction of a notorious moment from "Snow White" (Figure 14, 1995) provokes an equally uncertain response. Once again, the artist, who acknowledges the influences of Walt Disney and the great Victorian illustrators in her art, is taking an image of almost iconic familiarity and making it strange by making it personal; can we doubt that this is a real-world Snow White in the banal surroundings of a living-room? There may be no sign of the infamous apple, and the woman depicted is neither young nor beautiful, but Rego provides clues in her clutching at her throat and, in an allusion to his cultural domination, the unmistakable Disney colors of her dress. Having raised our expectations, Rego then thwarts them, for in gazing at this entranced woman, we find ourselves very far from the reassuring world of Disney. We note a straining awkwardness in her legs and her other hand clutching her skirt, which Rego explains very succinctly in terms that

---

1 Wendy Weitman and Kiki Smith, *Prints, Books & Things* (NY: Museum of Modern Art, 2003) 38.

surely reflect her own Catholic upbringing: "Look, even when they fall, they cover their knickers so they don't show their bums. She's more worried about showing herself than having swallowed the apple and choking."[1] Indeed, is this Snow White a "fallen" woman?

In an observation that reflects the thinking of many contemporary artists and writers who have chosen to revisit the fairy tale, the South African/Dutch artist Marlene Dumas states, "I use religious subjects as I use fairy-tale figures, in order to give my audience an easy starting point, a popular reference that relates to all times and that is familiar to most people."[2] However, in her *Snow White* series, the "popular reference" is quickly challenged and subverted by the obvious changes she makes to the story ("Snow White and the Broken Arm," Figure 15, 1988). Why is her arm broken—and who broke it? Why has a mortuary slab replaced the iconic glass coffin? What is the purpose of the Polaroid camera and pictures? Is this fairy-tale heroine sufficiently aware of her status to want to record this timeless moment? In what was surely a prophetic insight, Dumas has replaced the magic mirror with the instant gratification camera, which, through our current obsession with social media, has created the narcissistic fascination with "selfies."[3] Thus Dumas's use of the fairy tale may be seen as a reversion to one of its most crucial functions: through the freedom of fantasy to cast "reality" in a new and even disturbing light, with the goal of jolting us out of our complacency.[4] She describes her approach with surprising candor in a poem (rather startlingly entitled "Pornokitsch"), published in an exhibition catalogue:[5]

> The use of the fairy-tale functions
> as a concealment, a veiling of intentions.
> The viewer feels at home with the story
> satisfied that he knows what it's about.
> However, this feeling can't last forever,
> because slowly, the inconsistency of the elements

---

1 Paula Rego, quoted in "Paula Rego: 'You Punish People with Drawings,'" *The Guardian*, August 22, 2009.

2 Quoted from display caption for *Magdalena 4*, <http://www.tate.org.uk/art/artworks/dumas>.

3 "[A]n act usually carried out by girls aged 12-21, [which] involves taking photos of one's self while posing ..." <http://www.urbandictionary.com/php?term=selfies>.

4 We noted the absence of the huntsman in Smith's representation of Little Red Cap; neither Rego nor Dumas give any hint that the Prince will appear to save Snow White; in fact, he may have already come ... and gone.

5 *The Question of Human Pink*, 1989.

begins to dawn.
It's an emphemistic [*sic*] technique. A sugary way
to clothe impure motives.
Negativity and anxiety disguised with childlike humour,
while the politico-sexual attitudes bleed through at the edges.

For centuries, storytellers entranced our forbears with stories—some familiar, some strange; part truth, part fiction. Today, artists capture our attention with images of the classic fairy tale that, while immediately recognizable, are often unsettling—and frequently lacking the reassurance that "they all lived happily ever after."

Postscript

This is as good a place as any to comment on the intriguing surge of interest in the tale "Snow White." Many factors contribute to the popularity of one fairy tale and the obscurity of another. Indeed, to analyze the common characteristics that have elevated a certain group of tales into "classics" is to discover some important truths about our values—past and present—as a society. Currently, it seems that "Snow White" has caught the popular imagination in literary retellings and movies, artworks and advertising. Although it could be argued that the tale's prominence dates from 1937, when Walt Disney made *Snow White and the Seven Dwarfs* his first full-length animation, it has only been in more recent years that the tale has attracted such a sustained response in a variety of media. The question naturally arises: What features in the story have sparked this enthusiasm? Is it the intense mother/daughter relationship, with its overtones of sexual rivalry? Or is it the villainy of the Queen-stepmother, so driven in her pursuit of Youth and Beauty? The relevance of such questions to our own lives is obvious; fairy tales persist because they are about us.

THE STAGE

Dramatic representation of the fairy world can be found as far back as the sixteenth century in such well-known plays as *A Midsummer Night's Dream* (1592) and *The Tempest* (1610-11) by William Shakespeare. To track down the presence of the fairy *tale* on stage, we must turn to the remarkable success of pantomime in Victorian England, which was largely based on the fairy tales of the Grimms, Perrault, Andersen, and the Arabian Nights. In pantomime, however, the fairy tale is subjected to irreverences such as slapstick and *double entendre*; while intended primarily as Christmas season entertainment for children, pantomime's typical ingredients clearly cater to the adults in the audience as well. Cross-dressing is an essential part of the fun: the prince is played by a young woman (the more curvaceous the better) and the wicked witch or "dame" by a man, preferably a stand-up comedian with a talent for the risqué. Like the tale on which it is based, pantomime belongs to popular culture; it is as if the strolling players and mummers of earlier folk tradition eventually gave up their itinerant ways for the comforts of a permanent theatrical base but retained the allusive, localized, ad-libbing nature of their performance that harks back to the oral nature of the traditional fairy tale. For instance, it is customary to invite audience participation in the action on the stage, be it booing the villain or shouting encouragement to the prince. Clearly, the pantomime version of the fairy tale bears little resemblance to the original, which is in effect reduced to a framework on which to hang topical references—preferably scandalous—to politicians, royalty, and the rich-and-famous. Many of these characteristics are still to be found in the contemporary "fractured" fairy tale, the connection being clearly acknowledged in the *Fractured Fairy Tale Musicals* that have been a feature of the Toronto festive season for more than 16 years and have welcomed stars from the National Ballet, the Stratford Shakespeare Festival, the World Wrestling Federation, and *Canadian Idol*.

Although it doesn't strictly fall within the definition of a fairy tale, there is good reason for us to take note of the stage production of J.M. Barrie's *Peter Pan* (1904). Few people today are aware that this famous fantasy actually started out as a play, well before Barrie published the novel version (1911) or Disney the animated version (1953). The fact is that the stage show was an ambitious, expensive, and much-anticipated event that in certain important respects drew inspiration from pantomime. The part of Peter Pan has always been played by a woman, and Barrie reached again into pantomime's bag of tricks at the point in the play when Tinker Bell is dying; the opening night audience (primarily consisting of London high society!) were encouraged to clap their hands if they believed in fairies, thereby saving her life. After a few moments of silence, a storm of clapping shook the theater, which saved Tinker Bell's life and probably *Peter Pan*'s, too.

Curiously enough, a fairy tale provides the inspiration for a production that marks the transition between pantomime and the musical—and in the process, shifts the spotlight from England to the United States. As its title suggests, *Mr. Cinders* (1929) is an inversion of the Cinderella story (a notion clearly derived from pantomime) in which the Prince Charming character is now a spirited and unconventional American heiress and "Mr. Cinders" is Jim, the mistreated adopted son of minor English aristocrats. At this distance, it seems that the characterization itself is an implicit acknowledgement of where the musical's future lies.

Despite playing to sold-out houses, especially from the 1940s to the 1960s (the musical's Golden Age), the audience was necessarily limited to those who could afford the price of a ticket. As a consequence of this fact, and reflecting the rise of television as the dominant source of entertainment, the successful team of Richard Rodgers and Oscar Hammerstein II were persuaded to write an original musical specifically for the medium.[1] Faced with this challenge at a time when anxieties surrounding the Cold War were at their height, it is significant that they chose to base the project on the escapist fairy-tale world of *Cinderella*. It is also telling that Julie Andrews, whose participation was key, was at that time starring in the Broadway production of *My Fair Lady*, which might also be described as a "Cinderella story." When the CBS network broadcast the show, on March 31, 1957, the audience was in excess of 100 million—more than 60 per cent of the entire population of the United States—a vivid demonstration of how effective television could be in

---

1 Just as the pantomime is native to England, it might be said that the musical was born and raised in the United States. Once the television networks achieved continental coverage, the medium was in place to disseminate this whole new dimension of popular culture.

bringing the fairy tale to the people. Not surprisingly, there have since been two sub-sequent television versions, not to mention numerous stage adaptations, the most recent of which opened on Broadway in 2013, to positive reviews. However, the *New York Times* critic puts his finger on the challenge faced by all contemporary fairy-tale adaptations when he noted, "the knotty problem of being both traditional and up to date in a culture that has no tone to call its own[:] ... this 'Cinderella' wants to be reassuringly old-fashioned and refreshingly irreverent, sentimental and snarky, sincere and ironic, all at once."[1]

One other fairy-tale musical deserves mention, for reasons rather different from the high-profile *Cinderella*. *Once Upon a Mattress*, based on Hans Christian Ander-sen's tale "The Princess and the Pea," started life at an adult summer camp in Penn-sylvania,[2] and its subsequent success appears to have had more to do with popular rather than critical acclaim. The adaptation emphasizes humor over romance; Carol Burnett played the suffering princess in the original Broadway production (1959) and, later, the prince's overbearing mother, Queen Aggravain, in the third television adaptation (2005) made for *The Wonderful World of Disney*. Its "quasi-pantomimic" charm ensures frequent staging by school and community theater groups, which is arguably the most significant aspect of the fairy tale on the stage; it is, after all, one of the most democratic of art-forms.

We come close to the end of the twentieth century to find the next major stage production based on fairy tales. Stephen Sondheim and James Lapine's musical *Into the Woods* (1986) owes a minor debt to the pantomime tradition but is undeni-ably darker and more ironic in tone. As is customary with some recent fairy-tale retellings, the show questions and hypothesizes, even as it entertains: the book is a complex interweaving of several well-known tales that challenges the audience to be constantly aware of the contrast between this plot and that of the original tales. The whimsy that Barrie was so adept at exploiting in *Peter Pan* is long gone; this may be a musical about fairy tales, but its content and design as an art form are clearly directed at adults. There is a pleasing sense of returning the fairy tale to its origi-nal setting in the ambitious revivals of *Into the Woods* that took place outdoors, first in London ("with the ever-inviting greenery of Regent's Park providing a natural backdrop that no amount of money and scenic ingenuity could buy"[3]) and then in New York ("Central Park at night, when the moon rises and the wild things roam ...

---

1   Ben Brantley, "Gowns from the House of Sincere and Snark: 'Rodgers and Hammerstein's Cinderella' at Broadway Theater," *New York Times*, March 3, 2013.
2   Ken Mandelbaum "DVDs: Many Moons Ago: Once Upon A Mattress," January 5, 2006, <http://www.broadway.com/buzz/10918/dvds-many-moons-ago/>.
3   Matt Wolf, "Playing Sondheim in the Woods," *New York Times*, August 24, 2010.

the ideal and inevitable setting for stories of nature enchanted"[1]). Inside or out, the show continues to attract audiences; 27 years after its debut, there are plans afoot for a movie version, prospectively starring Meryl Streep and Johnny Depp, to be made by Disney Studios.

Given their well-earned reputation for getting the most out of their products, it should come as no surprise to find Disney transforming a musical into a movie or vice versa, for that matter. The pattern was established early on in his career: adaptation of a familiar story containing fantasy and magic, clear delineation between good and evil characters, emphasis on action and on song and dance, all blended together in a spectacle that was Disney's trademark. The effectiveness of this formula in his studio's new wave of fairy-tale animations of the final decades of the twentieth century has spilled over to their stage adaptations, exemplified in the movie of *Beauty and Beast* (1991) being followed by the Broadway version (1994-2007), which, despite closing to make way for the stage version of *The Little Mermaid*, remains the eighth longest-running show in Broadway's history. Success seems assured as yet another Disney movie takes its place on the stage.[2]

In bringing our discussion up to current times, we once again take the liberty of looking beyond the borders of the classic fairy tale in noting that three of the most publicized and successful stage productions of the last few years have had that same "crossover" appeal that Barrie pioneered over 100 years ago. In 2003 came *Wicked*, a musical based on Gregory Maguire's novel of the same name (1995), inspired by L. Frank Baum's fantasy/fairy tale *The Wonderful Wizard of Oz* (1900),[3] which might in some respects be regarded as the American equivalent to *Peter Pan*. Testifying to the appeal of what we may term the "submerged" fairy tale is another movie, *Billy Elliott* (2000), turned into *Billy Elliott the Musical* (2005), with songs by Sir Elton John. At first glance, this story of a miner's son who aspires to be a ballet dancer appears unlikely material for such a transition; however, the story's underlying motifs of both "The Ugly Duckling" and "Cinderella" may offer some explanation for its success. As we have seen elsewhere, our "real" world is, much more than we may think, interwoven with threads of fantasy, as a means of helping us cope with the wear-and-tear of daily life. Might this not be why fairy tales are still around, after all these years?

---

1 Review of "A Witch, a Wish and Fairy Tale Agony," *New York Times*, August 9, 2012.

2 *Snow White* (1979), *Beauty and the Beast* (1994), *The Little Mermaid* (2007), *Aladdin* (2014).

3 Both Baum's book and the better known movie (1939) helped inspire Andrew Lloyd Webber and Tim Rice's musical *The Wizard of Oz* (2011). It is a sign of the times that the young women who have been playing Dorothy in both the English and Canadian productions were chosen from a reality television show ("Over the Rainbow") designed for that specific purpose.

THE MOVIES

IT MAY SEEM HARD TO BELIEVE, BUT THERE *WERE* FAIRY-TALE MOVIES
before Disney—and some of them were made by Disney himself! The common
assumption is that Disney's association with fairy tale began with the making of
Snow White and the Seven Dwarfs in 1937, but in fact it goes back as far as 1922, when
his new and very small company Laugh-O-Gram Films released a series of fairy-
tale cartoons that included "Little Red Riding Hood," "Jack and the Beanstalk,"
"Puss in Boots," and "Cinderella." Disney was the first but not the only pioneer
in the field of animation; while his child-oriented knockabout versions deserve
credit for blazing the trail, the cartoons of Max Fleischer[1] in the 1930s and the
incomparable Tex Avery[2] in the 1940s both turned the "fracturing" of tales into
an art in its own right.[3] Indeed, the fairy tale must have struck the early animators
as the ideal vehicle for this new medium: short, fantastic, full of action, and in the
public domain. And since animation was developed as a *comic* medium, fairy-tale
adaptations were necessarily of the "fractured" variety, which in Disney's case laid
part of the groundwork for what would become the Disney world view. Be that as
it may, by the time Disney decided to tackle a feature-length fairy-tale animation,
he had a pretty good idea of what he was about.

---

1 Creator of Betty Boop, who is distinctly slinky as "Dizzy Red Riding Hood" (1931) and
   "Poor Cinderella" (1934).
2 Avery's claim to fractured fame rests primarily in "Red Hot Riding Hood" (1943) and
   "Swing Shift Cinderella" (1945). See Orenstein's fuller discussion, p. 178.
3 Many of these early "shorts" can be accessed on YouTube, <http://www.youtube.com>.

Once *Snow White and the Seven Dwarfs* was released, all that went before was simply overwhelmed. What has since been identified as "classic" Disney is in full view here: the fairy tale as romantic wish fulfillment, the dramatic struggle between good and evil (complete with the tried-and-true chase sequence), the scene-stealing secondary characters, and the song-and-dance numbers with their catchy tunes and memorable lyrics. The fact that such songs as "Some Day My Prince Will Come" and "Whistle While You Work" are still familiar, more than 75 years later, surely testifies to Disney's uncanny feel for the popular mood. In the decades—and the movies— that followed,[1] Disney laid the foundations for a media empire that has grown into what is arguably the most powerful force in popular culture that the world has ever known, to the extent that some critics have expressed concern at the organization's unparalleled reach and influence.

It is interesting to examine the process by which the name of Disney has become synonymous with fairy tale. Walt Disney has been criticized for his representation of the fairy tales, his departure from the central themes, and his "trivialization" of the tales, while, in more recent years, his portrayal of the female has come under particularly close scrutiny. In these respects, however, he (or his studio) has done what every successful storyteller, past or present, would do: adjusted his story to be reflective of his audience's expectations, for it is only through articulating their values, fears, and desires that his fairy-tale versions have achieved their lasting popularity.

Despite the enormous success of *Snow White* and *Cinderella* (1950), Disney's third fairy tale, *Sleeping Beauty* (1959) met with a much cooler reception, resulting in a 30-year hiatus before his studio's[2] next venture into fairy-tale animation. It was a period of profound social change that produced the counterculture of the 1960s and the rise of feminism and pop psychology. It also led to what some critics have described as the "Disney Renaissance" of the final decades of the twentieth century. The positive reception of *The Little Mermaid* (1989) was soon eclipsed by the acclaim for *Beauty and the Beast* (1991), both of which were notable for their recognition that times had changed: efforts were made to add some psychological depth to the characters and to address the gender stereotyping that characterized the earlier fairy-tale animations. Although, like its predecessor, *Beauty and the Beast* won several Grammy and Golden Globe awards, greater acclaim came from its being the first animated film to be nominated in the Best Picture category at the Academy Awards. (Oddly enough, it lost to another "Beauty and the Beast" variant, *Silence of the Lambs*.) Subsequent

---

1 We should note that in addition to the fairy tales, Disney released a number of other animated fantasies during this 22-year period, such as *Pinocchio* (1940), *Bambi* (1942), *Alice in Wonderland* (1951), and *Peter Pan* (1953).

2 Walt Disney died in 1966.

animations have maintained social awareness: the female characters in movies such as *The Princess and the Frog* (2009), *Tangled* (2010), and *Frozen* (2013) are uniformly feisty and determined, while their male counterparts have become ambiguous, more likely to need assistance than to give it. Gender politics may have been updated, but the musical format of the early fairy-tale animations has been reinstated—as effective now as it was then. More recently, other film companies have challenged the Disney dominance, but as we shall see, the Disney *imprimatur* remains a powerful creative force in the evolution of fairy-tale movies.

With the arrival of *Shrek* (2001), the fairy-tale movie underwent some major innovation. Like the Disney classics, it is an animation—but now we are in the brave new world of *computer* animation (CGI), the literally fantastic potential of which is still being explored. Visually, CGI films are often quite stunning; indeed, it can be argued that the popularity of fantasy movies in general can be attributed to the visual magic that this technology can provide. So detailed and convincing are these imaginary worlds that the adult visitor is as quickly caught up as the child; after all, is not this same technology revealing equivalent wonders in what we accept as the real world? Along with the new technology has come a new perspective, in marked contrast to the "conventional" Disney model in its ironic but affectionate irreverence toward the fairy-tale world—and how better to illustrate this "new perspective" than to point out that the ending of this "Beauty and the Beast" is marked *not* by the transformation of Shrek into a handsome prince but by the beautiful princess into a green ogress!

Another example of this kind of animation, designed to appeal to child and adult alike, is *Hoodwinked* (2005). Visual humor is abundant, but characterization and dialogue are clearly aimed at an older viewer more likely to appreciate satiric portrayals such as the tough-talking police chief or the indefatigable folksinger who recounts his entire existence in song. While the frame-story is that of a distinctly liberated Little Red Riding Hood, we are also shown the action from the point of view of several other characters. And as in *Shrek*, there is an array of equally "liberated" characters from other fairy tales (in *Hoodwinked* the Three Little Pigs turn up as sheriff's deputies, while Puss in Boots becomes a swashbuckling member of Shrek's inner circle, notwithstanding his history as ogre-killer), which naturally requires a familiarity with the world of fairy tale to get the joke. A more ambitious form of character liberation, which may well have influenced later productions such as the *Fables* comic books and the *Once Upon a Time* TV series, may be seen in the movie-makers' willingness to plunder the fantasy world at large in order to assemble an all-star cast; thus, in the first *Shrek* alone we encounter—among others—the Gingerbread Man, the Pied Piper, "Monsieur" Robin Hood, Peter Pan, Three Blind Mice, and the Big Bad Wolf (later to come into his own in the *Fables* comic book series as Bigby Wolf).

At the same time, the parodying of numerous instantly recognizable fairy-tale and fantasy characters clearly demands a more complex response on the part of the viewer in appreciating the ironic perspective.

Predictably, numerous sequels and spinoffs have followed the success of the original *Shrek* movie, along with an enthusiasm for live-action remakes—or, more accurately, *adaptations*—of "classic" fairy tales, which tend to fall into two broad categories: historical or contemporary. The choice has a bearing on the movie beyond the nature of its setting and costumes. Not surprisingly, the favored historical period is quasi-medieval, which is sufficiently distant to conjure the spirit of "once upon a time" and also permit a spectacular backdrop of dungeons and castles, swords and shields, and sumptuous costumes (which are rarely to be found in the tales themselves). A good example of this approach can be found in *Ever After: A Cinderella Story* (1998), which effectively combines humor, romance, and period trappings, with Leonardo da Vinci thrown in for good measure. It also looks to the gender-equal future in the exploits of its heroine who, in one strenuous role-reversing scene, is obliged to carry her prince out of trouble. More recent movies have placed a premium on the superstition and violence that played a part in medieval life, although we may suspect that inclusion of these elements has more to do with popular demand than with a desire for historical exactness. It is only in the heat of battle, after all, that the combined virtues of CGI and 3D can be fully enjoyed, which may be one reason why the romantic side of the fairy tale has become a secondary consideration. *Hansel and Gretel: Witch Hunters* (2013) and *Jack the Giant Slayer* (2013) both include a substantial helping of mayhem that has little or no basis in the original story, and there have been two versions of *Snow White* since 1997 that introduce violent aspects into the story,[1] with at least one other—a kung-fu version set in nineteenth-century China—in the works. And it's worth noting that in many of these movies, the live action is provided by well-known stars such as Drew Barrymore, Charlize Theron, and Ewan McGregor. While the financial rewards are undoubtedly a factor, we shouldn't underestimate the attraction of playing old-style heroes and villains, or—as far as the studios are concerned—of enhancing the popular appeal of their product.

In fact, fascination with evil is a striking feature of many fairy-tale films, and we do not have to look far beneath the surface of the tales themselves to find their darker sides. In the case of *Snow White*, Walt Disney was—somewhat surprisingly—the catalyst; his demonic stepmother Queen is an iconic example of storytelling instincts getting the better of any notion of sheltering young minds. Now the Disney studio is mining the same vein in *Maleficent* (a live-action adaptation, summer

---

1 *Snow White: A Tale of Terror* (1997); *Snow White and the Huntsman* (2012).

2014), which reflects the recent (and adult-oriented) interest in retelling a tale from the villain's point of view.[1] In fact, one additional attraction of the live-action tale may be the opportunity it provides the filmmaker to develop some theories on the psychopathology of the wicked character. For their part, viewers are divided between a voyeuristic desire to see unrestrained villainy in action and a need to know where such behavior is coming from. In *Snow White: A Tale of Terror* (1997), for instance, some effort is made to explain the stepmother's jealous rage by portraying Lille (Snow White) as a stubborn child. The wicked Queen in *Snow White and the Huntsman* (2012) is more enigmatic, more obsessed with her own inner demons, to the extent that her dark presence dominates the whole movie. Interestingly, this version follows *A Tale of Terror* in giving the new Queen a sinister brother with whom she has a close, possibly incestuous relationship. A similar question arises about the relationship between brother and sister in *Hansel and Gretel: Witch Hunters*, not least because these prototypical natural-born killers are bonded by the orgy of violence that accompanies their efforts to mete out justice.[2]

Fairy tales that have been given a contemporary setting often pursue the very different goal of exploring social and psychological crises relating to young people on the verge of adulthood. In other words, the conflict is personal rather than adversarial, the violence emotional rather than physical. The mood of these movies is more varied, from the teen comedy of *Sydney White* (2007), to the romantic drama of *Beastly* (2011), and the dark eroticism of *Sleeping Beauty* (2011). Common to these present-day adaptations seems to be a search for self: however sophisticated and complex modern life has become, the basic human need for love and understanding remains just beneath the busy surface.

Beyond direct adaptations there is a large group of movies that draws on fairy-tale narratives or motifs in order to tap into our deep-seated familiarity with these childhood stories, along with the pleasurable or frightening associations that they carry. For example, the unmistakable Cinderella motif surely played some part in the success of *Pretty Woman* (1990), while in *Cinderella Man* (2011), the title alone is an indication of the extent to which the tale has become part of our cultural idiom.[3] And can we not discern the outlines of "Beauty and the Beast" both in *Edward Scissorhands* (1990) and, more recently, in the *Twilight* series (2008-11), which is further enhanced by shades of "Little Red Riding Hood" (see p. 26, note 1)?

---

1 An example of this approach can be found in Neil Gaiman's retelling of "Snow White," p. 57.
2 Despite underwhelming critical reception, work is reportedly well under way on sequels for several of these movies.
3 "Cinderella Man" was in fact a nickname of the movie's central character, the American boxing champion James Braddock.

Certainly, the number of fairy-tale movies has grown considerably over the last quarter of a century, particularly if we include movies that make obvious allusion to fairy-tale motifs and elements. Although the results may vary widely, the endless *adaptability* of the fairy tale clearly continues to provide filmmakers with a rich source of material—a fact recognized as early as the end of the nineteenth century by the visionary Frenchman Georges Méliès, who made what is surely the first film version of "Cinderella" in 1899.[1] However, as noted above, it is important to remind ourselves that *all* fairy-tale movies are of necessity adaptations of what we may term the "classic" story.[2] It is not coincidental that one of the most faithful renditions of a fairy tale, Jean Cocteau's *Beauty and the Beast* (1946), was made in the first half of the twentieth century. Today, a filmmaker might well argue that it is no longer acceptable to interpret a tale so straightforwardly; in these postmodern times, there is an expectation of some ironic realignment that may take the form of humor, violence, or sexuality, to provoke a new interest in such "kids' stuff." Getting the audience's attention is still a challenge because of just how many voices are competing for that attention. Fairy tales lend themselves to such reworking because of their minimalism and flexibility—there are numerous versions, yet we can all relate to these stories, regardless of age or gender: the broader the audience, the more successful the movie.

---

1 Méliès's remarkable imagination and accomplishments were the subject of the award-winning children's book *The Invention of Hugo Cabret* (2007), which later became the equally successful movie *Hugo* (2011).

2 Given the variety of early literary sources, such as tales collected and embellished by such writers as Basile, Perrault, and the Brothers Grimm, it is problematic to refer to the "original" story.

TELEVISION

In one important respect, the fairy tale and television do not make a good match. It is stating the obvious to define the "classic" fairy tale as a short story with a highly structured (one might even say ritualistic) beginning, middle, and end. It is almost as obvious that this is not a shape that recommends itself to television programmers, for whom *continuity* is a key concept. Productions of individual tales have had some success, such as in Shelley Duvall's *Faerie Tale Theatre* (1982-87), but more recent adaptations of fairy tale for television have consistently chosen a serial approach, despite the apparent incompatibility. Many of the resulting stretchings and strainings are a direct consequence of this decision, since the open-ended, "to be continued" mantra of the episodic framework is of course inimical to the emphatic closure of the fairy tale.

That was not a concern for the cartoon, however, and at the outset we must take note of these early representations of the fairy tale that found a new home on television. *The Rocky and Bullwinkle Show* (ABC and NBC, 1959-64) produced a total of 91 four-minute segments of "fractured fairy tales" that were designed to appeal to both children and adults; the quality of animation was inferior to what had gone before, but the ironic tone and the tongue-in-cheek narration by Edward Everett Horton introduced a characteristic note of social satire that would resurface decades later in James Finn Garner's *Politically Correct Bedtime Stories* (see p. 76).

The various fairy-tale series that we examine in this section all in some way involve the issue of law and order, no doubt as the modern equivalent of the struggle between Good and Evil that animates many classic tales. They also attempt to counter the gender inequality typical of the traditional tale by transforming passive princesses into attorneys and law officers.

The first significant attempt to adapt a specific fairy tale to television was CBS's *Beauty and the Beast*, which ran from 1987 to 1990. Despite its realistic setting of contemporary New York (above and below ground), it remained faithful to the original story to the extent that it focussed on the developing relationship between Vincent, a gentle but beast-like man[1] who is a member of a mysterious community of outcasts living in tunnels beneath the city[2] and Catherine, a beautiful assistant district attorney who, like Beauty in the original tale, gradually discovers the meaning of "handsome is as handsome does." The show parts company from the tale in rejecting any physical transformation of Vincent, whose inner strength is clearly established; under his guidance, Catherine is motivated to abandon her high-society lifestyle to become a vigorous advocate for social justice.

In many respects, the show represented a quantum leap from what had gone before; at a time when the fairy tale was largely out of fashion (Disney hadn't produced a fairy-tale movie since *Sleeping Beauty* in 1959), it seemed little short of reckless to propose a TV series based on an adult interpretation of a fairy tale. It is of course a sign of the times that this Beauty is also a courageous lawyer fighting evil in the *metaphorical* underworld, while the *literal* underworld is depicted as a place of refuge and warmth, the home of a compassionate counterculture at odds with the callousness of modern life. Their bond evolves in highly romantic fashion—Vincent woos her with Shakespeare sonnets to the accompaniment of evocative background music—but ends at the beginning of the third season with Catherine's death at the hands of a criminal she is pursuing. On the mean streets of New York, "happily ever after" is a hard sell. It should be noted, however, that this crisis had more to do with the departure of the actress playing Catherine than with a philosophical decision to replace optimism with pessimism. Although the demands of serialization obliged the show to persevere for a time, the momentum was lost; the fairy tale was over.

Beauty and the Beast was revived in 2012, although with some significant changes. The main characters still carry the names Vincent and Catherine, but Vincent's beastliness is now psychological rather than physical: he is a former super-soldier whose condition is the result of genetic tampering rather than enchantment. Catherine has become a beautiful detective instead of a beautiful district attorney, the effect of which is to emphasize the police procedural aspect of the show. Predictably,

---

1 Both his character and his appearance clearly owe a debt to Cocteau's *La Belle et la Bête* (1946). Part of Vincent's "magic" is his extraordinary empathy which makes him aware when Catherine is in danger—or giving birth to his baby.

2 We may detect a parallel with the concept of Fabletown in the comic book series *Fables* (see p. 96).

the fantasy in this series relies more on the "rational" world of science fiction, making the flavor of the story quite different, although we are still eager to discover whether the relationship between Vincent and Catherine will have a happy ending. The roots of fairy tale go deep.

Even more firmly based as a police procedural is NBC's *Grimm* (2011). Handsome young detective Nick Burkhardt is "descended from an elite line of criminal profilers known as 'Grimms,' charged with keeping balance between humanity and the mythological creatures of the world."[1] As a result, he has the power to recognize the literally monstrous nature of the villains he pursues. The premise of the show is that fairy tales exist as warnings, which is certainly a hypothesis that pertains to some well-known tales such as "Little Red Riding Hood," "Rumpelstiltskin," or "Bluebeard." Unlike *Beauty and the Beast*, this series is not based on a single fairy tale, which means that the show has greater flexibility in plot development and less reliance on familiar fairy-tale characters. However, early episodes did offer modern interpretations of some classic tales: thus, the wicked witch in *Grimm*'s early "Hansel and Gretel" segment became a doctor who, working in a clinic catering to young street people, used her surgical skills to harvest organs from her patients and sell them on the black market.[2] One of the show's co-writers commented, "One of the challenges we faced in adapting 'Hansel and Gretel' into our own little repertoire of crime stories was firstly finding a crime that could live up to the morbidity of the original. I mean let's face it, cannibalism is a pretty high bar to reach …"[3] However, it would appear that the task of reworking individual tales proved problematic, presumably because the number of suitable well-known tales was limited, so the focus broadened to what might be termed a "folkloric" approach, embodied in the ancient "book of monsters" that Nick has inherited (along with much other Grimm paraphernalia) from his aunt. Consequently, the revelation of the villains' monstrous appearance (visible only to Nick) became the show's distinctive feature. The moment is undeniably dramatic and a triumph of special effects, but one may nevertheless question the justification for the name "Grimm" since the reference to fairy tale (let alone the famous brothers) is at times a tenuous one.

If *Grimm* looks to folk beliefs and superstitions for its inspiration, *Once Upon a Time* (2011) has stayed much closer to fairy tale, likewise embodied in a talismanic old book (this time containing fairy tales), the possession of an unmagical but

---

1 <http://www.nbc.com/grimm/about/>.

2 Is it coincidence that this is our second encounter with the issue of harvesting human organs? (See Garth Nix, "Hansel's Eyes," p. 49.) Or does it indicate an important source of the fairy tale's raw material: the inchoate fears and suspicions that, when mixed with a solid dose of imagination, turn into monsters?

3 Spiro Skentzos, <http://www.nbc.com/grimm/production-blog/>.

wise little boy named Henry. As its title suggests, *Once Upon a Time* adopts the generic approach much more aggressively than *Grimm*; not all fairy tales begin with these words, but that doesn't alter the fact that few phrases send a clearer signal of what to expect. The notion of the "liberated" fairy-tale character has already been discussed elsewhere (see the sections on comic books and movies), but nowhere is that concept better illustrated than in this television series. It is not surprising that many have seen similarities between this show and the *Fables* comic book series, most particularly in the wide variety of fairy-tale characters (as well as characters from well-known children's fantasies) who are involved in adventures that have little or nothing to do with the original narratives.[1] Along with familiar characters such as Rumpelstiltskin and Snow White, there are generic characters such as the Evil Queen and Prince Charming, as well as numerous "ordinary" types,[2] all of whom live shoulder-to-shoulder in Storybrooke (Maine). A further indication that *Once Upon a Time* has identifiable links to the world of the comic book is its adoption of the spinoff. We noted the phenomenon both in our discussion of comic books (see p. 95) and of movies (p. 115), and now we encounter it again in ABC's plans for *Once Upon a Time in Wonderland*, which, like *Fables* before it, finds inspiration beyond the borders of fairy tale, in this case in Lewis Carroll's masterpiece.

Because the real and the fantastic are so densely intertwined in the storyline, and because the familiar is so often rendered unfamiliar, the results can be disconcerting. While one has to admire the fertility of the writers' imaginations, that is also the problem. Drawing inspiration from all over the fantasy map is eventually going to create a kind of imaginative indigestion in the viewer, as Pinocchio meets Captain Hook and Rumpelstiltskin makes a deal with Sleeping Beauty. Although many of the names may be familiar, the relationships between them are not, so the viewer is in a constant state of adjustment and readjustment. No doubt in tacit acknowledgement of this fact, toward the end of the second season, a segment was broadcast in which the show's creators summarized the plot (an achievement in itself), which, while helpful, had the effect of encapsulating the problem. If the audience is not having a

---

1   In an intriguing if somewhat whimsical article (<http://www.comicbookresources. com/?page=article&id=35737>), Willingham expresses the view that *Once Upon a Time* "probably is ... influenced and at least in part inspired by 'Fables' ... but perhaps not on more than a 'this is the type of thing that's in the air these days' level." Which, given the unique history of "borrowing" that characterizes the fairy tale from earliest times, is arguably a very reasonable response.

2   In what appears an odd note of whimsy, one of these "ordinary mortals" bears the name Neal Cassidy, one of the Beat Generation immortalized in Jack Kerouac's *On the Road*.

hard time following the complexities of the plot, why would a show interrupt itself to untangle the narrative threads?[1]

Once Upon a Time's special effects are ambitious and often impressive; this series clearly set out to exploit the *visual* potential of these stories to a much greater extent than the other fairy-tale series we have examined, and given the popularity of movies that emphasized this aspect of fantasy, from *Lord of the Rings* to the *Harry Potter* series, one can assume that ABC felt justified in investing a good deal of money in the show.[2] The gamble seems to have paid off, since if audience ratings are anything to go by, the appetite for fairy tale on television is as healthy as in other media.

---

1 In this regard, *Once Upon a Time* is reminiscent of soap opera, whose similarly labyrinthine plots and open-ended storylines are regularly reviewed for confused viewers in several weekly publications dedicated to the purpose.

2 Not surprisingly, recent fairy-tale movies such as *Snow White and the Huntsman* and *Jack the Giant Killer* have also placed much emphasis on their visual appeal.

ADVERTISING

On the face of it, there is little to connect the worlds of fairy tale and consumer products. We are never told the name of the seed company that produced Jack's magic beans or the brand of shampoo that Rapunzel favored to protect against unusual wear and tear. At first glance, we might assume that the fantasy portal of "once upon a time" would be anathema to an advertiser—until we recognize the extent to which fantasy suffuses and influences our own daily lives, making the multicultural fairy tale an ideal vehicle for commercial exploitation in an increasingly global market.

While our contemporary media offer a plethora of fantasy worlds for our amusement and escape, whether science fiction, romance, or animation, there's no denying that the stem from which most of these variations have sprouted is the fairy tale. In many cultures, the fairy tale has become embedded in the process of growing up, aided and abetted by the educational system, which has embraced the tale as a means of promoting literacy, and by the television set, where the influence of Disney and others has made the tale a part of our social fabric. Consequently, its iconic characters and images have come to represent a pre-eminent frame of reference, which to the advertiser is the equivalent of the Holy Grail. As Bonner observes, "The language and motifs of the tales are internalized within the culture, rendering fairy tales sophisticated communication devices that influence consumer trends, lifestyle choices and gender models."[1]

---

1 Sarah Bonner, "Visualizing Little Red Riding Hood."

Thus, there is no mystery to the popularity of fairy tale in advertising; few images are more immediately recognizable in our culture than a glass slipper[1] or a girl in a red cloak. Moreover, that instant response is generally accompanied both by feelings of comfort and community, fairy tales being such a potent stimulus of childhood nostalgia, and also by the hope for transformation; no moment is more seductive than that in which the shoe fits the foot or the kiss awakens the girl. The association of such memories (real or imagined) with a particular product is therefore profound and persuasive; it also invites some arresting variations, as the following selection demonstrates.

The Amnesty International advertisement (Figure 16, 2009) takes the expectations of nostalgic "comfort and community" and turns them inside out, although it is important to note that the intent here is not to sell a product but to bring attention to an emotive social issue. Thus, although this advertisement is obviously based on "Little Red Riding Hood," it offers an object lesson in how broadly a fairy tale can be interpreted. Like the Anthropologie picture (see below), it includes just enough iconic images to ensure identification of the tale. Key to this ad is its timing; in order to focus the reader's attention on the message, the artist has taken only what is needed from the story. There is no wolf, just a claw mark on the woman's cheek. (What stage in the story does this image depict?) There is no young girl; in her place, a sophisticated (and manicured) young woman who seems a bit old for "Mom" to still be reading her tales. Is the change intended to suggest both mother *and* daughter, since the purpose of the ad is to condemn violence against *women*? How effectively this ad makes its point is one question; as far as its use of fairy tale is concerned, it surely underlines the extent to which the "classic" tales are woven into the very fabric of our lives—whatever language we speak.

Anthropologie describes itself as "a destination for women wanting a curated mix of clothing, accessories, gifts and home décor that reflects their personal style and fuels their lives' passions, from fashion to art to entertaining."[2] No obvious connection with fairy tale here, we might think[3]—but then we need to reflect on the impulses behind such concepts as "fashion" and "art" and perhaps "entertaining,"

---

1   As well-known shoe designer Stuart Weitzman observes, "What is every girl's first memory of shoes? Cinderella's glass slipper. When asked to recreate the iconic slipper for the new Broadway production, I jumped at the chance." Leah Melby, "Stuart Weitzman's Designing for Cinderella," *Elle*, <http://www.elle.com/news/fashion-style/stuart-weitzman-cinderella-broadway-shoe> February 11, 2013.

2   <http://www.anthropologie.com/anthro/help/ourstory.jsp>.

3   It must be pointed out that the transformative potential of fashion is first proposed in fairy tale, nowhere more dramatically than in Cinderella's grand entrance at the Prince's ball.

too. Central to the fairy-tale vision is the achievement of the *ultimate*, generally in the form of happiness, wealth, and beauty, so it isn't difficult to see the appeal for a retailer that specializes in providing the accoutrements for such an ideal world. We should note that Anthropologie's catalogue cover (Figure 17, November 2012) does not depict a particular episode in the story of Snow White. The concern is not so much with narrative accuracy as with memorable images—and so we have a striking collage of mirror, apple, and bewitched-but-chic heroine (an image that is surely intended to remind the potential Anthropologie customer of Kristen Stewart in *Snow White and the Huntsman*).[1] The fairy-tale motif is continued throughout the catalogue, with striking effect. The intent is clear: with artifacts and clothing supplied by Anthropologie, life is a fairy tale.

Life is very evidently *not* a fairy tale in the Snow White world as envisioned in the ad (Figure 18, 2007) for Ajuda de Mae ("Mother's Help"), a Portuguese organization whose mission is to provide support and guidance for needy young mothers. We could not be further from the artful romanticism of the fashion catalogue—or from Disney's blithe promise of marital bliss, which is surely implied by the iconic Snow White garb; now the camera's role is not to create fantasies but to strike a chord with working-class women struggling to come to terms with the fact that "happily ever after" is not an accurate description of their lives after the fairy tale ends.[2] This image is as frenetic in its detail as the Anthropologie image is calmly elegant in its sparseness: one tale, two very different perspectives.

The fact that many fairy tales (including a number of those currently considered "classics") contain a distinct sexual element comes as less of a surprise today than it might have 50 years ago. We are all familiar with the "wink-wink" jokes about what *really* went on between Snow White and the dwarves or between Little Red Riding Hood and the Wolf (Angela Carter had some thoughts about that, in her memorable retelling *The Company of Wolves*). Indeed, in tales such as "Rapunzel" or "Sun, Moon and Talia," an early version of "Sleeping Beauty,"[3] the sexuality is quite explicit. This aspect of fairy tale has of course proved irresistible to producers of erotica[4] and pornography, but on a more socially acceptable level, some advertisers have chosen to exploit the sexual content with a mildly cynical humor. In the Melissa: Bedtime Stories ad (Figure 19, 2007), one might be forgiven for wondering just what was being

---

1 The movie was released in June 2012; another Snow White movie, *Mirror, Mirror*, was released in March 2012.

2 It is surely no coincidence that photographer Dina Goldstein presents an almost identical scenario in "Snowy" (2009), in her series *Fallen Princesses* (<http://dinagoldstein.com/fallen-princesses/>).

3 Giambattista Basile, "Sun, Moon and Talia," in *The Pentamerone*, first published in 1634-36.

4 Ann Rice's *Sleeping Beauty Trilogy* (1983-85) is a case in point; see "Prose," p. 29, note 1.

advertised, but if the medium is indeed the message, what girl would not want a pair of shoes that promised the upper foot over a helpless prince?

A very different way of exploiting Rapunzel's crowning glory may be found in an advertisement (Figure 20, 2008) for Pantene's Anti-Breaking shampoo, which takes the form of urban re-enactments of the unusual means by which the eager prince reaches Rapunzel at the top of her tower. Clearly, the effectiveness of the marketing relies on familiarity with the tale; the distribution of free samples to (female) passersby carries the implication of both love and escape, which, for better or worse, has proved to be fairy tale's most potent promise. We should also note that Pantene returned to the allure of the fairy tale several years later by basing a campaign on the release of Disney's *Tangled* (2010), thereby benefitting from that company's fabled merchandising skills.

The advertisement for Brain Candy Toys (Figure 21, 2011) takes a novel approach to a familiar tale, as befits a company that takes play seriously! As Steve Wallace, the copywriter responsible for the advertisement points out, "We decided to use fairy tales in our campaign because they resonate with both children and adults, and are universally and immediately recognizable. We knew that we were going to use math equations to tell stories, so we had to make sure that we chose stories that were so entrenched in society that you don't need words to tell them." In response to our question as to whether he thought fairy tales could be used in an exclusively "adult" advertisement, Wallace was unequivocal: "Absolutely ... [A]ny creative people working in advertising would be amiss to not include fairy tales in their arsenal—no matter what client they're working for."[1]

Of all the different styles of graphic design in advertising, we are most comfortable with the cartoon approach, as exemplified in the Burger King ad (Figure 22, 2007), not least because it relocates the tale in the safe, well-defined context that we primarily associate with Walt Disney.[2] Within these reassuring stylistic bounds, the ad's appeal is based on parody, which is a familiar response to the fairy tale's characteristic unreality. A traumatic moment in the original tale is thus transformed into a reassuring scene of companionship and humor, as the wolf is able to satisfy his own appetite in a socially acceptable manner, aided and abetted by a quick-witted grandma who reckons that it's a much better idea for Mr. Wolf to sink his teeth into a Whopper rather than into her. And since the hamburger is the epitome of fast food, Burger King comes to the rescue as promptly as any woodcutter. Emboldened by our role as accomplices in this feast, we are amused rather than dismayed by Riding Hood's alarm;

---

1 Personal communication, November 22, 2012.

2 Burger King has associated itself with fairy tales on other occasions, most recently with a promotion for the movie *Hoodwinked Too! Hood vs. Evil* (2010).

after all, we think, if she'd got a move on instead of messing about picking flowers, she could have ordered her own burger and fries.

When we turn to fairy-tale advertisements in the electronic media, we find that many of the same criteria still apply. The nature of the message still governs the choice of image; for instance, the Sky Broadband series of fairy-tale spoofs (2010-11)[1] is generally set in Regency times, a period sufficiently fantastic in its own right to meet the fairy-tale world halfway. Upending the stereotype of the technologically challenged female, this modern princess gives her hopelessly behind-the-times prince a lesson on how to keep up with the demands of a highly connected world. New magic is replacing the old.

By contrast, the multi-layered Volvo ad (2012)[2] is set in the here-and-now: to the soundtrack of one of the few memorable fairy-tale songs outside the Disney canon,[3] a much-revised version of "Little Red Riding Hood" unfolds, the moral being that in the security provided by this brand of car, one need have no fear of the forest and its dangers. Safe in her child car seat, this latest red-hooded incarnation of a famous line demonstrates how much times have changed by indulging in a little howling of her own.

More pointed is the award-winning reworking of "The Three Little Pigs" by *The Guardian* newspaper (2012),[4] which superimposes the tale on the grim world of social protest. It is in equal measure absurd and disturbing; the rapid pace of news-style video and social media messaging results in our being overloaded with both information and emotion. The tale itself is undeniably violent, yet the juxtaposition of the bewildered fairy-tale characters and the tactical squads of the "real world" serves to underline the pent-up anger in our society, even as, in fantasy and fact, the desire for justice is paramount. Just how far from "once upon a time" are we?

As we have seen, the fairy tale has proved—through its universality, its recognizability, and its magic—to be a valuable resource for advertisers. We cannot conclude this discussion, however, without taking note of one other promotional campaign, since it pays tribute to the man (and his studio) who has been the most influential purveyor of fairy tales in the last 100 years and their most successful commercializer.

---

1 Sky Broadband, "The Princess and The Pea" TV advertisement, June 28, 2010, <http://www.youtube.com/watch?v=fFgvx-WvFgc>; Sky Broadband, "Frog Prince," March 30, 2011, <http://www.youtube.com/watch?v=2lgXK7lqPK4>.

2 Volvo, "Little Red Riding Hood," June 7, 2012 <www.youtube.com/watch?v=GeUwqp1Swil>. It seems that Volvo has no illusions about the power of fantasy, having also invested in some significant product placement in the popular *Twilight* movie series; Edward, the much-admired vampire, drives a model S60 ...

3 "L'il Red Riding Hood," attributed to Ronald Blackwell, recorded by Sam the Sham and the Pharaohs (1966), here sung by Laura Gibson. See Orenstein's discussion, p. 184.

4 <http://www.guardian.co.uk/media/video/2012/feb/29/open-journalism-three-little-pigs-advert>.

Its overall effect is to underline the Disney hegemony that his studio established as emphatically in image as the Brothers Grimm did in print. In a promotional campaign entitled the "Disney Dream Portrait Series," begun in 2007, the worlds of fantasy and stardom find their ultimate expression as celebrity photographer Annie Leibovitz, creator of iconic photographs of rock idols, movie stars, and royalty, uses her lens to reanimate Disney's fairy tale characters with a cast taken from the Who's Who of celebrity culture. In Leibovitz's lush photographs, the romantic dreams inspired by Disney's fairy-tale animations are embodied in the likes of Taylor Swift, Penelope Cruz, and David Beckham. The combination is irresistible, even for the stars themselves: actress Olivia Wilde, pictured as Disney's evil Queen in *Snow White* (2011), comments that it was natural to pair "some of the most iconic characters from all of our childhood with the photographer who is so good at capturing icons." Her co-star, Alec Baldwin (the Magic Mirror) reveals that of all celebrity photo-ops, the ultimate is "to be shot by Annie."[1] Elsewhere we have commented on the impact of Disney's fairy-tale movies on social attitudes and gender stereotypes; here, in Leibovitz's ravishing images, is evidence as to the nature of their attraction, for is not celebrity culture the closest that the modern world can get to the glamour of the fairy tale?

---

1 Quotations taken from video clips of the photography shoots found on "Photo Archive: Latest in the Annie Leibovitz Disney Dream Portrait Series Capturing Celebrities as Colorful Disney Characters," Ricky Brigante, <http://www.insidethemagic.net>.

NEW MEDIA

"Little Red Riding Hood was my first love. I felt that if I could have married Little Red Riding Hood, I should have known perfect bliss."[1]

—Charles Dickens

WE HABITUALLY ASSUME THAT THE TERM "POPULAR CULTURE" RE-fers to the contemporary scene—and yet as we have seen, it has a relevance for times past as well as the present. It might be argued that modern popular culture is based more on what is seen and heard than on what is written; it is a common belief that the book is giving way to the image. Another difference is the role of community: the stock image of the oral tale telling is—not surprisingly—one of the storyteller surrounded by a group of listeners. In the contemporary context, this is a relatively rare occurrence outside an elementary classroom. Furthermore, community as a concept has changed dramatically since the days of the folk tale; today, the term may well connote a *virtual* community established via social networks on the Internet. Further, one of the distinctive features of the oral tale telling is its dynamic participatory quality: effective tellers will adjust the narrative according to their own mood or that of their audience, so that the tale changes at every telling. With the establishment of literacy and the book, that opportunity for negotiation and feedback disappeared; the tale was immobilized in print. Currently, print is still with us, but in one medium at least, it's much less permanent; nobody with a computer is unfamiliar with the

---

1 Charles Dickens, "A Christmas Tree," in *Christmas Books and Reprinted Pieces* (New York: International Book Company, n.d.) 829.

"delete" key. This, combined with the spectacular rise of social media, has created an environment that is once again conducive to a virtual "participatory culture" restoring an immediacy to the fairy tale—and the status of a work-in-progress—that is in many ways reminiscent of its oral beginnings. In short, we have a progression here: first there was the communal informality surrounding the oral tale; then came literacy, which turned the tale into a solitary imaginative experience; and now, with the advent of social media, the collective and the personal exist side by side.

Thus, even as the creators of popular culture continue to adapt the fairy tale for established media such as the book, film, and television, the Internet has provided a forum for the long-silent majority to react to the professional tellers or simply to offer their own interpretations of familiar tales. There is no denying the creative challenge implicit in these short, strange narratives that we all know so well and yet find so elusive: what did Cinderella *really* think of her stepsisters? And how does Gretel go back to her life after the horrors of the gingerbread house? Some answers have been provided by writers and artists such as those represented in this book; others, equally valid if less expertly constructed, can be found on fan-fiction sites such as <http://www.fanfiction.net/book/Fairy-Tale/>, which are virtual tale-telling community workshops where tales are not only posted but reviewed and subsequently revised. The attraction of reinventing the fairy tale is reflected in the fact that as of July 2013, there were 4,478 submissions on this site alone.[1] Once again, the fairy tale belongs to us all.

The explosion of possibilities that has been afforded by the Internet has unquestionably changed the cultural products that are created and the way they are accessed and appreciated. Popular culture has often been associated with mass culture, thereby provoking negative connotations that stem from the traditional distinctions between "highbrow" and "lowbrow": the tastes of the educated and "cultured" as opposed to those of the "masses." However, popular culture theorist John Storey points out the difficulty with defining popular culture along class lines, since what appeals to one social group or another may shift in the course of time.[2] Today, the works of Shakespeare, for example, are commonly assumed to be "highbrow" art, accessible only to those who are highly educated. In fact, Shakespeare wrote equally for the working people, who could choose between *As You Like It* and the bear-baiting at the tavern across the street. An appreciation of opera and classical music likewise confers the status of being "cultured." Yet, once it was chosen as the BBC's

---

1 In May 2013, Amazon.com undertook to publish fan fiction in a venture entitled *Kindle Worlds* ("New stories inspired by books, shows, movies, comics, music, and games people love").

2 John Storey, *Cultural Theory and Popular Culture: An Introduction*, 5th ed. (New York: Pearson Longman, 2009) 7.

theme song for its coverage of the 1990 World Cup in Italy, Luciano Pavarotti's 1972 rendition of "Nessun Dorma" from Puccini's opera *Turandot* reached the top of the music "pop charts" in the United Kingdom. Subsequently, it became something of a sporting anthem, especially for soccer[1] and has been adapted by various artists, from pop singers to filmmakers.[2]

As we pointed out earlier, fairy tales have also crossed these same boundaries: having started out as popular oral entertainment for the illiterate, they were first written down in the seventeenth century by Basile and Perrault for the pleasure of the aristocracy, and then, with the publication of the Grimm Brothers' volumes, they became the cultural and educational property of middle-class children, until the advent of new technologies in the last century made their presence almost universal.

This discussion of the fairy tale and popular culture would not be complete, however, without some consideration of the tale's presence in video-gaming—that quintessential but controversial example of participatory culture made possible by the universal penetration of the Internet. And who better to introduce tale to game than the Disney organization, whose commercially successful and critically acclaimed "Kingdom Hearts" series makes use of its familiar fairy-tale characters. As one game reviewer observes, "it's easy to see how traditional folklore can be mapped onto an existing formula to enhance it."[3] Not surprisingly, popular Disney fairy-tale animations, such as *Beauty and the Beast*, have accompanying video games. However, the interest in the darker, violent side of fairy tales is certainly more conducive to the combat-oriented ethos of video gaming for older players. An advertisement for another popular game, "Fairytale Fights," makes this clear: "Fairytale Fights is a truly twisted hack'n'slash platform adventure where players assume the role of a much-loved fairytale character ... with action-packed combat and fairytale-style storylines."[4]

It is this role-playing aspect, together with multiplayer capability and narrative potential, that puts video gaming at the forefront of participatory culture. A popular "massively multiplayer online role-playing game" (MMORPG) is typically played by several hundred thousand participants throughout the world and, predictably, yields annual profits in the billion dollar range. Part of its equally "massive" appeal

---

1 "Nessun Dorma Put Football Back on Map," *The Telegraph*, September 7, 2007. Quoted in Storey, 8.

2 And one cannot ignore the performance of the same aria in 2007 by Paul Potts on the TV talent show *The X Factor*, which "went viral" on YouTube and, as of June 2013, had received almost 113 million hits.

3 "Fairy Tales and Video Games," October 28, 2009, <http://www.thegamereviews.com/article-1568-Fairy-Tales-and-Video-Games>.

4 *Playlogic International*, October 2009; Rated: Mature.

undoubtedly stems from immersion in a persistent virtual world (most often based on fantasy themes), the development and customization of the player's character, the very real social interaction within the game, the in-game culture, and the strong sense of membership—all of which combined have proven, unfortunately, to be addictive in some individuals. The benefits and burdens of this intense involvement have certainly come under scrutiny; however, of great interest culturally is the video game's potential as an art form.

Machinima (a combination of machine and cinema) is a unique artistic medium that has developed from the video game. It is a form of filmmaking derived from the manipulation of a favorite video game's engine or its core, which does not require any animation skills.[1] For example, Second Life, a free on-line 3D virtual world, is less about gaming than about providing the opportunity to participate and create. Its accessibility has allowed its "residents" to produce art, music, theater, and machinima. One notable exponent is Toxic Menges (Heidi Foster), who has created a number of fairy-tale machinima, such as "The Princess and the Pea" (2009) and "Little Red Riding Hood" (2010). As one fan puts it, the novelty is in the way a familiar "story idea might take on a new reality/perspective when created in a virtually constructed environment."[2] It seems that where there is enthusiasm and creativity—and the means to create and disseminate it—artistic production is bound to follow, transforming the fairy tale in the process.

The innovative work of the Belgian studio *Tale of Tales*[3] is aiming to take video games in a more artistic direction; its declared mission is "to create elegant and emotionally rich interactive entertainment," which will go beyond "the endless cycles of challenges and rewards" of the typical video game. The developers' efforts to turn theory into practice have resulted in *The Path* (2009) in which a single player engages in what is described as a psychological horror art game based on "Little Red Riding Hood." The game is less about winning and more about choosing: "The six protagonists [versions of Little Red Riding Hood] each have their own age and personality

---

1   Robert Jones, "From Shooting Monsters to Shooting Movies: Machinima and the Transformative Play of Video Game Fan Culture," in *Fan Fiction and Fan Communities in the Age of the Internet*, ed. Karen Hellekson and Kristina Busse (Jefferson, NC: McFarland and Company, 2006). Enthusiasm for this medium among creators and audiences has led not only to the establishment of the Academy of Machinima Arts and Science in 2002 and a yearly Machinima Film Festival (complete with awards) but also to the birth of a new fandom community.

2   "Monsters, Fairy Tales & the Magic of Machinima," *Magnum: The Machinima Review*, April 25, 2011, <http://www.magnummachinima.blogspot.ca>.

3   The company name is derived from Giambattista Basile's collection of fairy tales *Lo Cunto de li Cunti* (*The Tale of Tales*, 1634-36).

and allow the player to live through the tale in different ways ..."[1] As the developers explain, "We are not storytellers in the traditional sense of the word. In the sense that we know a story and we want to share it with you. [sic] Our work is more about exploring the narrative potential of a situation. We create only the situation. And the actual story emerges from playing, partially in the game, partially in the player's mind."[2] We may surmise that the many-layered texture of the game was inspired by different early versions of the tale—the young girl in "The Story of Grandmother," for instance, has little in common with Perrault's Little Red Riding Hood—but like a good storyteller, the game allows the player to find meaning in the tale.

It is precisely the universal familiarity with fairy tales—with particular narratives, characters, conventions—that creates this potential for dynamic interaction between source and audience. That it can mean different things to different people makes the fairy tale, as we have seen in the past and present, a rich source of creative energy.

---

1   <http://tale-of-tales.com/ThePath/>.
2   Mark Newheiser, "Michael Samyn and Auriea Harvey: Tale of Tales" (interview), *Adventure Classic Gaming*, April 7, 2009, <http://www.adventureclassicgaming.com/index.php/site/interviews/473>.

HAPPILY EVER AFTER

"The dream that you wish will come true"[1]

—Disney's Cinderella

IN THE SPRING OF 2013, WE WERE DOING OUR DUE EDITORIAL DILI-gence by attending a Broadway revival of Rodgers and Hammerstein's *Cinderella*[2] when, at the conclusion of the show, an unexpected postscript was added. After the cast had taken their bows, Prince Charming stepped forward and announced that the two winners of a "contest" should come up on the stage. When the young couple arrived, Prince Charming immediately handed the microphone to the man, who went down on one knee, produced a ring, and with great emotion asked his lady companion to marry him. Needless to say, the audience was quickly in tune with this unexpected confluence of Art and Life; after all, don't we all want our lives to be like a fairy tale?[3]

Ritual plays an important role in human society; it helps create order, connection to others, and, perhaps most importantly, the experience of transformation. In cultures far and wide, the wedding has established itself as not only the most significant ritual of a person's lifetime but also one that casts a spell upon us all, perhaps because the spectacle, familiar yet timeless, provides a moment of sublimity in a

---

1 From "A Dream Is a Wish Your Heart Makes" (1950), written and composed by Mack David, Al Hoffman, and Jerry Livingston, performed by Ilene Woods.
2 See discussion in "Stage" section, p. 112-13.
3 On further investigation, we discovered that this "contest" has taken place several times, with a winner on each occasion.

humdrum world. In effect, this once-upon-a-lifetime event, with its traditions and other-world solemnity, allows the couple to enter into a utopian dream world—to be transformed into Cinderella and Prince Charming and experience the prospect of a fairy-tale ending.

The lasting popularity of Disney's animated fairy tales and their promise that "Some day my prince will come" have certainly played a role in promoting this romantic association. Yet Life outdid Art in the most celebrated wedding of the twentieth century—that of Prince Charles and Lady Diana. Global media made it possible for an unprecedented 750 million people to watch as Diana arrived at St. Paul's Cathedral in a glass coach wearing an extravagantly decorated dress with a 25-foot train. As the Archbishop of Canterbury observed, "Here is the stuff of which fairy tales are made."[1] The associations with fairy tale went beyond the spectacle of the marriage ceremony, however; for many, Diana's life resembled that of Cinderella. Although she came from an old aristocratic family, her parents had divorced, and she dropped out of school at 16 and supported herself with odd jobs—house-cleaner, nanny, child-care aide—before she met Prince Charles and, at age 20, married him. This modern Cinderella became "the people's Princess," and the fantasy of the fairy tale was reaffirmed for millions around the globe.[2]

Today, marriage no longer carries the same symbolic weight as a social and sexual rite of passage nor, given the current rate of divorce, the guarantee of living "happily ever after," as became evident in the sad, all-too-human aftermath to that fairy-tale wedding of Charles and Diana. Nevertheless, for some its appeal remains undiminished; those who choose to honor the tradition often do so lavishly. It has been described "as one of the few recently democratized portals to re-enchantment in life," which "offers a temporary dream world for all in attendance."[3] This contemporary need for re-enchantment also partly explains our never-ending fascination with the fairy tale—not only creating and retelling it in every possible way—but also needing to live it, even if just for a day.

---

1   *The Guardian*, April 24, 1981.
2   Although there are doubtless other explanations for the statistic, the fact remains that in the decade following the royal wedding, there was "a record number of marriages in U.S. history." Cele Otnes and Elizabeth Pleck, *Cinderella Dreams: The Allure of the Lavish Wedding* (Berkeley: U of California P, 2003) 50.
3   Otnes and Pleck, 15

CRITICISM

DURING THE PAST FEW DECADES, THE BODY OF FAIRY-TALE SCHOLAR-ship has grown substantially, led by the work of distinguished critics such as Jack Zipes, Maria Tatar, and Marina Warner. Journals dedicated to the study and celebration of the fairy tale have been founded (*Marvels and Tales, Fairy Tale Review, Gramarye*), as have numerous websites, the best-known being Heidi Anne Heiner's <www.surlalune.com>.

In our selection of critical material included in this book, we have tried to show how the fairy tale is being reassessed for and by an evolving reader/viewership. The fairy tale has been around for a long time, but its enthusiastic annexation by popular culture may turn out to be a mixed blessing: while the tale has been freed from at least some of the bowdlerization and sentimentality it acquired as "children's literature," it may yet turn out to be a case of "out of the frying pan, into the fire" as the new tellers twist and stretch the tale to suit modern tastes. (On the other hand, it could of course be argued that this is the secret of its longevity!)

Seeing the tales for what they once were is, in Maria Tatar's view, a vital aspect of Terry Gilliam's film *The Brothers Grimm* (2005), which, she says, "… delivers a startling reminder that the narratives started out as adult entertainment …" In a world where so many labor under the misapprehension that Walt Disney is the father of fairy tale, that is an important corrective. Just how extensive a reach the Disney organization has in our culture is spelled out in an excerpt from *The Mouse that Roared: Disney and the End of Innocence* (2010), by Henry A. Giroux and Grace Pollock. While the authors do not refer specifically to Disney's fairy tales, they demonstrate very clearly the relationship between culture and big business; when we watch *Snow White and the Seven Dwarfs*, we are getting much more than a fairy tale.

What happens to a fairy tale when it is transformed from an oral to a literary or—more likely—a visual experience? That is a question Gail de Vos explores in "Folktales and the Comic Book Format" in which she argues that the comic book is in many respects the closest literary equivalent to *hearing* a fairy tale. For her part, Sarah Bonner chooses to examine contemporary artists' response to the fairy tale by focussing on one specific tale: "Little Red Riding Hood." Her article makes it clear that if intensity of image is any measure, the tale still has much to tell us about ourselves.

If it were necessary, following Bonner's discussion, to illustrate the extraordinary diversity of reaction to this fairy tale, the excerpt from Catherine Orenstein's book *Little Red Riding Hood Uncloaked: Sex, Morality and the Evolution of a Fairy Tale* (2003) should serve the purpose. Orenstein takes us into the *other* world of fairy-tale animation to show us how, under the tutelage of Tex Avery, the roles of little girl and wolf could be reversed—and how that reversal would prove prophetic of much that followed in both visual and literary interpretation.

Although Graeme McMillan's article "Another Bite of the Poisoned Apple: Why Does Pop Culture Love Fairy Tales Again?" dates from 2012 and therefore refers to movies that in terms of pop culture are already "so yesterday," it raises issues that are relevant to this book, such as the rediscovery of the tale as *adult* entertainment and its potential to satisfy both sides of the gender divide. This latter point is made even more explicit by the creators of the TV series *Once Upon a Time*, as Emily Rome demonstrates in her 2012 interview. It is a measure of the fairy tale's flexibility that what was condemned just 50 years ago for its archaic depiction of the female has now been transformed by writers, artists, and filmmakers into an often penetrating examination of current sexual attitudes and values.

At first glance, it may seem somewhat incongruous that the *Financial Times* should take an interest in fairy tale, as seen in this article, by Alex Fury until one reflects on the extent to which fantasy has permeated the business of our daily lives, whether through advertising or entertainment (see the previous section). Nowhere is this phenomenon more visible than in the world of *haute couture*, which explains the interest of a business-oriented newspaper.

Just as Gail de Vos explores the similarities between the oral tale and the comic book, Jessica Tiffin, in this excerpt from her book *Marvelous Geometry: Narrative and Metafiction in Modern Fairy Tale* (2009), compares the experience of listening to an oral folk tale with that of watching a fairy-tale film. She points out that in certain respects, the film provides a much more *communal* experience than does the literary text; however, there are forces at work in the production and presentation of a movie that divorce it almost completely from the intimacy and interaction of the oral tale-telling.

FAIRY TALES IN THE AGE OF TERROR: WHAT TERRY GILLIAM HELPS TO REMIND US ABOUT AN ANCIENT GENRE[1]

Maria Tatar

IN THE BROTHERS GRIMM [2005], TERRY GILLIAM INVITES US INTO the woods to witness the murder of Little Red Riding Hood in a setting of such breathtaking allure that we experience a double jolt—one administered by the girl's terrifying death and the other by the magnificent landscape in which she perishes. The dark blend of horror and fantasy onscreen is enough to make adults wonder anew just what were, and are, the "uses of enchantment," as Bruno Bettelheim called his book about why children need fairy tales. In an age when beauty has been separated from art, when horror has migrated into lowbrow entertainment, when cynicism has driven out wonder, and when the grand narrative style has given way to postmodern pastiche, we still hunger, especially in times of social and cultural crisis, for the primal and unforgiving emotional experience delivered by narratives like the ones told by our ancestors. There is transformative power in terror, as life has lately taught us, and we count on stories to keep us from forgetting that—a kind of story that has become harder, not easier, to find.

A film about fairy tales and about the two men who collected the traditional German tales that migrated across the Atlantic to become part of our folklore, *The Brothers Grimm* delivers a startling reminder that the narratives started out as adult entertainment—violent, bawdy, melodramatic improvisations that emerged in the evening hours, when ordinary chores engaged the labor of hands, leaving minds free to wander and wonder. Fairy tales, John Updike has proposed, were the television and pornography of an earlier age—part of a fund of popular culture (including jokes, gossip, news, advice, and folklore) that were told to the rhythms of spinning, weaving, repairing tools, and mending clothes.[2] The hearth, where all generations were present, including children, became the site at which miniature myths were stitched together, tales that took up in symbolic terms anxieties about death, loss, and the perils of daily life but also staged the triumph of the underdog. There Jack could slay the giant and escape with his treasured hen, Rapunzel could use her tears to restore the sight of the man who fathered her children, and Puss in Boots could

---

1 Published in *Slate*, September 22, 2005, <http://www.slate.com/articles/arts/culture-box/2005/09/fairy_tales_in_the_age_of_terror.html>.

2 "Fabian Italiane," review of Italo Calvino, *Italian Folktales*, 1980, in *Hugging the Shore: Essays and Criticism* (New York: Vintage, 1984) 662.

outwit an ogrelike monarch to advance the fortunes of his humble master. Beneath the horror was always the promise of revenge and restitution, the exquisite reassurance of a happily-ever-after.

Beauty, horror, wonders, violence, and magic have always tumbled thick and fast through fairy tales. Folk raconteurs gave their audiences what they wanted, indulging the desire for audacious eroticism, hyperbolic fantasies, and casual cruelty. For those gathered around the hearth, Little Red Riding Hood was not necessarily an innocent who strays from the forest path. In tales that formed part of an adult storytelling culture in premodern France, she unwittingly feasts on the flesh and blood of her grandmother, performs an elaborate striptease for the wolf, and manages to escape by telling the predatory beast that she needs to go outdoors to relieve herself. Firmly rooted in the familiar, she introduces us to the great existential mysteries, in a miniature and manageable form. Her irreverent behavior, effortless mobility, willingness to take detours, and daring resourcefulness modeled possibilities for those lingering at the fireside.

In the great migration of fairy tales from the fireside to the nursery that was finally accomplished in the course of the nineteenth century, "Little Red Riding Hood" was twisted, pretzel-like, into a cautionary tale, warning small children not only about the dangers of straying from the path but also about their own unruly desires. Charles Perrault's version of 1697 shows us a Little Red Cap who never emerges from the belly of the wolf, and her story becomes a platform for teaching children many lessons, among them the fact that "tame wolves / Are the most dangerous of all."

Framing fairy tales with platitudes about obedience (those efforts continue today in the anthologies of children's literature produced by William J. Bennett[1]) and settling them in the nursery could not strip them entirely of their power to shock and enthrall. If the Grimms took pains to eliminate raunchy folk humor from the narratives, they insisted on keeping the violence, in some cases intensifying it and surrounding its effects with an intoxicating verbal shimmer. J.R.R. Tolkien was fascinated by the "Juniper Tree," one of the more ghoulish tales in the collection, and referred to the scene in which a stepmother decapitates her stepson as "exquisite and tragic."[2] He was not alone; P.L. Travers, the author of *Mary Poppins*, found the story "beautiful,"[3] even though what follows the scene of decapitation is a description of how the boy is chopped into small pieces and served up to his father in a stew.

---

1 In volumes such as *The Book of Virtues for Young People: A Treasury of Great Moral Stories* (New York: Simon and Schuster, 1997) and *The Children's Book of Home and Family* (New York: Scholastic, 2003).

2 J.R.R. Tolkien, "On Fairy Stories," in *Tree and Leaf* (London: Unwin, 1964) 32.

3 P.L. Travers, "Only Connect," in *Only Connect: Readings in Children's Literature*, 2nd ed. (Toronto: Oxford UP, 1980) 201.

Disavowing the notion of fairy-tale whimsy, Tolkien and Travers are stirred by child-hood memories of how the violence in the stories can tear us apart but also restore us to life through the knowledge, wisdom, and experience they impart.

Fairy tales once elicited what Richard Wright has described as a "total emotional response." In *Black Boy*,[1] an autobiography of growing up in the Jim Crow South, Wright evokes the memory of having "Bluebeard and His Seven Wives" (a fairy tale whose implied audience is clearly adults) read to him by a schoolteacher named Ella: "My imagination blazed. The sensations the story aroused in me were never to leave me.... I hungered for the sharp, frightening, breathtaking, almost painful excitement that the story had given me." Like so many young fairy-tale protagonists, Wright found himself experiencing a shudder of pleasure and fear, standing "at the gate-way to a forbidden and enchanting land." And it was literally forbidden: Ella, who was boarding at his house, sneaked the story in, but this was long before Bettelheim had enlightened Americans about the therapeutic power of fairy tales to strengthen young superegos. For Wright, the maturational effect was a sound beating (Wright's grandmother denounced the tale as "devil's work") and a lifelong engagement with stories, whose power to change us—not least by frightening us into imagining al-ternate realities—had once overwhelmed him. Wright's experience gives us pause about our endless efforts to invent child-friendly fairy tales. Were our ancestors on to something when they included children in their communal storytelling practices?

Fairy tales have not vanished from the world of adults, but today they often take the form of cultural debris, fragments of once powerful narratives that find their way into our language to produce colorful turns of phrase. In the media, we read about a Goldilocks economy, about the Emperor's new clothes, and about Sleeping Beauty stocks. In popular send-ups of the classic plots, the purpose is usually to mock the values found in the earlier variants, whether it is the virtue of selfless industry or a lack of vanity. Julia Roberts plays a latter-day Cinderella who moves from rags to Ro-deo-Drive riches in *Pretty Woman* [1990]. Anne Sexton gives us a Snow White who is described as both "dumb bunny" and "lovely virgin" as she falls into her comatose state.[2] Not surprisingly, a parodic idea of wonder also gets enlisted to promote con-sumerist fantasies. Kim Cattrall makes her way through the cobblestone streets of Prague, wearing a red dress, red hooded cape, and red heels in search of a man with the good taste to drink Pepsi. This modern "use" of fairy tales depends on undercut-ting precisely their original power to give us a bite of reality, to confront us with monsters that seize us, and sink their teeth into our most vulnerable parts. In *The*

---

1 [Richard Wright, *Black Boy* (1945; New York: Harper Perennial Modern Classics, 1998).]
2 [Anne Sexton, "Snow White and the Seven Dwarves," in *The Complete Poems* (New York: Houghton Mifflin, 1981).]

Brothers Grimm, Gilliam gets us back to the raw emotional power of the originals, with his mirror queen, whose beautiful face shatters into pieces before our eyes, and with his gingerbread man, a gob of primal muck that emerges from a well to revel in chthonic glory as he swallows a child.

In a scene from *To the Lighthouse*,[1] Virginia Woolf captures the elusive hold that fairy tales have on modern sensibilities. When Mrs. Ramsey reads the Grimms' "Fisherman and His Wife" to her son, the tales of old are likened to "the bass gently accompanying a tune, which now and then ran up unexpectedly into the melody." The plots are still there, tugging on us as reminders of the hard-won wisdom that enabled our ancestors to cope with their collective anxieties and fantasies. They continue to haunt us, yet we never quite embrace them or abandon them completely.

Too anxious about the trackless future to trust in the clarifying energy of wandering in "once upon a time," we are in danger of losing our willingness to resurrect wondrous narratives that first transfix us with the terror they arouse, then engage our intellectual powers, provoking forms of curiosity that lead us to consider possibilities—what could be, what might be, what should be. These tales reveal the double face of wonder, restoring the pleasures of fascination, yet at the same time inciting us to reflect on the dark fears and desires embedded in that fascination. In returning us to the gnarled roots of the Grimms' tales, Terry Gilliam opens a gateway that takes us back to the enchantments of a long time ago but also leads us forward into the mysteries of the here and now, this time with an ancient road map in our hands.

---

1 [Virginia Woolf, *To the Lighthouse* (London: Hogarth, 1927).]

DISNEY AND THE POLITICS OF PUBLIC CULTURE[1]

Henry A. Giroux and Grace Pollock

> I think of a child's mind as a blank book. During the first years of his life, much will be written on the pages. The quality of that writing will affect his life profoundly.
>
> —Walt Disney[2]

IN THE POPULAR MIND, WALT DISNEY, BOTH THE MAN AND THE COM-pany, is synonymous with the notion of childhood innocence. As suburban America witnesses urban violence invading its own schools, homes, and neighborhoods, Disney becomes a symbol for the security and romance of the small-town America of yesteryear—a pristine never-never land in which children's fantasies come true, happiness reigns, and innocence is kept safe through the magic of pixie dust.

Of course, Walt realized that innocence as a cultural metaphor had to be associated with a particular rendering of childhood as well as a specific view of the American past, present, and future. In other words, Disney's view of innocence had to be constructed within particular maps of meaning in which children and adults could define themselves through a cultural language that offered them both modest pleasure and a coherent sense of identity. Nicholas Sammond has written a brilliant account of how the Walt Disney Company created a market niche for children's entertainment alongside scientific discourses—mainly sociology and psychology—that were being popularized from the 1930s to the 1960s in an attempt to define the "normal" child. One result of children being seen as "the crucible of ideal American culture" was the proliferation of media that aimed to "correct the way children are raised" so as to "eliminate a number of social ills."[3] In particular, Sammond suggests that the paternalistic image Walt Disney promoted of himself was key to the corporation's being seen as an expert parental substitute whose products implemented new, cutting-edge ideas of what was best for children and society more generally. The fact that most of those ideas regarding the generic American child were largely aimed at reinforcing dominant assumptions about gender, race, religion, and class is yet another paradox lying at the heart of Disney culture. Indeed, Walt Disney quickly saw

---

1 Chapter 1, *The Mouse that Roared: Disney and the End of Innocence* (Lanham, MD: Rowman and Littlefield, 2010) 17-21.

2 Walt Disney, cited in Jennifer J. Laabs, "Disney Helps Keep Kids in School," *Personnel Journal* (November 1992): 58.

3 Nicholas Sammond, *Babes in Tomorrowland: Walt Disney and the Making of the American Child, 1930-1960* (Durham, NC: Duke UP, 2005) 3.

the advantages to linking childhood innocence with home entertainment, which became the pedagogical vehicle to promote a set of values and practices that associated the safeguarding of childhood with a strong investment in the nuclear family, middle-class Protestant values, and the market as a sphere of consumption. Refusing to separate entertainment from education, Disney challenged the assumption that entertainment has little educational value and is simply about leisure. Walt understood that education is not confined to schools but embedded in the broader realm of popular culture and its mechanisms for the production of knowledge and values. In creating his ideal democracy of consumers, he also knew that the Walt Disney Company had to make products that were lively and enjoyable.

Walt's fusing of entertainment and education blurred the boundaries between public culture and commercial interests and found expression both in the various attractions that came to characterize theme parks, such as Disneyland and Disney World, and in the extended range of cultural and media outlets that shape everyday life. For decades, Hollywood films, radio stations, television networks, sports franchises, book publishers, and numerous daily newspapers all provided Disney with sites from which to promote its cultural pedagogy. Among Walt Disney's more lucrative insights—one that continues to distinguish the Disney corporation—was the realization that the educational field could be reconstructed and transformed through the mastery of new spaces for leisure, new electronic technologies, and new global markets. Pedagogy, for Disney, was not restricted to schooling, and schooling did not strictly define the contexts in which children could learn, make affective investments, and reconstruct their identities.

If we imagine the Walt Disney Company as a teaching machine whose power and influence can, in part, be measured by the number of people who come in contact with its goods, messages, values, and ideas, it becomes clear that Disney has now wielded for decades an enormous effect on the cultural life of several nations, especially with regard to the culture of children. In 1995, "more than 200 million people a year watch[ed] a Disney film or home video, 395 million watch[ed] a Disney TV show every week; 212 million listen[ed] or dance[d] to Disney music, records, tapes or compact discs…. More than 50 million people a year from all lands pass[ed] through the turnstiles of Disney theme parks."[1] In the company's 1997 annual report, Michael Eisner, former chairman and chief executive officer of the Walt Disney Company, claimed that during the week of November 2 to 8, 1997, Disney culture attracted the attention of the following numbers of people, mostly children:

---

1   Michael D. Eisner, "Planetized Entertainment," *New Perspectives Quarterly* 12, no. 4 (Fall 1995): 8.

During these seven days, 34.2 million people watched *The Wonderful World of Disney*, 3.3 million people turned on *One Saturday Morning*, 3.8 million subscribers viewed *The Disney Channel*, 2.8 million listened to *Radio Disney*, 793,000 visited Disney theme parks, 810,000 made a purchase at a Disney Store and nine million copies of *Beauty and the Beast: The Enchanted Christmas* were shipped to video stores across the country.[1]

Disney's success with brand licensing and cross-promotion of its hit television shows and films continues to exert a formidable influence on children and youth. In 2008, despite the economic recession, Disney had one of its most profitable years on record, generating $37.8 billion in sales.[2] The Disney website DisneyFairies.com, which helps very young computer users to generate fairy avatars, attracts more than one million daily visitors.[3] The tween franchises High School Musical and Hannah Montana helped to sell more than 33 million books.[4] The Disney Princess franchise, with its array of pink and gold items, is a "leading lifestyle brand" for six- to nine-year-old girls.[5] And Disney now claims to "fulfill the dreams of girls of any age, including brides-to-be," by selling bridal couture and home furnishings inspired by the "personality and style of each Disney Princess."[6] In 2007, Disney produced an estimated 40 per cent of all the licensed merchandise in the United States and Canada.[7] Marketing analysts now report that consumers around the world spend about 13 billion "person-hours" per year in contact with Disney's various brands.[8]

Disney's commercial success testifies to the crucial role that culture and en-

---

1 Michael D. Eisner, "Letter to Shareholders," in *The Walt Disney Company 1997 Annual Report* (Burbank, CA: Walt Disney Company, 1997) 3.
2 Robert Iger, "Letter to Shareholders, Part II," in *The Walt Disney Company 2008 Annual Report*, Disney Investor Relations, <http://corporate.disney.go.com/investors/annual_reports/2008/introduction/letterToShareholdersII.html> (accessed May 14, 2009).
3 Robert Iger, "Consumer Products, Part I," in *The Walt Disney Company 2007 Annual Report*, Disney Investor Relations, <http://corporate.disney.go.com/investors/annual_reports/2007/cp/part1.html> (accessed May 14, 2009).
4 Robert Iger, "Consumer Products, Part III," in *The Walt Disney Company 2007 Annual Report*, Disney Investor Relations, <http://corporate.disney.go.com/investors/annual_reports/2007/cp/part3.html> (accessed May 14, 2009).
5 Iger, "Consumer Products, Part I."
6 Iger, "Consumer Products, Part I."
7 "Disney's 2007 Holiday Best Sellers Top Consumer Wish Lists," Portfolio.com, January 9, 2008, <www.portfolio.com/resources/company-profiles/DIS/press/2008/01/09/disneys-2007-holiday-best-sellers-top-consumer-wish-lists> (accessed January 10, 2009).
8 Michael Santoli, "The Magic's Back: Disney's Bright Future," Smartmoney.com, February 26, 2008, <www.smartmoney.com/barrons/index.cfm?story=20080226-Walt-Disney-DIS&nav=RSS20> (accessed March 15, 2008).

tertainment play "in the structure and organization of late-modern society, in the processes of development of the global environment and in the disposition of its economic and material resources."[1] Disney's success represents, in part, the power of the culture industries to mediate and influence almost every aspect of our lives.[2] Corporate culture uses its power as an educational force to redefine the relationships between childhood and innocence, citizenship and consumption, civic values and commercial values. Both how and what young people learn, in a society in which power is increasingly held by megacorporations, raises serious concerns about what noncommodified public spheres exist to safeguard youth from the ravages of a market logic that provides neither a context for moral consideration, nor a language for defending vital social institutions and policies as a public good.

A vibrant democratic culture fulfills one of its most important functions when it views children as a social investment, whose worth and value cannot be measured exclusively in commercial and private terms. That is, a democratic culture provides the institutional and symbolic resources necessary for young people to develop their capacities to engage in critical thought, participate in power relations and policy decisions that affect their lives, and transform racial, social, and economic inequities that close down democratic social relations.[3]

The concept of democracy, when linked to the notion of social justice, refers to a society's obligation to create and maintain institutions that view education as a public asset and not merely a private good. The requirements of democratic citizenship necessitate vigilance in public affairs, criticism of public officials (and corporate interests), and participation in political decision making in the interest of expanding accountability, equality of opportunity, justice, and the public good. Such activity resists the privatizing impulses of corporations, which attempt to overshadow the demands of citizenship with the demands of commerce by replacing the notion of free and equal education as a right with the notion of restricted and income-based education as a commodity venture. The challenge democratic societies face with the rise of conglomerates such as Disney—with their profound interest in shaping all facets of youth culture—can be discerned in the crisis that has emerged around the very concept of childhood and the expanding role that corporate culture plays in shaping public education....

---

1 Stuart Hall, "The Centrality of Culture: Notes on the Cultural Revolutions of Our Time," in *Media and Cultural Regulation*, ed. Kenneth Thompson (Thousand Oaks, CA: Sage, 1997) 209.

2 On the influence of corporate media, see Robert W. McChesney, *Corporate Media and the Threat to Democracy* (New York: Seven Stories P, 1997), and Erik Barnouw et al., *Conglomerates and the Media* (New York: New P, 1997).

3 For an excellent analysis of the relationship between education and social justice, see R.W. Connell, *Schools and Social Justice* (Philadelphia: Temple UP, 1993).

FOLKTALES AND THE COMIC BOOK FORMAT[1]

Gail de Vos

The reading process in comics is an extension of text. In text alone the process of reading involves word-to-image conversion. Comics accelerate that by providing the image. When properly executed, it goes beyond conversion and speed and becomes a seamless whole. In every sense, this misnamed form of reading is entitled to be regarded as literature because the images are employed as a language. There is a recognizable relationship to the iconography and pictographs of oriental writing. When this language is employed as a conveyance of ideas and information, it separates itself from mindless visual entertainment. This makes comics a storytelling medium.

—Will Eisner (1996, 5)

WILL EISNER, IN HIS GROUND BREAKING WORK *GRAPHIC STORYTELL-ing*, points out that regardless of the various methods of transmitting a story incorporating any form of modern technology, there are only two major ways for it to be told: words (orally or written) and images. In comics, these two methods are combined (1996, 13). While Eisner defines a storyteller as the "writer or person in control of the narration" (1996, 6), I have always considered the term to mean an oral transmitter of a narrative. I will apply my denotation throughout this article, with the major focus on examples of retellings of traditional folktales in comic book format, particularly for the young adult reader. I became interested in the similarities between oral storytelling and the comic book format when conducting research on reworkings of traditional folktales for *New Tales for Old: Folktales as Literary Fictions for Young Adults* (1999). Reading folktales in this format made me realize that this was probably the closest literary genre to the oral art of telling a story. Both the comic book and the oral tale depend on dialogue and tone of voice, body language and gestures, and timing for an effective experience for the audience. Both of these storytelling forms require the audience to actively participate in the understanding of the story; the listening audience must decode the words and silences, the body language, and the voice to make their own images of the characters, the stage, and the action that is taking place in the tale. The

---

1 Revision and updating of "Storytelling, Folktales and the Comic Book Format," first published at <http://works.bepress.com/cgi/viewcontent.cgi?article=1027&context =gail_devos>.

strength of the oral tale is that each member of the audience uses his or her own experiences and background to create a story that is uniquely his or her own. In the comic book format, the reader must speculate on what happens in the gutters (the space between the panels) as well as read the visual cues to interpret the story, and as in the oral tale, the experience and background of the reader not only enrich the story but also individualize it.

This essay is not the first time that anyone has considered comic books in regards to traditional tales. In a study published in 1941, two psychiatrists conclude: "Comic books can probably be best understood if they are looked upon as an expression of the folklore of this age. They may be compared with the mythology, fairy tales and puppet shows, for example, of past ages" (cited in Levine 1992, 1372). A few years later, during the mid-1950s and the "comic book scare," several articles attempted to evaluate the dangers of comics by comparing them with fairy tales and other literature that preceded them, such as *Struwwelpeter*. Some of the critics noted structural and narrative similarities between comics and fairy tales and admitted that fairy tales also were cruel and perhaps inappropriate for children; however, since comic books were read more frequently than the traditional folktales, the quantity of comic consumption made the decisive difference.

Other critics rejected the comparison altogether on the grounds that such comparisons should not serve as justifications for the horror and cruelty in the comics. "Fairy tales take place in another remote world of 'once upon a time,' whereas the aim of horror series was to create a nauseous reality" (Jovanovic and Koch 1999, 112-13). Rolf Brednich, in 1976, reflected that there are numerous structural relationships between comics and oral narrative types, in particular, the fairy tale: "European folktales offer—as a sort of universal poetry—a great number of characters, constellations of characters, plots, and so forth, which have been taken over—whether consciously or unconsciously—by the producers of popular and 'trivial' literature" (1976, 47). His premise was that "comic book stories and folklore stories appeal to largely the same audience. Both are light entertainment that focus on the adventures of heroes who act outside the restrictions of the established authorities" (1976, 48).

Most of these critics compared the folktale to the superhero tale and paid no attention at all to the similarities of telling the same story both orally and in the graphic format. This, then, is the focus of this essay.

Eisner defines an image as the memory of an object or experience recorded either mechanically (photograph) or by hand (drawing): "In comics, images are generally impressionistic. Usually, they are rendered with economy in order to facilitate their usefulness as a language. Because experience precedes analysis, the intellectual digestive process is accelerated by the imagery provided in comics" (1996, 15). In his discussion of images as narrative tools, he speaks of the benefits of employing stereotypes in the comic book world. Stereotypes are also widely used in the world of folklore. They are the shorthand of human experience and allow for the engagement of the listener's imagination. Everyone knows what a beautiful princess looks and acts like, and so the storyteller does not have to stop or slow the telling of the tale to describe the characters or the setting (usually a castle, forest, or hut). In both the oral tale and the tale rendered in comic book form in comparison to a film or novel, there is not a great deal of time or space available to develop a character. Thus, the use of the stereotype, but, as Eisner points out, "the art of creating a stereotypical image for the purpose of storytelling requires a familiarity with the audience and a recognition that each society has its own ingrown set of accepted stereotypes" (1996, 19). This is what makes oral storytelling so powerful and the reading of comic books from other cultures so bewildering!

At the onset of the telling of a story, whether oral, written, or graphic, there is an understanding between the teller and the listener or reader. The teller expects that the audience will comprehend, while the audience expects that the author will deliver something that is comprehensible. In this agreement, the burden is on the teller. In comics, the reader is expected to understand things such as implied time, space, motion, sound, and emotions. In order to do this, a reader must not only draw on visceral reactions but also make use of an accumulation of experience as well as reasoning (1996, 49). Eisner claims the reader is an actor because of the importance of dialogue in the graphic format: "Where dialogue is not furnished, it requires that the storyteller depend on the reader's life experience to supply the speech that amplifies the intercourse between the actors. In depicting a silent sequence of interaction, the comic teller must be sure to employ gestures and postures easily identifiable with the dialogue being played out in a reader's mind" (1996, 57). Further on in his discussion about telling stories graphically, Eisner points out that subtle gestures or provocative postures are not easy to depict without the continuing movement afforded by film, and therefore the "telling" images are extracted from the flow of action and frozen in the image presented on the page (1996, 114). Gestures are hand, body, or face movements that aid in the communication process and must spring from strong, detailed images of the scenes, characters, and action in the story. In an oral tale, gestures are effective because they translate more directly into specific and powerful images in the listener's minds than do the words. They provide an important form of detailed visual information for the audience and must contribute to how the story is told. Gestures in comic books also aid in making the printed page and characters on it come alive.

The major difference between the print format and oral storytelling is that the latter transmits images primarily through sound. How the story sounds, however, depends on the individual's personal interpretation of the tale, the skill in which the storyteller tells the tale, and the listening experience and needs of the audience. Part of this skill also includes the effective use of body language and non-verbal communication cues. While the audience is listening to the sound of the words and decoding the images that are created in their minds, they are also reading the storyteller's gestures, facial expressions, and silences. I have found that it takes just as much fluency and exposure to the storytelling format on the part of the storyteller's audience to be effective listeners as it does for the readers of comics to effectively appreciate the story before them. When dialogue is present in the comic format, it appears in various types of sound balloons and fonts that guide the reader (actor) in hearing the conversations. Given the absence of sound, the dialogue in the balloons acts as a script to guide the reader in reciting it mentally. The style of the lettering and the emulation of accents are the clues enabling the reader to read it with the emotional nuances the comic teller intended. This is essential to the credibility of the imagery. There are commonly accepted lettering characteristics, which imply sound level and emotion (1996, 61).

Eisner also contends that in telling stories in a graphic medium, it is necessary to establish credibility and this is usually done in an economical prologue to the tale: "Stories built around a protagonist often depend on a prologue to quickly introduce him" (1996, 86). In oral storytelling, the function of this prologue is looked after in the opening to the story. The opening, often consisting of a brief anecdote that makes the story relevant to the audience or an explanation of something within the tale that the listener needs to know in order to appreciate or understand it better, creates the transition from the world of the listener into the world of the story. The told story, therefore, also employs a closing, which aids in the transition from the world of story back into the listener's real realm. These closings complete the circle that makes a story.

In order to clarify the similarities between the oral storytelling experience and the comic format one, I am going to draw on one of Eisner's own stories, "Street Magic" in *Minor Miracles* (2009), a collection of four stories set in the New York City of his youth. "Street Magic" is a story of survival magic for immigrant families new to New York. The splash page, similar in function to the introduction of a folktale, introduces the reader to the major characters, the setting, and the problem of the story. It contains a written prologue: "Immigrant families on our block believed they were in hostile territory. Survival skills were brought from the old country. They were kept as magic spells the family used when dealing with the predictable outrages of neighborhood life. They were not formally taught. They were learned by emulating older and more experienced family members. Cousin Mersh, for instance, was an authority on the application of street magic" (2009, 19). Eisner does not work with the traditional comic book framed panels to tell his story; the reader needs to follow two or three sequential vignettes on each page. The experienced reader knows how to follow the sequence of the illustrations or panels as well as the sequence of speakers and the rate of their speech. This aspect of reading comics is perhaps the most frustrating to those not familiar or comfortable with the format. Eisner's style in this particular story makes this easy for all readers since there are only a few illustrations on each page. Experienced comic book readers also know that the shape of sound balloons as well as the content offers clues to the reader. There are regular dialogue balloons, directed at the reader as if the reader is sitting on the steps with the speakers. Other shapes inform the reader if the dialogue is internal or electronically transmitted, and so on. The splash page contains just one illustration: Cousin Mersh is walking hand-in-hand with a young boy who is listening to Mersh tell him to "Keep your mouth shut and stay close by me … This is an enemy block" (2009, 19). Comic books use panels and the turning of pages to add pauses and to elicit drama much in the same way as a storyteller does: to arouse interest and intensify emotional responses to the story. The reader knows the two boys are going into possible danger but will not know what happens next until the page is turned.

The next two pages transport the reader to the steps of a tenement building where three louts (easy to recognize by their body language, dress, and method of speech) are watching the two boys approach. The reader, through the dialogue of the three bullies, discovers their plan. They had beaten up Cousin Mersh before and are looking for a way to enliven the process for today. The gang leader decides to conduct a lottery. Two pieces of paper are put in a hat and Cousin Mersh is to draw one out. If he chooses the one that says "guilty," the bullies will give him another beating. If he chooses the one that is blank, however, he will be left alone. The bullies are delighted with their plan for they have surreptitiously written "guilty" on both pieces of paper. The reader's last image before the page is turned is that of Cousin Mersh and his charge walking up to the three smug bullies on the steps. On the next two pages, their plan is put into effect, and the final image here is of Cousin Mersh selecting a piece of paper from the hat with his cousin fearfully looking on and the three bullies totally pleased with themselves and the situation. The page is turned and the reader, along with the three bullies, waits in anticipation as Cousin Mersh opens the selected piece of paper and reads it. Before any of the spectators, including the reader, can see what is on the piece of paper, Cousin Mersh swallows it. He then confronts the bemused trio: "So, now … open up the other paper! … What does it say?" (2009, 25). "Guilty" is the answer! We turn the page to see the two heroes walking away in victory after claiming that the blank piece of paper must have been the one that was swallowed! The final two "panels" have Cousin Mersh explaining the street magic to the young boy and ends with a caveat: "Keep walking! Don't look back" (2009, 26).

The story is told visually but employs the oral storyteller's toolkit of sound (how the words are presented in the sound balloons for the "actor" to say out loud includes pitch, volume, and rate of speech); gesture and body language (facial expressions and non-verbal body clues of all the characters); timing (exemplified by the number of panels on each page and the turning of it); and stereotypes (the reader immediately recognizes the role of all the characters in this story). The only information that is given outside of the comic book format is Eisner's written prologue, putting the situation into context. He points out that this magic has been transported from the old world. And to me, the magic was not only the minor miracle of Mersh's escape from a beating but the incorporation of an old tale for a new audience. I immediately recognized the Jewish folktale that it was based on, "The Rabbi and the Inquisitor." How many readers would realize that this particular story in this collection was not reminiscent of the comic book elder but of a tale well-employed? It was certainly not recognized in the numerous reviews when the graphic novel was released.

Eisner states in his Foreword that these tales, "while they are apocryphal, they were nevertheless distilled from my remembrance of those that were the common property of our family" (2009, 2). These minor miracles, he continues, are a sort of cultural inheritance and similar themes can be found in classical Yiddish folklore and in old German folktales (2009, 3). One version of the traditional tale can be found in Ausubel's *A Treasury of Jewish Folklore* (1948, 36) and Sherman's *A Sampler of Jewish American Folklore* (1992, 101-02). In her note on the folktale, Josepha Sherman states that this story is known to her in both a Jewish version and in a non-Jewish variant. The idea of rigged lots with a clever person overcoming the fact that both papers have been marked "guilty" (or, in the case of a non-literate culture, both pebbles painted black) by swallowing one of the lots is a common folkloric "gimmick" throughout the world. Most of the time, the gambler is risking his own life, though, not the life of a whole community as well, and often the gambler is guilty, a rogue managing to escape justice (1992, 187).

We turn now to see how other folktales have fared in the contemporary comic book and graphic novel format. The term graphic novel is used fairly loosely here in that it also refers to anthologies of stories, reprints of serialized comic issues, and the stand-alone novel. "Graphic novels are printed on better-quality paper and bound more carefully, often in hard-cover. The extended lifespan and traditional book shape give graphic novels a certain legitimacy that their flimsier comic brethren never had" (Long, 1997, 15). In their article on folklore in comic books, Banks and Wein state that "the use of folklore in comic books can range from wholesale reproductions to imaginative variations and alterations of well-known folk narratives, from the subtle inclusion of motifs, references, and particularly, folk beliefs, in story-lines and characterizations, to the blatant reintroduction of stock folkloric characters" (1998, n.p.). They cite the appearance of Thomas the Rhymer from Scottish ballads, Loki, and the parliament of rooks in the *Sandman* series as examples of the inclusions of references into storylines. They assert that numerous comic book creators borrow the themes and ideas from folklore and folklore theory for the development of their narratives. Their article analyses three series published by DC Comics that have a heavy dependence on folklore within their storyline, characterization, illustration, and incidental dialogue—*Swamp Thing, The Sandman,* and *Hellblazer.* Neil Gaiman, author of *The Sandman,* has indicated that his reference tools include J.G. Frazer, Joseph Campbell, and Andrew Lang among other "popular" standard sources of folklore for the lay reader. Banks and Wein remark that these are sources that "the average reader wanting information about folk religion and ritual finds in general bookstores and reads with pleasure" (1998, n.p.). They discuss Gaiman's use of the Jewish folklore character Lilith to demonstrate that many of his sources went beyond the more popular ones as well. There are few readers who would understand the role of such a character in the traditional literature since Lilith is only mentioned once in the Hebrew Bible and is developed as a character only in its Apocrypha and in the rabbinical commentary, the Aggadah. They also briefly discuss Gaiman's series as "a journey through folklore, myth, legend, and imagination where archetypal motifs are continually brought to the fore" (1998, n.p.).

Mike Mignola frequently incorporates folklore in a similar manner in his Hellboy universe with his continuous references to folklore motifs and tales embracing folklore from all corners of the globe. An early example is "The Corpse," found in *Hellboy: The Chained Coffin and Others* (1998), an almost flawless reworking of the traditional Irish tale "Teig O'Kane." The splash page contains an excerpt from the poem "The Fairies" by William Allingham, placing the story in context. Upon turning the page, the reader is introduced to the crisis of a changeling invading the household of a family in Ireland. This changeling presents the rationale for Hellboy to appear in the story. The rather weak traditional protagonist will not do for a hero of a Hellboy tale! It is not until the seventh page of the story that Mignola actually moves into the traditional tale: the scene is set, the reader is immersed in the Irish tale, and, other than for the appearances of the changeling in the illustrations, the story now mirrors the story structure of the traditional tale, with a few divergent elements to build suspense and give Hellboy a more active role.

There has been a conspicuous resurgence in the reworking of fairy tales since the onset of Bill Willingham's successful series, *Fables,* and subsequent offshoots from the series, *Jack of Fables, The Fairest,* and *Cinderella.* The Vertigo series, first published in 2002 and written for a mature audience, effectively weaves well-known characters, storylines, and motifs into a new world of Willingham's own making. Willingham's notable knowledge and respect for folklore transforms and reconstructs the traditional characters and their roles in a contemporary setting. The *Fables* characters have been fleshed out, "... given form, drapery, adornment that at once marks them as contiguous with their fairy-tale selves, and lends them a verisimilitude that allows them to pass unquestioned into human society, both ours and the fictional New York of the series" (Zolkover 2008, 42). Non-human characters live at the Farm where, along with survival, a primary anxiety is keeping the Mundys (ordinary or "mundane" humans) ignorant of their existence. A recent crossover series, that combines this title with Peter Carey's literary comic book series *The Unwritten*, firmly establishes these folklore characters as important contenders in contemporary popular culture as does the *Fables* universe role-playing video game, *The Wolf Among Us*.

Zenescope publications, in their multi-titled series *Grimms' Fairy Tales*, have also reimagined the most familiar folklore characters, but the illustrations of their female lead characters have infuriated many potential readers who boycott the entire set of spinoff titles. The primary series, first published in 2005, incorporates a frame story for each of the reworked tales. Dr. Sela Mathers, a professor of literature, uses the tales to edify individuals about their life choices. Her frustration with the ignoring of her lessons turns her to dispense justice instead of offering clues to these irresponsible folks. Other folktale-related spinoffs include Marvel's two four-issue series, *Spider-Man Fairy Tales* and *X-Men Fairy Tales* and Archie Comics' single issue title *Betty & Veronica in Snow White and the Riverdale Dwarfs* and their compilation *Betty and Veronica Storybook*. *Max Hamm: Fairy Tale Detective* is another delightful series, playing with both traditional tales and the *noir* detective genre. Other creative reworkings of the traditional tales extending the story by placing it in a new setting include *Seven Sons* by Alexander Grecian and Riley Rossmo. In this adaptation, the tale of the seven identical Chinese brothers is moved to the early North American west to explore themes of racism and settlement issues. Shannon and Dean Hale, with illustrations by Nathan Hale, similarly shift the setting in their adaptation of "Rapunzel" in their two graphic novels *Rapunzel's Revenge* and *Calamity Jack* to a fantastical Wild West. Steve Sheinkin's *Rabbi Harvey* series of short stories is also set in the American west. In this series the title character either retells a Jewish folktale to aid his community or is an active character in one of the reworked tales.

There are countless folktale characters who step out of their traditional tales to manifest themselves in a multiplicity of comic book titles. For instance, Baba Yaga, the infamous witch from Russian folklore, appears in *Sandman*, *Hellboy*, *Fables*, *The Books of Magic*, the *Grimm Fairy Tales* universe, and Marvel's *Earth-616*, among other comic book series. These types of appearances are too numerous to list but provide entertainment for comic book readers who know their folklore.

Along with the reworkings of the tales and characters from the realm of folktale, there has also been a renaissance in the publishing of the tales, slightly tweaked, in comic book anthologies. Strawberry Publishers have recently released an anthology of Grimms' tales, *Erstwhile: Untold Tales from the Brothers Grimm*, by Gina Biggs, Louisa Roy and Elle Skinner (2012). The illustrations are simple, reminiscent of manga, and the tellings are straightforward. It is refreshing to find stories other than the most popular canon. Editor Chris Duffy recently published *Fairy Tale Comics: Classic Tales Told by Extraordinary Cartoonists* (2013) with 17 folk and fairy tales reimagined, although frequently truncated, in this recent collection from First Second in the companion to their 2011 title *Nursery Rhyme Comics*. The stories range from six to eight pages which may be responsible for their truncated state in which the folk tradition of three repetitions is often ignored. Most of the included tales originate with the Grimms but there are a few surprising exceptions: "The Prince and the Tortoise," adapted from Jean-Charles Mardus's translation of Arabian Nights (1001 Nights), and "Baba Yaga" and "The King and His Storyteller," adapted by Craig Thompson from Petrus Alphonsi's medieval collection of tales. First Second's anthology has a direct connection to an earlier fairy-tale anthology edited by Art Spiegelman and Françoise Mouly. In *Little Lit: Folklore & Fairy Tale Funnies* (2006), Spiegelman and Mouly present a wide variety of familiar and not so familiar tales adapted by comic book creators not principally known for their child-friendly content work.

After almost two decades of research into the appearance and adaptation of folktales and folklore motifs in the comic book format, I realize that I have just begun to scratch the surface.

Works Cited

Ausubel, Nathan. 1948. *A Treasury of Jewish Folklore*. New York: Crown.

Banks, Amanda Carson, and Elizabeth Wein. 1998. "Folklore and the Comic Book: The Traditional Meets the Popular." <http://www.temple.edu/isllc/newfolk/comics1.html>.

Brednich, Rolf Wilhelm. 1976. "Comic Strips as a Subject of Folk Narrative Research." *Folklore Today*: 45-55.

de Vos, Gail. 2010. "Folklore in Comics." In *Encyclopedia of Comic Books and Graphic Novels*, Volume 1, ed. M. Keith Booker. Santa Barbara, CA: Greenwood. 220-23.

de Vos, Gail, and Anna Altmann. 1999. *New Tales for Old: Folktales as Literary Fictions for Young Adults*. Santa Barbara, CA: Libraries Unlimited.

Eisner, Will. *Graphic Storytelling*. 1996. Tamarac, FL: Poorhouse P.

Eisner, Will. *Minor Miracles*. 2009. New York: W.W. Norton.

Jovanovic, Goran, and Ulrich Koch. 1999. "Trash Literature and Fairy Tales: The Comics Debate in Germany: Against Dirt and Rubbish, Pictorial Idiotism, and Cultural Analphabetism." In *Pulp Demons: International Dimensions of the Postwar Anti-Comics Campaign*, ed. John A. Lent. Madison: Associated University Presses. 93-129.

Levine, Lawrence W. 1992. "The Folklore of Industrial Society: Popular Culture and Its Audiences." *American Historical Review* 97: 1369-99.

Long, Everitt. 1997. "Reading, Writing and Rendering the World in Neil Gaiman's *The Sandman*." Master of Arts Thesis, University of Western Ontario. <http://www.nlc-bnc.ca.login.ezproxy.library.ualberta.ca/obj/s4/f2/dsk2/tape15?PQDD_0013/MQ32492.pdf>.

Sherman, Josepha. 1992. *A Sampler of Jewish American Folklore*. Little Rock: August House.

Zolkover, Adam. 2008. "Corporealizing Fairy Tales: The Body, the Bawdy, and the Carnivalesque in the Comic Book Fables." *Marvels & Tales: Journal of Fairy-Tale Studies* 22.1: 38-51.

VISUALIZING LITTLE RED RIDING HOOD[1]

Sarah Bonner

IN RECENT YEARS CONTEMPORARY ARTISTS HAVE BEEN APPROPRIAT-
ing and reinventing traditional fairy tales. Subverting and interrogating received
meanings, artists are challenging the traditional parameters of the tales that convey
ideas of gender role and racial identity. The fairy tale is being translated from literary text into visual culture. The artists recoding the tales address shifts in cultural
attitude, predominantly engaging with issues of identity and discrimination. In this
paper I intend to examine the visual development of "Little Red Riding Hood." I will
address the manner in which the literary tale has been adopted by contemporary
artists; how the visual responds to the textual; and examine the implicated cultural
attitudes embedded in reiterations of the tale.

Critical literature dedicated to the field of fairy-tale study is wide and in depth;
various frameworks are utilized from historical and ideological to Marxist and feminist. Critics of the fairy tale predominately analyze the literary versions, and there
is little evidence of any research into the visual interpretations of the tales. Where
visual analysis occurs, the subject is illustration or popular culture; this paper intends to extend this analysis into the forum of fine art. Critic Jack Zipes is widely
published and employs a socio-historical framework for analyzing the development
and significance of the tales. Writing from a Marxist viewpoint, he believes the fairy
tale embodies the shifting cultural codes of history which can be interpreted, in
turn, as documents that record processes of social production. Zipes asserts that
fairy tales are instrumental in gender politics and identity construction, legitimizing
the genre as relevant in the current period as it was for pre-literate society. His analysis of "Little Red Riding Hood" illustrations provides a sound basis for continuing
research into the visualizing of the tale. Where Zipes comments on ideologies conveyed by fairy tales, Catherine Orenstein, with particular reference to "Little Red
Riding Hood" [see "Red Hot Riding Hood," p. 178] explores the history and cultural
impact of the tale. Orenstein examines broadly cultural incidences of the tale from
cartoons and porn to films and advertising, focusing closely on the construction and
interpretation of gender. The critics' commentary on the various interpretations of
"Little Red Riding Hood" evidences the commonality of the tale in popular culture,
that, translated, emphasizes its continued relevance on an individual and social level.

---

1 An earlier version of this article appeared in *Moveable Type* (a publication of The Post-
   graduate Society of the Department of English Language and Literature at University
   College, London), 2006.

The morality and meaning of fairy tales has undergone rigorous analysis not least within the field of psychoanalysis. Bruno Bettelheim, a Freudian psychoanalyst of the genre, believed that fairy tales were instrumental in developing children's identity. For Bettelheim, children were able to locate, in the text, answers to their own trials and tribulations. Psychoanalysis constitutes significant research in this field; however, it operates a closed system, preferring universalities over individualities. Freud's patriarchal meta-narrative favours boys' development rather than girls' and tends to ignore subjectivity as a whole in childhood development. Bettelheim's discoveries have come under close scrutiny by contemporary artists informing their interpretation of the "Little Red Riding Hood" tale. Flouting the prescribed constraints of fairy-tale psychoanalysis, artists have sought a freedom of interpretation found in narrative analysis such as Roland Barthes's understanding of the relationship between text and image.

Critical analysis of the literary genre is consistent and the critics mentioned above have informed my understanding of "Little Red Riding Hood." However, my main ambition is to understand how contemporary artists are appropriating the tale and to what end. The text and image are intimately related, yet I propose that the image contains qualities that release interpretation from the strictures of tradition, making them more relevant and immediate in contemporary society.

The tale "Little Red Riding Hood" has sustained continued analysis and appropriation, making it a forum for interrogation. References to the tale are abundant, indicating its presence in our cultural unconscious, and Maria Tatar identifies the tale as a place to "work through anxieties about gender, identity, sexuality and violence."[1] Catherine Orenstein in her 2002 study *Little Red Riding Hood Uncloaked* suggests that the tale

> embodies complex and fundamental human concerns. [Red Riding Hood's] tale speaks to enduring themes of family, morality, growing up, growing old, of lighting out into the world, and of the relationships between the sexes. It brings together archetypal opposites, through which it explores the boundaries of culture, class, and especially, what it means to be a man or a woman. The girl and the wolf inhabit a place, call it the forest or call it the human psyche, where the spectrum of human sagas converges and where their social and cultural meanings play out.[2]

---

1 See Maria Tatar, *The Hard Facts of the Grimm's Fairy Tales* (Oxford: Princeton UP, 2003).

2 Catherine Orenstein, *Little Red Riding Hood Uncloaked: Sex, Morality and the Evolution of a Fairy Tale* (New York: Basic Books, 2002) 8.

Orenstein's observation highlights the relevance and endurance of the tale, and despite undergoing a succession of interpretations, it remains recognizable through the repeated use of specific tropes, namely the red hood and the wolf.

"Little Red Riding Hood" has undergone progressive development, yet is known mainly from two literary sources: the 1697 version by Charles Perrault (1628-1703) contained in his collection *Contes du temps passé (Tales of Olden Times)* published under his son's name Pierre Darmancourt; and the collection by Jacob (1785-1863) and Wilhelm (1786-1859) Grimm, *Die Kinder- und Hausmärchen (Children's and Household Tales)* first published in 1812. The basic format of the tale is familiar: Little Red Riding Hood is sent by her mother to her grandmother's house with a basket of goodies; her mother warns her not to stray from the path nor dally on the journey. In the woods Red Riding Hood meets the wolf who finds out where she is going and races off to beat her there, and the girl continues on her journey. Arriving first at grandmother's house, the wolf eats the woman and dons her clothes to fool Red Riding Hood. When the girl arrives at the house, the wolf continues his deception with the ultimate intention to eat the girl. The traditional repartee ensues until— "Grandmother dear, what big teeth you have!" "The better to eat you with!"[1]—thus sealing Red Riding Hood's fate. Whether the girl is eaten (as Perrault would have it) or is eaten but saved (according to the Grimms), the message is one of obedience or punishment. In response to feminist accusations of the tale being "an unfortunate source of negative stereotypes,"[2] recent versions of the tale illustrate empowerment or complicity. A comedic interpretation of such empowerment can be found in Roald Dahl's "Little Red Riding Hood and the Wolf"; when under threat from the wolf, "the small girl smiles. One eyelid flickers. / She whips a pistol from her knickers. / She aims it at the creature's head / And *bang bang bang*, she shoots him dead."[3]

The visual fairy tale has been widely developed in the twentieth century with the advancement of film and animation technologies. The improved technology has also meant an expanded dissemination of the fairy tale. As society becomes increasingly visually oriented, culture is becoming saturated with fairy-tale references. The language and motifs of the tales are so internalized that fairy tales have become sophisticated communications devices influencing consumer trends, entertainment and leisure, and most significantly lifestyle choices [and] roles in society, gender expectations, and identity models.

1 Charles Perrault, *Perrault's Fairy Tales*, trans. A.E. Johnson (New York: Dover, 1969).
2 K. Stone, "Feminist Approaches to the Interpretation of Fairy Tales." In *Fairy Tales & Society: Illusion, Allusion and Paradigm*, ed. Ruth B. Bottigheimer (Philadelphia: U of Pennsylvania P, 1986) 229.
3 Roald Dahl, *Revolting Rhymes* (London: Penguin, 1982) 40.

The translation from text to image relies on the repeated use of tropes particular to "Little Red Riding Hood." The presence of the wolf and red hood is sufficient to identify the tale to the reader/viewer. Where the written text demands an investment of time and offers an accumulated meaning, the image, in contrast, imposes a direct communication; the presence of a red hood immediately identifies the tale to our cultural unconscious. The simplicity of these motifs belies the complex history and interpretation that lend the tale its meaning; and despite changing historical contexts, these tropes endure. One effect of the adoption into visual media is that fairy-tale significance is underestimated, rendered invisible by their very ubiquity.

The visual aspect of the literary fairy tale began with the inclusion of illustrations printed alongside the text. At this juncture a visual language was introduced to the tales. The broad print dissemination ensured the association and consumption of the accompanying image, effectively creating a visual language, a series of motifs immediately recognizable to the viewer. The illustrator's selection of significant scenes has served to internalize the images in a collective unconscious to the extent that the images can exist without the text as reference. Jack Zipes has written extensively on the fairy-tale genre and has published a volume dedicated to the development of "Little Red Riding Hood," examining the processes of appropriation and change over the last three hundred years.[1] Zipes tracks progressive versions from Perrault's new literary version of 1697 to contemporary reworkings of the tale.[2] The illustrations accompanying the tale are also examined. A chronological assessment shows the wolf's changing character: an early illustration by Gustav Doré of 1862 shows a realistic representation of the animal; late-1800 versions render the wolf more dandified, "civilized" in a jacket and standing on his hind legs. Other depictions show the wolf as a harmless and friendly dog, and middle twentieth-century images render the meeting cartoon-like. The adherence to the text by specific plot events means the visual image can communicate immediately and directly with the audience, often working on a subconscious level internalizing the moralistic or gendered messages imposed by the texts.

Through these illustrations the fairy tale can be reduced to a series of key scenes: the departure of Little Red Riding Hood with appropriate finger-wagging from her mother; the meeting with the wolf in the woods; the wolf in grandmother disguise;

---

1 Jack Zipes, *The Trials and Tribulations of Little Red Riding Hood* (London: Routledge, 1993).

2 There is evidence of the Red Riding Hood tale type pre-dating Perrault's literary version. Research has been made into the tale development in the middle ages; see particularly J.M. Ziolkowski, "A Fairy Tale from before Fairy Tales: Egbert of Leige's 'De puella a lupellis seruata' and the Medieval Background of 'Little Red Riding Hood,'" *Speculum* 67, no. 3 (1992): 549-75.

and the discourse between the girl and the wolf. Each image is so strongly attached to the text the meaning is implicit and in fact enhanced due to the direct way in which images communicate with the viewer. The familiarity of the fairy tale fundamentally underpins this visual recognition, the illustration relies on the text and reinforces its meaning. The image sequence delivers the story relying on the internalized tale and the strength of the symbolism embodied by the text—thus, Little Red Riding Hood, the wolf, and the red cape all feature to confirm the tale to the reader/viewer.

Despite the strength of these images, however, the illustrations are rarely viewed separately from the text. The relationship between the textual and visual is intimate and reciprocal. Until recently these illustrations have been the only images associated with the fairy tale. Currently, however, visual references to the tales have saturated contemporary culture; for example, the Chanel No. 5 fragrance advertisement campaign of 1998 presents Estella Warren dressed as a movie starlet complete with red satin cape sneaking out for the night in Paris leaving a subdued and tamed wolf. The idea of Little Red Riding Hood deviating from the straight and narrow is picked up in this campaign; she is cast as sexy and knowing, surpassing even the sly wolf. Representing the male, this wolf has been castrated of his traditional power, succumbing to the prowess embodied by the girl's sexuality, enhanced, of course, with the potency of Chanel No. 5. The motifs of the tale are active despite the distortions made to the traditional formulation.[1] The language of fairy tales lends itself ideally to visual representation.

Print dissemination and broad televisual coverage has ensured the internalization of the texts serving to fix the meaning of the image. This fixed meaning was of particular interest to French philosopher Roland Barthes. In his essay *The Rhetoric of the Image*, he analyzes the role of text as a method of *anchoring* possible meanings; Barthes suggests that the linguistic message is used "to counter the terror of uncertain signs"[2] found in images. Through selected illustrations the fairy tale is reduced to a series of images depicting key points in the traditional narrative such as Doré's illustration of the showdown between the girl and the wolf. For Barthes, Doré's depiction of Red Riding Hood in bed with the wolf could have any number of interpretations, not least the potential sexual relationship between the pair. The text, according to his theory, counters the *terror* of this image by qualifying its meaning, establishing a recommended reading for this depiction. Each image is strongly attached to the text and the meaning understood as it is linked to a known narrative.

---

1   The distortions are just that, however. The campaign seems to invert the traditional tale apparently empowering the female, yet her dress and attitude cast her as a male fantasy—sex appeal is reduced to market value.
2   R. Barthes, *Image Music Text* (London: Fontana P, 1977) 39.

Without this anchorage, however, anxiety is embedded in images that are physically independent of text. It is precisely this situation of image without text that contemporary artists exploit in their engagement with fairy tales. Barthes discusses the image absent of text [by] stating in a footnote that "images without words can certainly be found in certain cartoons, but by way of a paradox; the absence of words always covers an enigmatic intention."[1] The absence of words enables artists to fundamentally challenge prescribed meanings. "Enigmatic intention" provides a textual loophole, allowing artists to use fairy tales, unrestricted by specific textual direction, yet retaining a textual memory through the use of familiar tropes. As repositories of identity conventions, the fairy tale, in this case "Little Red Riding Hood," offers a forum that artists can use in order to incisively critique shifts in cultural attitude. Barthes's *anxiety* of a non-textualized image renews the conscious reception of the tale and activates the potential for change.

The main concern of this paper, that is little analyzed, is the appropriation of fairy tales by fine artists. Just as radical revisions in the literary fairy tale have occurred since the 1970s, more recently subversions have emerged from the fine art forum.[2] Within popular culture, such as advertising and films, the adoption of fairy tales has increased and is now infiltrating the high culture of fine art. Taking the traditional fairy tale, artists are reviewing and reinventing the tales in both parody and critique. The tales appropriated are radically challenged to articulate late twentieth-century mores.

Artists Gérard Rancinan, Paula Rego, and Kiki Smith have all produced significant bodies of work, referencing fairy tales that respond, via subversion, to recent cultural pressures, specifically identity construction. Addressing their work on "Little Red Riding Hood," a dialogue of identity and discrimination engages the viewer, challenging their experience of fairy tales and introducing cultural revelations.

Rancinan is one of a number of contemporary artists that are appropriating and interpreting fairy tales. As one of a series of five fairy-tale inspired works, Rancinan's interpretation of "Little Red Riding Hood" (Fig. 1) engages the literary tale and fundamentally subverts meaning. Surrounded by blood-spattered hanging sheets and dangling from a hook, Red Riding Hood is cast as a cross-dressing male ballet dancer watched by a wolf behind bars. The traditional tale echoes through the motifs; and Rancinan, through selection and inversion (female cast male, wild animal caged), renders meaning ambiguous. Referencing the violence attributed to this tale in particular, Rancinan upsets and unsettles the formulaic and saccharine portrayal

---

1 Ibid 38.
2 Particular authors offering dark feminist re-readings of the traditional tale types are Angela Carter, Tanith Lee, and Anne Sexton.

of fairy tales as offered and made familiar by Disney in the twentieth century. This contemporary image rendered like a crime scene abandons the forest, instead suspending the ominous relationship between Red Riding Hood and the wolf against a backdrop of polythene sheeting. Barthes's anxiety returns as questions are more abundant than answers. This ambiguity and violence is sustained in other artists' work, particularly in Paula Rego's *Little Red Riding Hood Suite* (2003), and finds direct root in the tale itself.

Fig. 1: Gérard Rancinan, *Red Riding Hood*, 2003.

In her work Rego frequently appropriates fairy tales and "Snow White" and "Pinocchio" have both featured in a number of explorations. Interested in exploring and subverting accepted power relations, the artist's work is suited to re-visioning fairy tales to redress gender and societal inequalities. In her *Little Red Riding Hood Suite* (Figs. 2 to 7) she fundamentally undermines the traditional tale by relying on its endurance and familiarity. Instead of the wolf eating the girl, and the woodcutter saving the day, Rego engineers an alternative tale that responds to current ideas of role and status in society.

The suite comprises six images and is executed in pastels; the detail is contained in the characters rather than the surroundings. This device serves to focus the viewer's attention on the cast, playing on the motifs of the tale fixed neither to time nor

Fig. 2: Paula Rego, *Happy Family—Mother,*
Red Riding Hood and Grandmother, 2003.

Fig. 3: Paula Rego, *Little Red Riding Hood*
on the Edge, 2003.

place. The deliberately stark grounds activate a fluid positioning of the tale; whether in the nineteenth or twenty-first century, for Rego the relationship of the cast is central to understanding the tale. The first image we come across is Little Red Riding Hood and her mother embracing, [while] in the background the grandmother is featured looking on (Fig. 2). Embarking on her journey Red Riding Hood is introduced proper[ly] in the second image (Fig. 3). Complete with red hood and matching nail varnish, she is seen crouching down, turning as if she has been disturbed. Enter the wolf (Fig. 4). Here Rego opts to make human the beast rather than personify the wolf as illustrators have elected.

The wolf is imaged as a man standing dressed in a dated and effeminate exercise outfit replete with sweatband. Rego has posed the wolf with hands on hips, yet he is unbalanced with legs crossed. Despite his wild and unkempt appearance, his prowess is negated by his exaggerated stance and attire. In this piece the wolf imposes no threat or beastly presence, a quality that is carried over into the next work which sees the wolf disguised as Little Red Riding Hood's grandmother (Fig. 5). The girl is positioned, albeit obediently, by his/her feet but with arms crossed and an expression of scepticism as he "chats her up." Here Little Red Riding Hood looks to be in control of the situation, bored but allowing the wolf to play out his role. In the next image, however, it becomes apparent that, in fact, the wolf has succeeded in eating the girl as he is found, stomach distended, lying on the red coat (Fig. 6). The scene shows us

Fig. 4: Paula Rego, *The Wolf*, 2003.

Fig. 5: Paula Rego, *The Wolf Chats Up Red Riding Hood*, 2003.

Little Red Riding Hood's mother prodding his stomach with a pitchfork in revenge. In the final image of the series it is revealed that the mother has triumphed over the wolf as she poses sporting a new wolf skin muffler (Fig. 7).

In this series Rego adheres to the plot laid down by Perrault, sacrificing the girl to the wolf, but rejects the ending devised by the Grimms whereby the girl and grandmother survive. The artist inverts the traditional tale by activating the role of the mother. A psychoanalytical reading of the tale comments on the mother's agency, or lack thereof. Bruno Bettelheim suggests that in the literary tale the mother is represented both as herself and as the grandmother which effectively renders the figure absent or invalid. Red Riding Hood acts alone throughout the tale without the authority of the mother figure. For Bettelheim the girl is sexualized by the (grand) mother with the gift of the red hood. The girl's journey is conflicted with a duality of obedience and seduction; the gift of the hood is really the gift of sexual maturity. According to Bettelheim, "[w]hether it is Mother or Grandmother—this mother once removed—it is fatal for the young girl if this older woman abdicates her own attractiveness to males and transfers it to the daughter by giving her a too attractive red cloak."[1] Thus a psychoanalytical reading of Perrault sexualizes the girl; the Grimm

---

1 B. Bettelheim, *The Uses of Enchantment: The Meaning and Importance of Fairy Tales* (London: Penguin, 1975) 173.

Fig. 6: Paula Rego, *Mother Takes Revenge,* 2003.

Fig. 7: Paula Rego, *Mother Wears the Wolf's Pelt,* 2003.

version, however, alleviates, to some extent, the anxiety of Red Riding Hood's predicament by the inclusion of the father figure embodied by the male rescuer. With this reading the sexualizing of the girl is initiated through seduction and consumption, but incomplete due to parental intervention and the escape from the wolf's belly. A feminist re-reading of this version of the tale recognizes the gender oppressive message subjecting females into positions of weakness. This is embedded in the idea of the mother abandoning the girl to the woods, the grandmother's impotence through age/illness, and the ultimate rescue by the adult male. Rego's interpretation sees the tale as told from the mother's point of view, thus challenging the psychoanalytical readings and empowering the female figure.

The presentation of the suite takes directly from the traditional process of illustrating the tales; the artist has selected the plot indicators from the revised tale and has created a series of scenes akin to theatre. The images are spare and the characters occupy an empty stage. Rego has exploited the capacity of the tale to tell itself without relying on extra descriptive material. She relies on the audience to be able to read the text through the images, and the viewer is comforted by recognizing the story as it unfolds. Yet the subversion occurs in the finale when Rego offers two endings, one in which the mother overcomes the wolf/male in an act of revenge, without the intervention of a male rescuer; or an alternative reading, where the mother overcomes both the beast as male *and* the girl as youth. For Rego, the absence of the daughter means the mother's individual identity is asserted as present, rather than the traditional position of absence. The fact that the mother in the final scene is dressed in red with her own version of a red hood and the addition of the wolf skin muffler reinforces the message, contrary to psychoanalytical fairy-tale interpretation, that age itself implies a knowledge, strength, and cunning ensuring the survival of the fittest.

Rego provides an alternative version to the "Little Red Riding Hood" tale, retaining the basic plot formulation and cast as established by the literary tradition. In contrast, the artist Kiki Smith transcends the parameters of the literary tradition [by] projecting the tale beyond the familiar ending, instigating a parallel reading of the events. By appropriating the protagonists of the traditional text, Smith is able to interrogate her characters, specifically Red Riding Hood and the wolf, examining their identity, role, and relationship. Her installation and sculptural work responds to the traditional literary text whilst taking inspiration from recent literary subversions of the tale that promote the complicity of the girl and wolf, and the cultural climate today that is concerned with alienation and difference.

As an overarching theme the artist examines the lynchpin relationship between the girl and the wolf. This relationship has invited much scrutiny from the authors themselves, the readers, the illustrators, and the critics. As the tale develops, the relationship between the girl and wolf evolves, and their initial encounter has been described as friendly, threatening, flirtatious, and sexual. Zipes argues that the relationship between the girl and wolf is based on rape and violence. He attributes this to the patriarchal societies that witnessed the genesis of the genre's literary form, specifically the versions of Perrault and the Grimms. The cultural context is essential in the reading of this tale, affecting the authors' description, the reading, and the visual imaging of the relationship. Yet every perceived meaning of the tale is hinged on the initial encounter of Little Red Riding Hood and the wolf, which then informs the subsequent events that take place. Gender roles are conveyed at this point, the wolf is always cast as male and the seducer, Little Red Riding Hood is at once the innocent girl, the *femme fatale*, and also the inevitable fallen woman. Recent visual responses to the tale have focused on this relationship exploring the textual manifestations of the girl and wolf.

Smith appears to reject the relationship based on violence and sex; instead she explores the idea of difference, discrimination, and the resulting complicity. In her work the girl and wolf join together and eventually become each other. Both can be classed as *other* in comparison to the dominant human male; this position of difference in turn engenders discrimination. Smith highlights the idea that the pair are actually similar rather than different, that imposed textual categories of primitive/civilized, animal/human, male/female are misleading as opposites and are actually intrinsic to each other. The rejection of these opposites can be seen in the identity trauma that is at the core of her work; a "no-man's-land" in terms of identity and belonging. *Daughter* (1999) is a four-foot high sculpture of a girl wearing the tell-tale red cape and hood (Fig. 8). Despite the fact that she is immediately identifiable as Little Red Riding Hood, there remains an uncertainty as her face sprouts hair suggesting a morphing bestiality, invoking both the werewolf myth and the freakish bearded lady of the circus arena. In this work Smith undermines the clear-cut definitions of wolf and girl as given in the literary tale, instead inviting the possibility of duality.

Fig. 8: Kiki Smith, *Daughter*, 1999.

By her difference *Daughter* is made a spectacle as something other. The viewer is challenged to accommodate and reconcile what we know of Little Red Riding Hood and the wolf. The opposites of predator and prey embodied in *Daughter* force the viewers to review their experience of the tale and, to an extent, themselves [by] recognizing the equal presence of innocence and the malign. From this work the artist imagines that Little Red Riding Hood and the wolf have come together as outcasts and given birth to *Daughter*. Helaine Posner suggests that "their improbable offspring becomes the embodiment of male, female, and animal characteristics, the unique progeny of disparate beings."[1] In *Daughter* unification is found to challenge the parameters of good and evil predicated in the traditional Grimm tale.

---

1   H. Posner, "Once Upon a Time ..." in the exhibition catalogue *Kiki Smith: Telling Tales* (New York: International Center of Photography, 2001) 10.

Continuing with the theme of girl and wolf joined by difference Smith's *Gang of Girls and Pack of Wolves* (1999) explores the companionship of the two and their inevitable complicity (Fig. 9). The work is composed of a series of paintings on glass measuring almost fifty feet in length and depicts images of girls and wolves, collaborating as outcasts. In this work Smith combines "Little Red Riding Hood" with analysis of Saint Genevieve, the patron saint of Paris. Genevieve, a poor shepherd's daughter, is identified by her company of wolves and lambs living harmoniously and thus symbolizing her "virtue and gentility."[1] *Gang of Girls and Pack of Wolves* is sig-

Fig. 9: Kiki Smith, *Gang of Girls and Pack of Wolves*, 1999.

nificant for its depiction of acceptance and tolerance; the artist offers a message of inclusion rather than discrimination. Smith critiques the social codes of difference that reinforce marginalization and perpetuate the fear and threat of otherness, a notion that has particular resonance in race and class debates.

The symbiotic partnership shown in *Gang of Girls and Pack of Wolves* reaches a fully metamorphosed state in Smith's work *Rapture* (2001) (Fig. 10). In this bronze sculpture we are witness to the life-size event of a woman stepping out of a wolf's belly, emerging as if born of the beast. Returning to the symbolism of "Little Red Riding Hood," it is inevitable that we make the link here; the wolf is present and although the girl and hood are absent, the event of a women being released from the belly of a wolf recalls the Grimm tale, where the woodcutter saves the girl and her grandmother from the stomach of the wolf.

1   W. Weitman, *Kiki Smith: Prints, Books and Things* (New York: The Museum of Modern Art, 2003) 27.

Fig. 10: Kiki Smith, *Rapture*, 1999.

Just as Smith projects the tale of "Little Red Riding Hood" in *Daughter*, *Rapture* extends the Grimm version to include the belief that describes the consuming of the girl as symbolic of initial sexual experience and maturation. Zipes identifies the themes of sexuality and violence as intrinsic to the tale, from the meeting in the woods to the wolf's consuming of the girl.[1] In *Rapture*, Smith explores this idea, revising the release of girl and grandmother from the wolf's stomach whilst referencing this interpretation in the title of the piece. Traditionally the crime of *rapt* meant forceful abduction or seduction, and by the same root come the words rape and rapture.[2] "Little Red Riding Hood" has been received as symbolic of sexual initiation, and the etymological root of the word rapture introduces the sexual violence found in the literary versions of the tale. Susan Brownmiller suggests that "Red Riding

---

1 Jack Zipes, *The Trials and Tribulations of Little Red Riding Hood* (London: Routledge, 1993).
2 C. Orenstein, *Little Red Riding Hood Uncloaked: Sex, Morality and the Evolution of a Fairy Tale* (New York: Basic Books, 2002) 150.

Hood is a parable of rape,"[1] yet in Smith's *Rapture* the meaning is ambiguous, sex and rebirth are implicit, equally so, the violence via killing, sacrifice, or metamorphosis.

The three artists addressed above deal with the fairy tale in different ways. Rancinan and Rego both deal with gender and violence in their images. Rancinan's bloodspattered sheeting is an obvious reference, whereas Rego only alludes to violence in the last image where the mother sports a new wolf skin muffler, having killed the wolf herself (relating her to Dahl's gun-toting heroine). Rancinan and Rego also adopt a theatrical presentation; Rego uses this method to confirm the tale to the audience via familiar scenes and motifs. Rancinan, in contrast, confounds interpretation with his scene of grace and horror. Predominantly referencing gender, Rego redirects the traditional tale's focus to the mother, and Rancinan acts in dissent by casting the girl as an adult male. For Rancinan sexuality is questioned by his depiction of a transvestite Red Riding Hood, a concession, perhaps, to the implicit deviant sexualized coupling of the girl and the wolf in the traditional tale.

In contrast, Smith's appropriation of the tale diffuses notions of violence and, to an extent, the assertion of particular gendered roles. Smith projects beyond the confines of the tale and explores possibilities of difference. The main theme in her work is the complicity between the girl and the wolf; at times they are joined as one, elsewhere they are comfortable companions. Gender distinction is either undone or left open in Smith's pieces; *Rapture* may represent the sexual woman released from the wolf's belly, or alternatively present the metamorphosis of the wolf into woman. Where Rego is indebted to the Grimm tale, Smith is more closely related to the feminist writing of Angela Carter. Unlike Rancinan, Smith removes overt references of violence from her work; instead her focus is on alienation, questioning what makes difference.

Where Rego subverts from within the familiar tale, Smith extends beyond the established parameters, and Rancinan inverts the conformity of gender and power from the traditional tales. All three artists have variously utilized "Little Red Riding Hood" to explore and revise the narrative; undermine ideas of gender conventions; or interrogate changing attitudes of identity and discrimination. These artists challenge the parameters of the traditional texts favouring recent literary revisions and their potential for change. As the fairy tale conveys ideologies of identity, the artists employ them to penetrate, subvert, and change the traditional values they represent. To visualize the fairy tale is to recognize the potential for change in keeping with today's morality and value expectations. Fairy tales are reused for their didactic value to illustrate and record shifts in cultural attitude.

---

1   [Quoted in] J. Zipes (ed.), *Don't Bet on the Prince: Contemporary Feminist Fairy Tales in North America & England* (London: Scholar Press, 1993) 232.

And they all lived happily ever after? Little Red Riding Hood's story is embedded in our cultural unconscious, and its endurance signifies its continuing relevance and interest to artists, critics, and audiences of popular culture. The potential for change embodied in the fairy tale is recognized by artists who add their interpretation to a heritage of adjustment. Appropriated into visual culture, the fairy tale reaches a far wider audience than the literary text. The artists cited here consciously subvert the traditional literature, utilizing a visual format to analyze contemporary societal mores.

Copyright Credits

© Gérard Rancinan—copyright the artist, <http://www.rancinan.com>
© Paula Rego images—copyright the artist, photography courtesy of Marlborough Fine Art (London) Ltd., <http://www.marlboroughfineart.com/>
Kiki Smith, *Daughter*, 1999
  Nepal paper, bubble wrap, methyl cellulose and hair, 48 x 15 x 10" (121.9 x 38.1 x 25.4 cm)
  © Kiki Smith, Courtesy PaceWildenstein, New York
  Photo By: Ellen Page Wilson/Courtesy PaceWildenstein, New York
Kiki Smith, *Gang of Girls and Pack of Wolves*, 1999
  fired paint on glass with brass and lead, 69-3/8 x 53-3/4" (176.2 x 136.5 cm), 12 glass sheets, each installation dimensions variable
  © Kiki Smith, Courtesy PaceWildenstein, New York
  Photo By: Ellen Page Wilson/Courtesy PaceWildenstein, New York
Kiki Smith, *Rapture*, 2001
  Bronze, 67-1/4" x 62" x 26-1/4" (170.8 cm x 157.5 cm x 66.7 cm)
  © Kiki Smith, Courtesy PaceWildenstein, New York
  Photo By: Richard-Max Tremblay/Courtesy PaceWildenstein, New York

Bibliography

Anwell, Maggie. "Lolita Meets the Werewolf: The Company of Wolves." In *The Female Gaze: Women as Viewers of Popular Culture*, ed. L. Gammon and M. Marshment. London: The Women's P, 1988. 76-85.
Bacchilega, Cristina. *Postmodern Fairy Tales: Gender and Narrative Strategies*. Philadelphia: U of Pennsylvania P, 1997.
Barthes, R. *Image Music Text*. London: Fontana P, 1977.
Bettelheim, Bruno. *The Uses of Enchantment: The Meaning and Importance of Fairy Tales*. London: Penguin, 1975, 1976.
Carter, Angela. *The Bloody Chamber*. London: Vintage, 1979.

Dahl, Roald. *Revolting Rhymes*. London: Penguin, 1982.

Perrault, Charles. *Perrault's Fairy Tales*. Trans. A.E. Johnson. New York: Dover, 1969.

Jones, Amelia (ed.). *The Feminism and Visual Culture Reader*. London: Routledge, 2003.

Jones, Steven S. "On Analyzing Fairy Tales: 'Little Red Riding Hood' Revisited." *Western Folklore* 46.2 (1987): 97-106.

Lee, Tanith. *Red as Blood or Tales from the Sisters Grimmer*. New York: Daw Books, 1983.

Mills, Margaret. "Feminist Theory and the Study of Folklore: A Twenty-Year Trajectory toward Theory." *Western Folklore* 52.2/4 (1993): 173-92.

Orenstein, C. *Little Red Riding Hood Uncloaked: Sex, Morality and the Evolution of a Fairy Tale*. New York: Basic Books, 2002.

Rowe, Karen E. "Feminism & Fairy Tales." *Don't Bet on the Prince: Contemporary Feminist Fairy Tales in North America & England*, ed. Jack Zipes. London: Scholar P, 1993. 209-26.

Sexton, Anne. *Transformations*. New York: Mariner Books, 1971.

Smith, K., and H. Posner. *Telling Tales*. New York: International Center of Photography, 2001.

Stone, Kay F. "Feminist Approaches to the Interpretation of Fairy Tales." *Fairy Tales & Society: Illusion, Allusion and Paradigm*, ed. Ruth B. Bottigheimer. Philadelphia: U of Pennsylvania P, 1986. 229-36.

Tatar, Maria. *The Hard Facts of the Grimm's Fairy Tales*. 2nd ed. Oxford: Princeton UP, 2003.

Warner, Marina. *From the Beast to the Blonde: On Fairy Tales and Their Tellers*. London: Vintage, 1994.

Weitman, W. *Kiki Smith: Prints, Books and Things*. New York: The Museum of Modern Art, 2003. 1-34.

Ziolkowski, Jan M. "A Fairy Tale from before Fairy Tales: Egbert of Liege's 'De puella a lupellis seruata' and the Medieval Background of 'Little Red Riding Hood.'" *Speculum* 67.3 (1992): 549-75.

Zipes, Jack (ed.). *Don't Bet on the Prince: Contemporary Feminist Fairy Tales in North America & England*. London: Scholar P, 1993.

_____. "A Second Gaze at Little Red Riding Hood's Trials and Tribulations." *Don't Bet on the Prince: Contemporary Feminist Fairy Tales in North America & England*, ed. Jack Zipes. London: Scholar P, 1993. 227-60.

_____. *The Trials and Tribulations of Little Red Riding Hood*. London: Routledge, 1993.

T RIDING HOOD: A BABE IN THE WOODS[1]

)renstein

WHEN THE GRIMM BROTHERS TURNED "LITTLE RED RIDING HOOD" into a children's tale for Victorian audiences of the nineteenth century, the heroine became the embodiment of innocence. She lost all traces of her earlier French sexuality. Not until the twentieth century was the bowdlerized Red Riding Hood defrocked, so to speak, and redressed. Or, in the hands of the legendary animator Tex Avery, simply defrocked. Avery brought the heroine and her wolf from the European forest to the Hollywood nightclub and transformed the fairy tale into a caricature of American courtship. In his *Red Hot Riding Hood*, released in 1943, the sweet heroine of storybook tradition—who in Perrault's seventeenth-century original had served up a warning about the dangers of promiscuity—became her own symbolic opposite: a Hollywood stripper.

Red Hot Riding Hood begins on the corner of Hollywood and Vine, the legendary spot of history's most famous nightclubs, where the wolf, dressed to the nines in top hat and tails, arrives for an evening of carousing. Grandma's house is now a bordello around the corner, a penthouse apartment lit up by a neon sign: "Grandma's Joint— come up and see me." (A neon hand with a wiggling finger, à la Mae West, invites the passerby upstairs.) And on stage at the Sunset Strip, a chic nightclub that advertises "30 gorgeous girls, no cover," Red Hot Riding Hood steps into the spotlight, all dolled up in make-up and cape—which she quickly tosses aside, along with her basket. No kid anymore, this Red's a buxom bombshell in a short (*very* short) red strapless number. She launches into her song and dance—"Hey Daddy, you better get the best for me"—which sends the wolf, seated in the audience, into a frenzy. He hoots and howls, claps and whistles, and employs a clapping and whistling machine to amplify his appreciation. "Hey Daddy! Hi Paw! Say now *Father*," Red goes on, undulating her hips and shaking her fanny. The wolf's eyes pop out (literally—they fly across the room), his tongue unrolls like a red carpet, and he rises in the air and stiffens into a full body erection.

As soon as Red finishes her routine, the wolf snakes a long arm onto the stage to whip her to his table. "Fly away with me to the Riviera," he says in a smarmy French accent. But after he follows Red to Grandma's Joint, the tables turn. Granny, a hot old dame in a slinky red dress, is besotted. Now *she* whistles and levitates and hoots, as she chases him from door to door with puckered lips. "*That's* a wolf! *Whoo hoo!*"

---

1 From *Little Red Riding Hood Uncloaked: Sex, Morality, and the Evolution of a Fairy Tale* (New York: Basic Books, 2003) 112-29.

"Little Red Riding Hood" was apparently Avery's favorite fairy tale. He repeatedly returned to it, or some semblance of it, throughout the 1930s and 1940s, transforming the tale into a full-scale romance, told in multiple episodes. In *Little Red Walking Hood*, the first of Avery's flirtations with the tale in 1937, he gave Red the body of a little girl but the demeanor of a grown woman. She trots along the boulevard, as the wolf—here a pool hall city slicker, all oily charm and questionable intentions—drives slowly behind her in a shiny black car, throwing out pick-up lines as fast as his lips can animate. She eventually interrupts the narrative to commiserate with the women in the audience about lascivious male behavior.

In *The Bear's Tale* (1940), Avery cast Red as a smart-mouthed, freckle-faced kid from Brooklyn. She teams up with Goldilocks to defeat the wolf by leaning over a split-screen line that separates their plots: "Hello, Goldie! This is Red Ridin' Hood. I just found a note from that skunk the Wolf…." (She hands over the note.) In *Little Rural Riding Hood* (1949), the last of Avery's pseudo-fairy-tale burlesques, he drew a gangly, toothy redhead as the country cousin of Red Hot Riding Hood. She opens and closes doors with her long, unsightly toes, and puckers her enormous, almost snout-like lips.

Of all Avery's variations on this theme, however, *Red Hot Riding Hood* gave him his guiding stars. The buxom redhead and the wolf quickly outgrew the plot that inspired them, becoming recurrent characters in numerous animated shorts. Avery placed the couple not only in his "Red Riding Hood" send-ups, but also in other fairy-tale cartoons. The heroine of *Swing Shift Cinderella* (1945) is really Red Hot all over again. She appears in the familiar nightclub set, with the same upswept red hair, gyrating the same va-va-voom figure. She wears the same revealing outfit, only this time it's conjured up by her fairy godmother. (Red: "You do wave a mean wand, don't you old girl?") And of course, as in her first appearance in *Red Hot Riding Hood*, she is paired up with the same eternally aroused wolf, who falls into throes of ecstasy at her song and dance. This time the tune goes, "Oh Wolfie, ain't you the one!"

Avery placed Red Hot and her wolf in cartoon parodies of other genres as well, including *The Shooting of Dan McGoo* (1945), his mock western, *Wild and Wolfy* (1945), and *Uncle Tom's Cabin* (1947). In his last spoof on the couple, *Little Rural Riding Hood*, inspired by the Jean de La Fontaine fable about a country mouse and a city mouse, Red is again a dancer at the same nightclub, this time performing for two wolves: a hormone-crazed country bumpkin and a supercilious urbane Romeo (who later falls for Red Hot's homely country cousin).

For Avery, the characters of *Red Hot Riding Hood* transcended the fairy tale. The showgirl and her lascivious pursuer were not just a girl and a wolf, but the characters and symbols of the human sexual drama. His heroine is a sex object. His wolf, stiffening and levitating at the sight of her, is the penis personified.

Such gags were not unusual in the cartoons of an earlier era. Avery's Red Riding Hood riffs were only incidentally for children. They were pre-television, shown in theaters before the main attraction for a general audience. Children went to movies, too, but they were an afterthought for Avery. Like other cartoonists working at this time, Avery incorporated details of American life during the war into his animations. In *Blitzwolf*, released in 1942, the three little pigs face their old enemy the wolf, who has now taken on the persona of Adolph Hitler (a break from his trademark role as lascivious nightclub suitor, and a startling contrast to the Nazi interpretation of the wolf as the marauding Jew). Avery's Swing Shift Cinderella is a nod to Rosie the Riveter; she has to flee the nightclub to be on time for her midnight job—the "swing shift" at the Lockheed factory. And his Red Hot Riding Hood is obviously modeled on the pin-up girls who raised the "morale" of World War II soldiers.

Avery subverted the prevailing standards of animation set by Walt Disney, whose *Snow White and the Seven Dwarfs* became the first full-length feature cartoon in 1937. While Disney revered the Grimms' tradition, Avery disrupted his plots with running gags, ridiculed fairy-tale clichés, and blended Old Europe with contemporary America wherever he found a way to make it funny (as in the tavern called "Ye Old Beere Joint"). He mixed and matched tales, provided unorthodox settings, and produced self-aware characters who frequently interrupt the narrative to comment on the plot or make a statement to the audience, completely rupturing any suspension of disbelief. *Red Hot Riding Hood* begins with a traditional Euro-Disney landscape and the conventional storybook plot. ("Good evening, kiddies," the off-screen narrator intones.) But then the characters rebel and demand that it be done a new way. (The narrator agrees and obligingly begins again.) In *Little Red Walking Hood*, the girl and the wolf suspend animation to wait for a pair of late moviegoers to seat themselves; the fictitious offenders' "silhouettes" appear realistically on the screen. Above all, Avery worked in opposition to Disney's saccharine sweetness, epitomized by the bleached heroine of Disney's *Snow White*.

Avery's endless, obvious visual metaphors for sexual excitement earned him the scrutiny of US government censors. He was known to create salacious sequences that he knew would be cut, hoping to distract them from the sex gags that he truly wanted to keep—though not always successfully. In the publicly released version of *Red Hot Riding Hood*, the wolf is driven mad by the attentions of Red Hot's grandma and vows to kill himself if he ever sees another woman. He shoots himself when Red Hot appears on stage again, and his ghost rises to cheer her striptease on. But the original version that Avery animated, struck by the Hays Office for its explicit theme of bestiality, was much racier. In that version, sent to GIs abroad but not shown to civilian audiences, Grandma and the wolf are married in a shotgun wedding (with Red sitting in the seat of an antiaircraft gun pointed at the wolf's back). They appear in the next scene back at the Sunset Strip, for Red's last act, with a litter of howling wolf pups in tow.

Avery's *Red Hot Riding Hood* captured a changing vision of the American woman in the 1930s and 1940s. She was not only more frankly sexual, but also tougher and more self-reliant than the demure woman of the Victorian era. In Avery's animations, the roles of sex object (even stripper) and self-reliant heroine are not mutually exclusive. His Red Riding Hood, no matter which of his cartoons she appears in, can take care of herself: She is easily able to fend off her suitor with a literal cold shoulder (drawn as a snowball in *Little Red Walking Hood*) or to give his ardor a lights-out by hitting him over the head with a nightclub table lamp (in *Red Hot Riding Hood*).

Avery's contemporary, the humorist James Thurber, also captured this new street-smart quality of American womanhood (minus Avery's explicit sexuality) in a cartoon adaptation of "Little Red Riding Hood" that appeared in his *Fables for Our Time and Famous Poems* in 1939. "It is not so easy to fool little girls nowadays as it used to be," reads the moral beneath his drawing of a no-nonsense heroine, arms akimbo, who regards the tongue-wagging wolf who waits for her in bed with evident annoyance. Thurber's cartoon, like Avery's animations, reflects changes in the lives of American women from the 1920s through the 1940s that sparked new ideas and attitudes. Among those changes: Suffragettes won the vote, bras replaced corsets, and women began wearing pants—finally following the advice of nineteenth-century dress reformer Amelia Bloomer. Amelia Earhart flew solo across the Atlantic in 1932; the Gibson Girl gave way to the flapper, who stepped aside for Rosie the Riveter; the "new woman" went to work, wore lipstick, and smoked cigarettes; and in Hollywood, female stars like Joan Crawford and Bette Davis made names for themselves playing tough femmes fatales.

Avery's and Thurber's work capture some of the sexual and political attitudes of this era, with its revolutionized manners. Avery's Red Hot Riding Hood is the new leading lady—she's a sexpot, sure, but no pushover. She's a cross between Rita Hayworth (the market-savvy redheaded sex goddess who dyed her hair and hid her Spanish heritage to become an "Anglo" star) and Mae West, who herself trafficked in fairy tales, but also restaged and rewrote them. West's one-liners captured the public imagination and entered the language as clichés for the same reason that Avery's cartoons became famous: because they put the fairy tale in twentieth-century terms. "I used to be Snow White," West once famously quipped. "But I drifted."

Tex Avery's *Red Hot Riding Hood*, with its wartime pin-up girl heroine, captured a slice of American history and gave new meaning to the fairy tale as a courtship story. It also heralded the onset of a specific new role for Little Red Riding Hood. In twentieth-century pop culture, she increasingly conveyed adult female ideals and represented a new and growing demographic: the single woman. "*Miss* Riding-hood," as Avery's wolf calls her. Of the best-known fairy-tale heroines, only Red Riding Hood remains unattached at tale's end—there's no wedding, no prince, not even a brother or two. Thus, over the next decades, as fairy tales became increasingly devoted to expressing feminine ideals, she developed a significance very different from that of other fairy-tale heroines, who underwent their own transitions at the time.

It's no secret that today's best-known fairy-tale protagonists are female: Cinderella, Snow White, Rapunzel, Sleeping Beauty, and Red Riding Hood, to name just a few. These heroines act amongst a cast of banal male foils. The men are simply fathers, beasts, dwarfs or princes, all interchangeable and usually illustrated as one and the same from tale to tale. In Stephen Sondheim's Broadway musical *Into the Woods*, the Prince Charmings of two interwoven fairy tales swap places without so much as a ripple in the plot. In an illustration from the book adaptation of the musical, they wear matching outfits in matching colors, just as they share a common name and common romantic mission. ("And how do *you* manage a visit?" says one to the other.)

In these fairy tales, the heroines make decisions that illustrate the expectations of women in real life, while the male figures are simply metaphors for punishment (misbehave and you'll meet a wolf) and reward (a prince in the end—if you're good!).

But what a contrast today's feminine fairy tale is to the genre's past. The brothers Grimm, who were prolific collectors, penned twice as many male as female leads. Looking over their table of contents can befuddle the modern reader: Hans my Hedgehog? King Thrushbeard? Where have these tales of male adventure gone? The answer: They have lost out in the game of editorial selection. As folklorist Kay Stone observed, most children's storybooks contain only a handful of the original 212 stories that appear in the Grimms' complete *Children's and Household Tales*—and nearly all of those that survive feature female-driven plots.[1] Tales with female leads are also far more likely to be made into movies. Disney's *Snow White and the Seven Dwarfs*, an overnight success in 1937, along with *Cinderella* in 1950, established the fairy-tale heroine as a collective role model for every girl and woman aspiring to be a wife and mother. Disney's Snow White gives the dwarfs' bachelor pad a spring cleaning, singing "Whistle While You Work" as she washes dishes, sweeps floors, dusts cobwebs, and scrubs clothing with the assistance of birds, deer, rabbits, and other forest fauna. In a similar scene in Disney's later *Cinderella*, mice and birds assist the heroine by sewing a gown for the ball while she finishes cleaning house and dressing her stepsisters—chores that anticipate her life as happy housewife to Prince Charming.

---

1 [See, for example, Kay Stone, "Things Walt Disney Never Told Us" (1975), in *Some Day Your Witch Will Come* (Detroit: Wayne State University, 2008).]

These two movies, like the new twentieth-century feminized fairy tale in general, captured the allure of marriage and domesticity that became the dominant ideal for women after the war. In the 1950s, the age of newlyweds dropped, as did the age of first motherhood, and divorce rates plummeted. Men returned to their jobs, and Rosie the Riveter was urged back into the home. With the family as the center of American life, managing the household became the preoccupation of women's lives. Despite new labor-saving appliances, the number of hours devoted to housework increased. Child care took up twice as much time as it had in the 1920s. Joan Crawford posed for pictures mopping floors. Ozzie and Harriet acted out an idealized version of their real-life marriage on TV. And during this time, American culture produced a parallel ideal in fiction: the "fairy-tale wedding"—a romanticized union that in fact has nothing whatsoever to do with the forced matrimonial trades behind Charles Perrault's seventeenth-century fairy tales—which never existed before the twentieth century.

Yet if America idealized the family, behind the trimmed hedges and driveways of suburbia the reality of mid-century life was more complex, as scholars like Stephanie Coontz have thoroughly documented.[1] Despite the cult of domesticity and the prudery of Ozzie and Harriet, the 1950s were a time of new sexual freedoms. Terms like "going steady" and "petting" (or even "heavy petting") came about to describe them. Teenage girls got pregnant, were sent away to have their babies, and came back "rehabilitated." The number of pregnant brides skyrocketed—though with the appearance of better methods of birth control (particularly the pill in 1960) premarital sex became less risky. And alongside the glorified housewife, there was increasingly the woman who did not go straight from father's to husband's arms. Living on her own, she navigated the double standards of the age. This is the demographic that Red Riding Hood, the single heroine, rose to serve.

As Sleeping Beauty, Cinderella, and Snow White marched down the aisle, mid-century pop culture depictions of Little Red Riding Hood seem as if meant to illustrate Helen Gurley Brown's 1962 bestseller *Sex and the Single Girl*. In advertising of the time she is cast as a femme fatale, hawking liquor, make-up, and fast cars. Ripe, young "riding hood red" lipstick would "bring the wolves out," Max Factor promised in a poster-sized ad appearing in *Vogue* magazine in 1953 that radically transformed the tale's traditional warning against speaking to strangers. On one side of the spread a red-hooded, red-nailed vixen smiles coyly as she applies a bright shade of red lipstick. On the opposite page, a background shot shows a forest, with a company of

---

1 [See, for example, Stephanie Coontz, *The Way We Never Were: American Families and the Nostalgia Trap* (New York: Basic Books, 1992) and Stephanie Coontz, *The Way We Really Are: Coming to Terms with America's Changing Families* (New York: Basic Books, 1997).]

Gregory Peck look-alikes peering out from behind the trees, grinning comically lecherous grins. "Wear Riding Hood Red at your own sweet risk…. We warn you, you're going to be followed!" says the ad copy: "It's a rich, succulent red that turns the most innocent look into a tantalizing invitation." A 1962 advertisement in *The New Yorker* similarly cast Red as a glamorous femme fatale: this time, on her way to Grandma's in her "little red Hertz." Her car is a racy convertible; her hood now a high-fashion item that might have come from Dior; her coy come-hither smile and sidelong glance is almost identical to that of the Max Factor model. And, "Without red, nothing doing," says a 1983 ad for Johnny Walker red label, which shows a wolf bypassing a girl dressed in white. Who wants to buy a drink for bleached goody-two-shoes?

In pop music, Sam the Sham and the Pharaohs also echoed the new popular version of the tale as a courtship dance and the heroine's new availability—both social and sexual. In their 1966 smash hit "Lil' Red Riding Hood"—which could easily have been the theme song for Madison Avenue ads or for Avery's *Red Hot Riding Hood*—the wolf pursues the girl not in search of a meal but in hopes of a date. This time it is *he* who notices what big eyes—not to mention full lips—that the heroine, now a "big girl," has. "Owoo! Little Red Riding Hood—you sure are looking good!"

As Sam the Sham and the ads of Madison Avenue suggest, the new grown-up Red Riding Hood has a suitor; indeed, she may bring out as many wolves as she pleases—but she is defined by her independence from them. Brown's *Sex and the Single Girl*, which described the prototype of the *Cosmo Girl*, offers an insight into the sort of woman who might purchase Max Factor's ripe young "riding hood red" lipstick. Brown's advice, though in opposition to some of the coming ideas of feminism, nevertheless stands in stark contrast to the clichés of 1950s gender stereotypes and epitomizes the sort of power that at the time was available to single women—as "gold-diggers" and flirts. During a woman's best years, Brown counseled, "You don't need a husband," just a man, and men "are often cheaper emotionally and a lot more fun by the bunch." She advised flirtation with butchers to get a better side of beef, and counseled single women against having an affair with only one married man—though there was nothing wrong with dating *many*.[1]

Fast-forward to the end of the twentieth century, when a 1998 television spot crafted by Luc Besson for Chanel No. 5 perfume updates the heroine's commercial sex appeal. This time, Red is a Parisian beauty (model Estella Warren …) who calls her own shots. She sashays through a mansion in a red satin bustier-and-petticoats number—reminiscent of the outfit worn by Avery's Red Hot. In her vault, bottles

---

1 [Helen Gurley Brown, *Sex and the Single Girl* (New York: Bernard Geis Associates, 1962) 2].

of Chanel No. 5 perfume, stacked ceiling high and wall to wall like bricks of gold, signify her incredible stock of sex appeal, here defined as scent. After dabbing her pulse points, she dons a shiny red satin cloak and heads for the door, where she turns at the last moment and places a finger to her lips to shush a howling wolf—her house pet. Subdued, he sits obediently as she flips her hood over her head and with a smile heads out the door to the Paris skyline for a night on the town with a different set of wolves. "Share the fantasy," exhorts the legendary Chanel tag line.

In just thirty seconds the Chanel ad inverts the tale's traditional message: The admonition to obedience has been redirected—now *he* is tamed—and instead of the womanizing wolf, this time it's the heroine who goes on the prowl. But has the message *really* changed? Although Chanel's "Little Red Riding Hood" has tamed her wolf, her implicit lesson is hardly different from that of Max Factor's femme fatale in 1953: namely, that sexual appeal—or lack thereof—is the source of female power and value, whether in the perfume vault or in the open market of dating and mating.

The sultry single woman has been one of Little Red Riding Hood's great twentieth-century roles, whether *Red Hot* or "ripe, young" or just a fantasy in a perfumed red dress. Chased by a pack of smitten bachelors in the cartoons of Tex Avery, the croonings of Sam the Sham, or the ad copy of Max Factor, by mid-century our heroine emerged as an icon of feminine availability: the image of woman as man desires her, distinguished by her ability to turn his head (or make him levitate, steam, and lose his eyeballs) and always desirous of a romantic romp.

But while the popular understanding of the tale as a parable of puppy love endures into the present day, this version of the story as a romance, crafted by men like Avery, Luc Besson, and the executives of Madison Avenue, contrasts sharply with the way women in the latter half of the twentieth century retold the fairy tale. Far from romantic fun and games, feminists cast Red Riding Hood's encounter with the wolf in a far more sinister light.

ANOTHER BITE OF THE POISONED APPLE: WHY DOES POP CULTURE LOVE FAIRY TALES AGAIN?[1]

Graeme McMillan

SNOW WHITE AND THE HUNTSMAN—A SOMEWHAT MODERNIZED TAKE on the familiar fairy tale featuring *Twilight's* Kristen Stewart as the titular Snow in conflict with Charlize Theron's demonic Evil Queen—hits theaters this Friday, something that you may already know if you'd seen the commercials on television while watching ABC's *Once Upon a Time*, the show that features *Big Love's* Gennifer Goodwin as Snow White in conflict with Lana Parrilla's melodramatic Evil Queen. Of course, *Snow White and The Huntsman* is the second Snow White movie released this year; in March, we had *Mirror Mirror*, in which Lily Collins's Snow had to deal with Julia Roberts's bitchy Evil Queen. (Disney, meanwhile, just shelved its own Snow White movie last week.) Clearly, a trend is underway.

It's not just a *Snow White* trend, though; the director of the original *Twilight*—there's that name again—Catherine Hardwicke followed up her über-successful love story about a girl and a vampire with an updated *Red Riding Hood*, a love story about a girl and a werewolf. Later this year, *The Golden Compass'* Philip Pullman is releasing his own versions of stories such as Cinderella, Rapunzel and, yes, Snow White made famous by the Brothers Grimm. DC Comics' *Fables*, celebrating its tenth anniversary this year, has become the biggest success for the publisher's Vertigo imprint since Neil Gaiman's *Sandman* in the 1990s, spawning multiple spin-off series, graphic novels and even a prose novel. NBC's *Grimm* (a series about supernatural menaces that is loosely based, in part, on the Grimm stories) has just been renewed for a second season. And Bryan Singer's *Jack the Giant Killer* is scheduled to be released in March 2013. Pop culture of all kinds, it seems, is banking on fairy tales as the official Next Big Thing, raising the obvious question: How did *that* happen?

It's a question that perplexes many; in March, as *Mirror Mirror* was preparing to be ignored by audiences nationwide, the *New York Times'* Terrence Rafferty argued that the genre was out of step with today's world:

> The world from which fairy tales and folk tales emerged has largely vanished, and although it pleases us to think of these stark, simple, fantastic narratives as timeless, they aren't. Thanks to video games, computer graphics and the

---

1 Published in *Time Entertainment*, May 30, 2012, TIME.com <http://entertainment.time .com/2012/05/30/another-bite-of-the-poisoned-apple-why-does-pop-culture -love-fairy-tales-again/>.

general awfulness of everyday life, fantasies of all kinds have had a resurgence in the past few years But the social realities on which the original fairy tales depend are almost incomprehensibly alien to 21st-century sensibilities; they reek of feudalism. And the lessons they're supposed to teach our young don't have much force these days. Kids learn to be skeptical almost before they've been taught anything to be skeptical of.[1]

That last point may have been disproved by a February survey in the United Kingdom which revealed that one in four British parents wouldn't read fairy tales to their children until they were five years old because they were too scary. That same poll backed up the idea that the stories were also too old-fashioned for their intended audience: 52% of the 2,000 adults surveyed admitted that they thought that Cinderella set a bad example to children because she did housework all day. (Never mind that that is supposed to be a bad thing in the story itself; maybe the survey should've asked the parents whether or not they remembered what actually happened in the stories.)

But, of course, none of these modern fairy tale movies, television shows or comics are for children, as the *Snow White and The Huntsman* trailer makes clear with its grime, violence and self-important menace.[2]

Whether it's the look of that trailer (or *Red Riding Hood*, which offered a slightly more colorful aesthetic), or the extra-marital affairs and primetime soap operatics of *Once Upon a Time*, there's one thing that today's fairy tale revivals want you to think: *These aren't the sanitized fairy tales of the Disney Princesses. These are the same stories for grown-ups.* In that respect, they could be seen as returning to their roots as folktales shared by adults that often (and somewhat gleefully) included sex or any amount of shameless, tasteless violence and grisly death in order to maintain the audience's attention. As Neil Gaiman once wrote, "Wilhelm and Jacob Grimm, to pick two writers who had a lot to do with the matter, did not set out to collect the stories that bear their name in order to entertain children."[3] The censorship and selective editing to make the stories more suitable for younger ears came from market forces throughout the years.

Gennifer Goodwin, star of *Once Upon a Time*, has a theory as to why adults need fairy tales today. Talking during an appearance at the Paley Center earlier this year, she explained "I understand why society, especially American society, is gravitating

---

1   Published in *The New York Times*, March 21, 2012, <http://www.nytimes.com/2012/03/25 /movies/mirror-mirror-grimm-and-hollywood-love-for-fairy-tales.html>.

2   [You can see the trailer at <http://www.youtube.com/watch?v=55Dq2psogSw>.]

3   [Neil Gaiman, "Happily Ever After," *The Guardian*, October 13, 2007, <http://www. theguardian.com/books/2007/oct/13/film.fiction>.]

toward fairy tales given our economy. We've been exploring the world of witches and wizards for years. We've been exploring the world of vampires for years. Clearly the public—I mean, I feel like all of this was ushered in by Harry Potter—in my own fannish beliefs [sic]. But the world has been responding in the last 10, 12, 15 years very strongly to fantasy. I think it's always a reflection to where we are as a society."

It's a nice theory to consider, and it definitely has merit, but I suspect that there's more to the trend of reviving fairy tales than simply an escape from the everyday world. (After all, doesn't *all* fiction offer that kind of release valve?) That said, pop culture has historically developed a tendency to infantilize the audience, something that may have reached its zenith with Hollywood's reliance on superheroes. It's tempting to draw parallels between the mainstreaming of superheroes and the apparent mainstreaming of fairy tales—Is the Pullman book going to offer the same kind of literary legitimacy that Michael Chabon's *The Amazing Adventures of Kavalier and Clay* did for comic books, for example?—but there's another trend that the most well-known fairy tales tie into, one that could also explain their current popularity beyond the superhero connection.

Maria Tatar, who chairs the Program in Folklore and Mythology at Harvard University, put her finger on a potential lure of fairy tales as pop culture source material in a piece for the *New Yorker* earlier this year: "Boy heroes clearly had a hard time surviving the nineteenth-century migration of fairy tales from the communal hearth into the nursery, when oral storytelling traditions, under the pressures of urbanization and industrialization, lost their cross-generational appeal," she wrote. "Once mothers, nannies, and domestics were in charge of telling stories at bedtime, it seems they favored tales with female heroines."[1]

It's true; with the exception of a few stories—Jack and the Beanstalk, Hansel and Gretel—fairy tales tend to focus on the females. Not only do we get female heroes and villains—even if the heroes tend to be somewhat passive at least at the start of their stories—but we also get objectified males who work more as personifications of the goal than as individual characters. They don't even have real names; they're all Prince Charming, which leads to the fun meta-joke in *Fables* wherein each heroine's Prince Charming is the same man, a lothario who has worked his way around all the female characters before the story has started and been discarded in disgust by them all. Alyssa Rosenberg, cultural critic for *The Atlantic* and *ThinkProgress*, wrote once that one of the strengths of *Once Upon a Time* was that "[t]he show doesn't hammer it in obsessively, but it is nice to spend time in an environment where the normal

---

1   [Maria Tatar, "Cinderfellas: The Long-Lost Fairy Tales," *The New Yorker*, March 16, 2012, <http://www.newyorker.com/online/blogs/books/2012/03/long-lost-fairy-tales.html>.]

assumptions about who controls things are flipped."[1] The same could arguably be said of most of the new breed of fairy tale projects.

For decades, science fiction and fantasy have proven to be the dominant genres in terms of money making, but they've constantly been accused of being too male-centric or overly reliant on male power fantasies. That's been shifting slowly as shows like *Buffy* and, more importantly, movies like *The Hunger Games* and, yes, the *Twilight Saga* demonstrate the audience hunger for female-led fantasy projects (and, perhaps as importantly for the executives, that hunger can produce as much money as male-dominated traditional projects). The very idea of, maybe not feminist fantasy, but *female-led* fantasy, at least, feels like it answers a particular need to broaden the focus of, and audience for, some of the most financially successful films and television shows.

Fairy tales become a triple treat in terms of appeal for pop culture creators. First, they're firmly in the fantasy genre, and so provide a particularly successful kind of eye-candy-esque escapism. They're also filled with the kind of nostalgic appeal and familiarity to anyone who encountered them as a kid—which, thanks to Disney, is most likely everyone who'll be seeing the new project—that makes them a much easier sell to the audience. But what fairy tales have as a sub-genre that potentially gives them an edge over superheroes or *Star Trek* revivals is that they theoretically appeal to both genders equally thanks to the female leads and focus of the story and the male-centric appeal of violence, special effect spectacle and action. On paper, at least, that's a magical combination.

Whether that magic on paper translates to reality, however, remains to be seen. *Red Riding Hood* and the more traditional, much campier *Mirror Mirror* both flopped at the box office, suggesting that while the appeal seems simple, the execution is anything but. *Once Upon a Time* and *Grimm* both found varying amounts of favor with television audiences—enough to return for another year, at least—but both also hid their "fairy tale-ness" within other existing, successful genres, making it harder to estimate how much appeal the source material actually had. Given that uneven win/lose ratio, it's possible that *Snow White and the Huntsman* will be looked upon as the project that will prove whether or not fairy tales hold enough mass appeal to escape the pop culture purgatory of being considered a passing fad. Here's hoping that the combination of star power, special effects and frowning proves as potent for fairy tales as it did for superheroes in *Avengers* just a few weeks ago.

---

1   [Alyssa Rosenberg, "Why 'Once Upon a Time' Works Better Than 'Grimm,'" *Think-Progress*, January 27, 2012, <http://thinkprogress.org/alyssa/2012/01/27/412472/why-once-upon-a-time-works-better-than-grimm/>.]

"ONCE UPON A TIME" TEAM: WE SHOW WOMEN WHO AREN'T AFRAID OF POWER[1]

Emily Rome

IN THEIR OFFICE JUST DOWN THE ROAD FROM WALT DISNEY STUDIOS, "Once Upon a Time" writers Adam Horowitz and Edward Kitsis paper their walls with their own past ("Tron: Legacy" and "Lost" posters) as well as their influences ("Snow White and the Seven Dwarfs" and a large, light-up poster of George Lucas's Death Star). "Star Wars," Horowitz says, is "one of the most iconic pieces of story-telling ever. It was inventing a fairy tale that also felt like it had always been around." Fairy tale invention and reinvention are the duo's focus goal these days as they break the story for the first season finale of "Once Upon a Time." Tonight's episode, mean-while, is "Skin Deep," which takes on the tale of "Beauty and the Beast" and reveals more about how much Mr. Gold/Rumpelstiltskin remembers of his life in Fairy Tale Land. During an interview with Hero Complex writer Emily Rome, the tandem talk-ed about the future of the show.

ER: Do you two feel like human encyclopedias of fairy tales now? Are you fairy tale experts after all the research you've had to do for the show?

EK: I can honestly say that Adam and I feel that we are experts in nothing.

AH: Actually, I feel like the Blue Fairy [laughs]. No, I would say that we feel certainly immersed in the world but part of the fun of the show for us was taking these stories that were so formative for us and saying, "What's our spin on them? What's the stuff we don't know about them? Let's not retell them. Let's find something new."

EK: There's definitely people that know way more about fairy tales than we do, but we love to just kind of get in and say what's our spin on "Well, why did Grumpy become Grumpy?"

ER: When writing your characters, how do you decide how much to turn to the original fairy tales versus the Disney version?

EK: Sometimes it's what's most iconic. The reason we chose to open up the pilot with Snow White was because if you were going to show a curse that took away a happy ending, take away the happiest of them all, which is Snow White being woken up in a coffin. So for us there are certain iconic touchstones, like Cinderella with a glass slipper. But how she got the glass slipper, we chose

---

1 Published in the *Los Angeles Times*, February 12, 2012, <http://herocomplex.latimes.com/ tv/once-upon-a-time-team-we-show-women-who-arent-afraid-of-power/>.

Rumpelstiltskin to have kill her fairy godmother. That's the part of the story you didn't know.

AH: We're sort of trying to build out our own world and use these characters as the jumping off point for telling this larger story that we're trying to tell about what is essentially a new fairy tale character—the child of Snow White and Prince Charming, Emma Swan, and how she gets embroiled in this huge battle of good versus evil.

ER: Tell me about the choice to have a lot of the costumes, like Cinderella's and Belle's in Sunday's episode, be so influenced by their costumes in the Disney animated movies.

EK: We call it fairy tale couture. Eduardo Castro, who did "Ugly Betty," does all our costumes. They're one part Disney and two parts Alexander McQueen. We're always trying to do something a little forward with them. I think that we use Disney because when Adam and I were growing up, that's what inspired us. Because they inspire us and because we love them and they're iconic. We are Disney, so we can use them. It's really cool to be able to kind of get to play in that sandbox that Disney's allowed us to. Just personally as a fan, if I'm watching a show I would rather see Grumpy and Sneezy and Bashful than three names we made up.

ER: How different would the show be if it were on another network?

AH: It's funny because it's the only place we took it. We've been working with ABC/Disney for many years now. I guess it's a good thing they went ahead with it, because if they didn't, I'm not sure where we could have done it with the same amount of latitude that we've been given. The brand management people at the Walt Disney Company have been great. From when we first pitched the idea, they've been very supportive of allowing us to play with their icons and kind of re-invent them.

EK: I mean, we killed a dwarf. We had a pregnant Snow White. We had Cinderella promising somebody her first-born. So they've been really great in allowing us that freedom.

ER: Tell me about your approach to the Evil Queen Regina. There are some moments when you feel sympathetic toward her, but she's also this despicable villain. How do you decide how much to stay true to the traditional, straight evil villain versus making her more complex?

EK: We have a phrase that you'll see in later episodes, "Evil's not born—it's made." What we love about Regina is she's very tortured. And you understand that there's a hidden pain inside her that is causing her to do these things. We're just not going to reveal it till the end of the season.

ER: So by the end of the season we'll learn what made her so evil?

AH: Prior to the end of the season, well before the finale. That question of being evil, what happened between her and Snow that we've kind of hinted throughout the season is one that we see a few things before the finale.

EK: Episode 18, I believe.

ER: As we've moved beyond Prince Phillip saving Aurora and are now post-Ariel, post-Belle, post-Tiana, with modern fairy tales the damsel in distress-type female characters are a thing of the past. Is that type of character something you're actively trying to avoid and turn on its head?

AH: I'd say from the first scenes of the pilot, that's what we were trying to do. Snow White pulls out a sword. We did not want to have the damsel in distress. We did not want to have the princess who needs saving.

EK: The perfect example is how they met. Snow meets Charming because she steals from him and then knocks him out. We weren't interested in writing damsels in distress. We were interested in writing really tough women [who] were not afraid to use power because we feel like that's what's relevant today and that's what's interesting as writers.

ER: You also have women in the three lead roles, something you don't see very often on TV.

AH: I don't think we consciously set out to do it that way. It's one of those things where it was a very organic process of developing the story for the show, and it became—it's very much a story about mothers.

EK: In the way that "Lost" was about fathers. It's a family dynamic. Fairy tales are about family, so for us it just felt natural. It's funny because our wives will watch an episode and be like, "How do you write that? Why aren't you that at home? Why aren't you that understanding at home?"

ER: You have an interesting relationship between Mary Margaret and Emma, who are actually mother and daughter but often act more like sisters. How do you figure out that kind of relationship when a mother and daughter are the same age?

AH: That was one of the fun things for us, saying, "What do you do when a mother and daughter are contemporaries?" It's a fascinating thing for writers to explore.

EK: Mary Margaret will very much act like Emma's mom in certain situations, and in other situations you see Emma being her big sister. Emma has always been looking for home, but because she's never had one, she doesn't know what it is when she finds it. She comes in very tough, walls up and Henry's the first one to poke at it. You're going to see as the season goes by so does Mary Margaret.

ER: In episode 7, "The Heart Is a Lonely Hunter," we finally got to see a Storybrooke character remember who he was in Fairy Tale Land. As we see more of those realizations on the show, how are you going to make each one uniquely rewarding for the audience?

EK: That's what keeps us up at night!

AH: Telling that story relatively early in the season was a way for us to tell the audience, "This is what can happen here."

EK: And that it's real. It's not in Henry's head. Don't worry—we're not going to wake up and Henry's going to say "You were there, and you were there, and you were there." It's real.

ER: How long do we have to wait until another character remembers?

AH: All I'll say is as a viewer, I'd be pissed if it was a really long time. There's hints of it coming soon. There are levels of seepage that occur.

EK: Levels of awaking for different moments.

ER: Can you tell me what the visual effects budget is like on "Once"?

AH: There is no budget. It's all done with magic.

ER: I thought magic always comes with a price! Isn't that what Rumpelstiltskin says?

EK: Yes, it does! We're not a cheap show. But we're not the most expensive show.

ER: There have been mixed reactions to the quality of the effects on the show. I don't think a lot of people are really fooled into thinking any of the green screen is real, but you do completely create this great mystical world.

AH: It's one of those things where when you're a first season show and you're hoping to be more than a first season show, you learn what works and what doesn't work.

EK: Sometimes your ambition doesn't match technology. And then you say, "Well, do we lower our ambition or do we go for it?" And sometimes when you go for it, there are effects that are much more successful than others.

AH: We give [Zoic Studios, which does the show's visual effects] a big screen-possible task each week, and they really kind of push the limits. Everyone—not just on the effects level but on every department of the show from the story to the costumes to everything—everybody is learning and growing as they move forward and hopefully we're getting better.

ER: I wanted to ask about the inevitable comparisons to Bill Willingham's comic series, "Fables." Did you see the post he wrote about "Once" and "Fables"?

AH: He actually sent that to us before [he published it]. He was really lovely.

ER: Many suspicious of the similarities point out that ABC was developing a pilot for "Fables" back in 2008.

EK: We had no idea about the "Fables" development when we started our show. Things are developed every year. But immediately when our show came out, of course the boards lit up with "How dare they, those thieves! How dare they take public domain characters—" We think that Bill Willingham, what he did on "Fables" is amazing, the scope and the characters. It's amazing, but what's even more amazing about him is that he was generous to us. At an early time when we felt like there were villagers ready to knock down our door, he stepped in front and said, "It's OK. There can be two different things." And I truly think that now, after seeing 11 episodes, people realize that there is probably still room for a "Fables" TV show out there that can still exist in the same world as "Grimm" and "Once."

ER: So you think "Fables" could still [be] developed and picked up while "Once" is on the air?

EK: Sure, why not? They're two totally different things. If "Chicago Hope" and "ER"[1] can exist at the same time, I don't see why not.

ER: The promo for the "Beauty and the Beast" story in Sunday's episode says, "It's different when the beast really is a monster." Where did the idea for this take and to have Rumpelstiltskin be the beast come from?

AH: For us it's like, "Who's the character on the show who thinks he's a monster?" Rumpelstiltskin. You've seen him enjoy being the monster in episode four when he's stealing babies. And you've seen him as the village coward in episode eight. For us it was natural to use that as a way to really learn more about the character.

ER: It's still unclear whether Mr. Gold remembers his life as Rumpelstiltskin in Fairy Tale Land. When will we find out just how much he knows?

EK: You know what? I would be so pissed if I watched this weekend and that wasn't answered. I want to know what that guy knows, and I just hope to God that I get it Sunday night, but you know, that would mean I don't watch the Grammys, but I guess I can TiVo[2] the Grammys.

ER: What was your approach to Belle's character?

AH: With Belle, it's not just that she's beautiful, which she is, but she's a beautiful soul in every way. And it's what happens when you put that up against one of the darkest elements of our show. For us that was really exciting to kind of explore.

ER: Tell me about casting "Lost" alum Emilie de Ravin as Belle.

AH: We love Emilie. We were so thrilled that she wanted to do it. All those qualities about Belle being smart and empowered and strong, those are all things that Emilie embodies, and we're really excited for people to see her take on the character.

EK: We loved writing for her on "Lost." There's such a strength to her. The way she would have those scenes with John Locke and never be frightened of him.

AH: It's only natural to put her next to the Beast.

---

1 [Hospital shows.]
2 [An on-demand service for recording television programs, available only in the United States at time of publication of this book.]

ER: Is there something more to Emma's last name? Is there an ugly duckling or swan princess connection for her?

EK: We chose the name because it's the metaphor for her journey, to become the swan. And right now I don't think she is. The funny thing about Emma is theoretically, if she truly believed what's going on, she's a princess. But if you told Emma Swan she was a princess she'd ... laugh at you.

ER: What were your favorite fairy tales growing up?

EK: "Peter Pan." The ability to not grow up is still to this day what I want. I love the magic of that. I love the magic of leaving through a windowsill and going to a place called Neverland and never having to grow up.

AH: My favorite was "Snow White." It was the first one I ever heard of, it was the first one I ever saw. I think it was the first time I was ever terrified. The first time I was introduced to such a magical world.

EK: But honestly, I think one of our favorite fairy tales is "Star Wars." What better fairy tale is there than a young orphan learning that he has a special power to rise up and take down the evil forces?

AH: To me, it's one of the most iconic pieces of storytelling ever. It was inventing a fairy tale that also felt like it had always been around.

ER: Mary Margaret says in the pilot that stories are "a way for us to deal with our world." Do you think that's what it boils down to or do you have any other theories on why these fairy tales continue to capture our interest?

AH: It's a way for us to deal with the world, and I would also say they're also the first stories we hear. I've got twin daughters who are three and I'm starting to read to them. They'll start reciting "Rapunzel" to me. It's how they're starting to understand how to communicate.

EK: For us, "Lost" was about redemption, and "Once" is about hope. Fairy tales are a way to deal with our world, but also as dark as they are, they give us a little bit of sunlight. It's interesting because in 1937, "Snow White" came out in the height of the Depression. So, why now? Look at the times we're in. To us fairy tales are like a lottery ticket. Why do [you] buy a lottery ticket? So you win so much money you can tell your boss to go to hell and you can retire to an island that you just bought. Isn't that Cinderella's story? But through that journey you have to realize there aren't shortcuts. There are these morality tales that have to be told. That's what's fun about fairy tales—they're kind of like CliffsNotes[1] for life.

---

1 [A series of student study guides.]

THE FAIREST OF THEM ALL [1]

Alex Fury

WHEN *MIRROR MIRROR: THE UNTOLD ADVENTURES OF SNOW WHITE* opens in cinemas across Europe and the United States in the next couple of weeks, the costumes worn by its stars will be just as influential as the ones they wear on the red carpet. For the fashion world is having a fairy tale moment. Not only is *Once Upon a Time*, ABC's twist on Snow White, currently on TV, and *Snow White and the Huntsman*, with Kristen Stewart, set for summer release, there's also an emphasis on the dressed-up and romantic carrying through from spring/summer collections such as Alexander McQueen's, to autumn/winter.

The grand, bullion-encrusted capes shown for autumn/winter at Dolce & Gabbana, Versace's slinky chainmail evening dresses and the ravaged rococo ballgowns at Giles in London could slip seamlessly into either of these films, give or take a smattering of medieval-inspired embroidery and the odd hint of armour.

And there are plenty more fairy tale films on the way next year and beyond, including Guillermo del Toro's take on *Beauty and the Beast*, *Maleficent*, with Angelina Jolie as Sleeping Beauty's nemesis, *Jack the Giant Killer*, and *Hansel and Gretel: Witch Hunters*, a sequel of sorts to the classic tale.

Essentially, fashion is the ultimate fairy tale—every show is a Cinderella story, transforming the models from mere mortals into a designer's fantasy. Or maybe that should be Snow White. After all, the story of a woman perpetually questioning who is the fairest, with a watchful and even vengeful eye on the competition, has a wry parallel in the youth-obsessed, beauty-fixated fashion industry.

Over the past few years contemporary fashion and Hollywood's interpretation of tales Grimm and not-so-grim have come closer and closer together. From haute couture to high street, fashion has increased its levels of fantasy and the fairy tales themselves become more real. Kristen Stewart, who plays the heroine in *Snow White and the Huntsman*, is according to the film's costume designer, Colleen Atwood, "Much less kind of princess-y and more of a 'badass' girl." On the other hand, last September's Rodarte show, with its puffed-sleeve evening gowns by designers Kate and Laura Mulleavy, was an unashamedly girlie paean to Disney princess dresses.

Haute couture is the source for many of the clothes that real-life princesses and 21st-century crowned heads wear, as well as being a designer's playground when it comes to experimentation and fly-by-the-seat-of-your-pants invention. "Mr. Dior

---

1 Published in the *Financial Times*, March 23, 2012, <http://www.ft.com/cms/s/2 /12e9297e-6f7d-11e1-b368-00144feab49a.html#axzz2b6Hn1c2x>.

said he wanted to 'make women dream,'" says Bill Gaytten, head designer at Christian Dior. "That fantasy element is important. You want the clothes to inspire as well as empower." Cue, for example, Dior's millefeuille ruffled and embroidered evening wear.

Valentino's haute couture show in January by Maria Grazia Chiuri and PierPaolo Piccioli featured watered toile de jouy taffetas inspired by Marie Antoinette's "fairy tale" of pastoral femininity at Versailles—reinterpreted in quintessentially Valentino vein by an army of 40 seamstresses in the company's Alta Moda studio in Piazza Mignanelli, Rome.

Fairy tales aren't something you necessarily associate with Jean Paul Gaultier— for whom denim and fur figure as frequently as tulle and taffeta. But, as Gaultier says, "All creation is fantasy." He has taken his turn at the Snow White story, creating costumes for French choreographer Angelin Preljocaj's Sadler's Wells staging of the ballet in May. "Angelin knew that he wanted to present *Snow White* as quite sensual and dark, as the fairy tales often are," says Gaultier. "But he gave me creative freedom for the costumes." The results, from Snow White's plissé slip of chiffon to the Wicked Queen's crimson and black slash of ombre silk, over underwear-as-outerwear constructions, are classic Gaultier.

The darkness of fairy tales is possibly what draws fashion to them: the doomed heroine, of course, but also the evil queen or stepmother who, truth be told, is much more fun to dress. "I like something when it has a very definite undertone of something that's quite dark or evil," says British designer Gareth Pugh, whose designs frequently have a gothic, fairy tale edge. Kate and Laura Mulleavy sought the same effect when designing their costumes for Darren Aronofsky's *Black Swan* (2011). "The story of *Swan Lake* unfolds as a tale of the transformation of the maiden into a swan," say the designers. "We were inspired by the idea of metamorphosis, specifically the dichotomy between perfection and decay."

It's not only in the high drama worlds of haute couture and out-there costume design that fashion is in thrall to the idea of fairy tale. "The notion of fashion as a fairy tale plays a big part in our planning," says Judd Crane, Selfridges director of womenswear. "It's about shopping as art." Think about it: with the Shoe Galleries, Selfridges has the largest women's footwear department of any store in the world—35,000 square feet of retail retifism. Could there be anything more Cinderella than that?

MAGICAL ILLUSION: FAIRY-TALE FILM[1]

Jessica Tiffin

FILM VERSIONS OF FAIRY TALE ARE INEVITABLE, GIVEN THE EXTREME adaptability shown by fairy-tale structures across the centuries, and its ability to continually reinvent its voices, settings, and message as well as its medium of expression. As with the adaptation of oral folktale into written literature, the adaptation of written literature into film brings with it the possibilities and the constraints of the new medium: if writing and the printed book reinvented the oral tale, cinema's impact on literary storytelling is perhaps even more profound. Film is a vitally different form of expression from the book, and its creation—technical, massively expensive, requiring the input and skills of a large and diverse body of contributors—hugely exaggerates the importance of technology in the transmission of cultural artifacts. This leap in the complexity of the process is enabled by the concomitant leap in audience: the twentieth century saw the development of the mass market, the ability of texts to reach more people more easily than ever before. The distance from the cozy oral storyteller in a small circle of listeners could not be greater. With the new costs and new audience naturally come new constraints on the narrative, which must be adapted to its viewers on a far broader and less personal scale to provide the necessary mass appeal which will recoup the enormous costs of production. Film thus has a dual nature as an exciting and powerfully visual form of artistic expression but also as a medium operating within the consumerist paradigm of modern mass culture. Both film-as-art and film-as-product retain the potential to offer an essentially self-reflexive notion of narrative, metafiction given new expression by a new technology.

From the earliest days of cinema, in texts such as the experimental fairy-tale films of Georges Méliès, fairy-tale film has been extremely successful. Fairy-tale motifs adapt easily to the visual, and fairy tale's clear, simplified narratives are also far more conveniently adaptable to the time-scale of a film than are the detailed textures and events of a novel. This thematic simplicity also possibly explains why fairy-tale film has become strongly associated with the particular film medium of animation, a form which similarly refuses to reflect a realistically textured world. On the narrative level, fairy-tale film offers an obvious articulation of the classic Hollywood "fairy-tale" plot, which relies heavily on the comedic marriage resolution and on wish fulfillment and utopian impulses that empower the underdog. The close fit between film and fairy tale is also in some ways inevitable given folkloric narrative's long

---

1 Chapter 6. *Marvelous Geometry: Narrative and Metafiction in Modern Fairy Tales* (Detroit: Wayne State UP, 2009) 179-88.

history of happy interaction with theatrical as well as literary forms. Following the adaptation of folklore into the French aristocratic pursuits of the eighteenth century, fairy-tale motifs seem to have spread rapidly to the theater, ballet, and opera. The heyday of fairy-tale ballet in the nineteenth century saw the creation of such classics as *Sleeping Beauty*, *Swan Lake*, and *The Nutcracker*, all with recognizable fairy-tale themes. In opera, fairy-tale awareness, although expanded into a more complex narrative, informs operas such as Mozart's *The Magic Flute*, Verdi's *Vakula the Smith*, and Puccini's *Turandot*.

As a symbolic genre, fairy tale has strong visual and dramatic potential. It is also obvious that the simple, ritualistic formulae of fairy tale would work well in ritualistic traditions, most notably ballet and opera, which are artistic productions whose meaning is expressed via a powerful system of structural codes (song, movement) rather than a process of realistic representation. Suzanne Rahn writes, "Like fairy tales, ballets are constructed as highly formalized narratives which make extensive use of repetition and tell their stories primarily through the physical actions of their characters" (in Zipes, *Oxford Companion* 34). In the twentieth century, the successful use of fairy tale in the Broadway musical follows a similar pattern; Stephen Sondheim's 1986 musical *Into the Woods*, for example, explores the dangerous gap between fairy tale and real life in a manner similar to [Terry] Pratchett's *Witches Abroad* [published in 1991]. Again, the musical is an artificial form whose encodings—the stock romantic characters, the likelihood of any character to break into song or dance at any moment—have very little to do with reality. Disney's characteristic blending of the fairy tale and the musical is a good illustration of these similarities; films such as *Beauty and the Beast* not only use the musical format but also refer constantly to the Hollywood musical.

However, theater, ballet, and other live art forms face an inherent logical problem in visually representing the marvelous, relying on stylization or at times unconvincing mechanisms to pretend to the magical; Tolkien, typically, claims that "Fantasy … hardly ever succeeds in Drama…. Fantastic forms are not to be counterfeited" (49). This is in many ways an anachronistic view in the age of CGI (computer-generated imagery), and the verisimilitude of magical spectacle in film has seen a steady increase over the last hundred years, culminating in the giant leaps made by computer imagery in influential films such as Peter Jackson's three-film version of *The Lord of the Rings*. Cinema's tricky camera is thus ultimately able to overcome the difficulties of nonreal representation, harnessing fairy tale's symbolic qualities to provide a rich visual texture. The contributions of special effects and CGI have made possible visual enchantments Tolkien could not have imagined, but the film/fairy tale fit is more profound than that; even in the early days of the medium, cinema has always been the site of magic. While apparently offering the real, it is a fertile ground for trickery, in which apparently real objects may disappear, reappear, change size or orientation, change shape—in fact, the whole of the special effects man's box of tricks; David Galef's discussion of Jean Cocteau's *La Belle et la Bête* offers a detailed and interesting analysis of this kind of magical cinematic function. The authority of the camera is such that the impossible takes on the same status as the realistic, which is in any case a good working definition of magic.

On a more fundamental level, the magical paradigm of fairy tale finds echoes in the magic of the film experience even without special effects, in film's ability to create the apparent three-dimensionality of the real on a flat, unmoving screen, through the trickery of light and image. Film powerfully realizes the transcendence over reality with which magical narrative is intrinsically concerned. This is, of course, another aspect of the debate André Bazin has called "the quarrel over realism in art" that arises from ongoing technical refinement; he suggests that the eye of the camera has the power to satisfy "our obsession with realism" and "our appetite for illusion" (12). Photography and film are particularly suited to the depiction of the fantastic because they are able to produce "a hallucination that is also a fact" (16); to blur, in fact, the boundaries between fiction and mimesis, although in a way which seldom denies its own illusion to produce the frame break which would signal metafictional play.

In addition to this, the absorbing effect of the film experience—the immersion of the viewer in a constructed reality—parallels the more traditional folk storytelling experience. Jack Zipes formulates a general theory of fairy-tale film, commenting on the importance of the storyteller's ability to create a new, removed, and absorbing reality for his or her audience. He suggests, "A magic folk tale concerned not only the miraculous turn of events in the story but also the magical play of words by the teller as performer.... Telling a magic folk tale was and is not unlike performing a magic trick, and depending on the art of the storyteller, listeners are placed under a spell. They are ... transcending reality for a brief moment, to be transported to extraordinary realms of experience" (*Happily Ever After* 63). In this characterization, cinema, like fairy tale, is a form of illusion, its viewers willingly suspending disbelief in order to surpass reality and experience the magical. Zipes notes the association between early filmmakers and stage magic—"magic lantern shows, magician's tricks, shadow theatres, animation devices ..." (68). The filmmaker becomes the magician, the showman with the power of technological marvels, exerting the same spell as the storyteller, but with new, spectacular special effects.

The interaction of film and fairy tale does not, however, constitute an unproblematical romance. While the magic of film may parallel some aspects of fairy tale, at the same time a visual medium can be crippling to the kind of imaginative exercise usually required of the reader by almost any magical narrative. Tolkien goes as far as to deny the validity even of illustrated literary fairy tale: "The radical distinction between all art (including drama) that offers a *visible* presentation and true literature is that it imposes one visible form. Literature works from mind to mind and is thus more progenitive" (80). In this context, film's presentation of realism is a problem as well as a strength. The recording eye of the camera intrinsically designates its objects as real, and the effect of watching a film is that of immersion in a highly detailed reality. In contrast, most forms of fantasy, fairy tale included, work on evocation, rather than being explicit; the process of imaginative interaction with the fantasy requires a tailoring of the fantasy world to the psychological reality of the individual. Film, in its extreme visuality, operates directly against this; a fairy-tale medium, in its meta-fictional awareness of craftedness, is specifically not realistic, and it may be jarring to have realistic representation on screen. Donald P. Haase's discussion of Neil Jordan's *The Company of Wolves* raises the same point: "The one-dimensionality, the depth-lessness, and the abstract style (Lüthi 4-36) of the fairy tale do not require the auditor or reader to envision a specific reality, and thereby they encourage imaginative belief in an unreal world. In the fairy tale, then, *not seeing* is believing" (90). Yet film paradoxically offers the potential for sending strong signals through visual details of setting and costume—the presence of self-conscious medievalism in a fairy-tale film, together with details of fairy-tale landscapes (forests, mountains, castles) may effectively signal the unreality of long ago and far away. Thus fairy-tale films such as *The Company of Wolves* and *The Grimm Brothers' Snow White* feature particularly vast and Gothic stretches of forest, while *Ever After* makes effective use of medieval castles, sweeping landscapes, and beautiful costumes. Cocteau's unexplained surrealist images in the Beast's castle, and Jordan's dense use of apparently disconnected symbol (animals, roses, etc.) fulfill the same function. In this deliberate symbolic texturing, once again, fairy-tale film has the potential to realize visually the meta-fictional strategy at the heart of its structures despite its illusory offering of realism.

Film and the Folk Voice

> A real fairy tale, a tale in its true function, is a tale within a circle of listeners.
> —Karel Capek in Warner, *From the Beast to the Blonde* 17

There are various thematic matches between film and fairy-tale narrative, but cinematic versions of fairy tale can be seen to offer their own pitfalls and drawbacks. While the power of the film medium in modern society has provided a fertile new ground for fairy-tale cultural and ideological production, the medium of film offers problems as well as possibilities for fairy tale. One of the most insidious tendencies has been that of the powerful new visual medium rooted firmly in modern technological popular culture, to supplant all other versions, and in so doing, to deliberately claim the folk voice originally excluded by the adaptation of fairy tale into a literary form. While parallel in many ways to the process by which oral folktale became written fairy tale, the adaptation from written fairy tale into fairy-tale film is more problematical precisely because of the power of the film medium, and the striking fit between some narrative aspects of fairy tale and the narrative function of film. To unwrap the dangers of this process will require examination of the uneasy, contested spaces of folk culture, popular culture, and mass culture.

As one of the more powerful and pervasive forms of popular culture in the twentieth and twenty-first century, film offers an interesting context for the folk voice of fairy tale. Although the folktale has been replaced gradually with the literary fairy tale in the last few centuries, film versions of fairy tale tend to flirt superficially and self-consciously with the folk voice. As the most prevalent cinematic experience in Western culture, Hollywood film caters to a popular market, offering both entertainment and the opportunity to participate in a popular awareness of actors and film which centers on the Hollywood star system. Although a form of mass culture in its reliance on the budgets of wealthy studios, and the resulting need to commodify film in order to fill cinema seats, film functions in modern Western culture as a group and social activity whose audience participates in an essentially nonliterary popular culture. Walter Ong argues for a modern notion of "secondary orality," a development through literacy into a kind of postliteracy under technology; he points out that "the drive towards group sense and towards participatory activities, towards 'happenings,' which mysteriously emerges out of modern electronic technological cultures is strikingly similar to certain drives in preliterate cultures" (*Rhetoric, Romance, and Technology* 284). The cinema experience offers far more of group participation than reading a written text. This inheres not only in the simultaneous experience of the film text, with shared reactions such as laughter, but also in the social activity around a common interest in film genres or specific stars, meeting to view a film, the discussion which often takes place either before or afterward over drinks or a meal. The experience of a home viewing of the video or DVD version of a film is an even more pronounced version of this communality. This is in many ways a superficial restoration of the communal folk experience of storytelling, in some senses reversing the historical translation of the oral folk voice into a written form experienced only by the individual, and reinstating it as shared cultural artifact. It also underlines the restitution offered the form after its appropriation by written narrative, and thus a social elite; Zipes comments that popular fairy-tale film "actually returns the fairy tale to the majority of people" (*Fairy Tale as Myth* 83).

However, while a film is certainly more communal than a single individual reading a book, it is not a true folk culture. The group may share the experience, but it is not *produced* from within the group, nor does the production come from a source which has the same status—here defined economically—as group members. Likewise, interaction with the film narrative cannot equal the folk experience since film is a one-way process. The film modifies the experience of the viewer, but the film is not a genuine oral voice and cannot in its turn be modified in response to the audience, other than on the macrolevel represented by the research done by a studio's marketing arm before the next film is made. Walter Benjamin suggests, in fact, that the reproduction of mass images ultimately denies the authenticity of the artistic object, its ability to transfer value, and that film "is inconceivable without its destructive, cathartic effect, that is, the liquidation of the traditional value of the cultural heritage" (II); the denial of tradition in this formulation speaks directly to the divide between folk and mass culture. Film may imitate folk culture, but if it functions as a true form of modern folk culture, it is within a somewhat radically restructured notion of "folk," and, indeed, of "culture."

In keeping with film's apparently transparent offer of itself as a substitute oral and folk tradition, many fairy-tale films rely heavily on an explicit evocation of the folk voice in order to frame and contextualize their narratives. In apparently receiving the story from the physical presence or voice of an onscreen narrator, the viewer is able to participate in the removal of the tale from literary capture, placing him or herself in the position of audience to an oral storyteller. The self-conscious recognition of viewer as "listener" taps into a notion of orality which is both artificial and idealized. The purpose here is only partially to participate in the metafictional play of crafted tale and its self-conscious pleasures; it is also to access the notions of communality and trust which inhere in modern notions of orality. Thus many Disney films begin with a voice-over giving the initial scenario of the tale in traditional fairy-tale form: "Once upon a time." This is usually accompanied by static images that characterize tale as artifact—*Sleeping Beauty*'s medieval stills, *Beauty and the Beast*'s stained-glass windows, the Grecian vases of *Hercules*. At the same time, many of Disney's films characteristically hedge their bets: the voice-over may well be associated with stills that strongly associate the tale with the written tradition, in the form of a beautifully calligraphed and illuminated book whose pages are turned as the voice-over progresses (*Sleeping Beauty, Snow White*). As well as invoking the nostalgic memory of the parent-to-child oral voice and the familiar form of the literary fairy tale, this also claims the historical status of literature—generally, in its association with literacy and education *higher* than that of the oral tale—for the film. The use of this motif in Dreamworks' *Shrek* was notable for its acute and cynical insight into the actual status of the original tale as written narrative—*Shrek*'s voice reads out the dragon-slaying fairy tale, after which the camera pulls back to reveal that the book is being used as toilet paper. This nods ironically to the fact that film versions of fairy tale have all but replaced the written, but the film's ideological project affirms the status of the film version in its suggestion that they *should* replace the written, which entrenches the outdated and reactionary social assumptions the film sets out to upset.

It is important to note, however, that invocation of the oral and literary are not sustained through most fairy-tale films, which quickly give way to the immersing experience of the moving image. The result is effectively to overwrite the literary and the oral with the cinematic. Jack Zipes picks up on this erasure in readings of fairy-tale film which generally rely on the characterization of modern fairy tale within a somewhat totalitarian sense of the culture industry. He argues that film has "silenced the personal and communal voice of the oral magic tales and obfuscated the personal voice of literary fairy-tale narratives"; it focuses on image rather than text, distances its audience, and transforms traditional tales into standardized units of mass production (*Happily Ever After* 69). In this characterization, rather as the upper classes appropriated folk narrative in the seventeenth and eighteenth centuries, the folk voice in the twentieth and twenty-first centuries is colonized by a ruling monolith, although one that is commercial rather than aristocratic. Such a colonization entails, in Baudrillard's terms, an actual *re-creation* of a spurious notion of orality; simultaneously, its commercial aspect redefines the awareness of artifact central to metafictional storytelling as, effectively, awareness of *product*. Zipes's characterization of fairy tale as "secular instructive narratives" offering "strategies of intervention within the civilising process" (*Happily Ever After* 65) becomes more sinister when, rather than reflecting the mores and beliefs of the folk culture, fairy tales are used to reflect the conservative and market-driven ideologies of large companies marketing consumer culture. Such characterizations of mass cultural productions sound a note of alarm in their sense of a production elite which seeks to duplicate and usurp the popular or folk voice. Zipes's argument implies that any claim of nostalgic orality or literariness in fairy-tale film is entirely spurious; logically, the elements of self-conscious play that I suggest are present become in his terms a cynical appropriation of fairy tale's metafictional project by what are effectively market forces. He is, of course, engaging in cultural criticism firmly in the mode of the Frankfurt School, and more specifically Adorno and Horkheimer, who suggest that modern consumer culture is a process of the deliberate discouragement of imaginative or intellectual response to the cultural products of the mass market. Instead, the receiver of such artifacts is lulled, via strategies such as nostalgia, familiarity, and superficial novelty, into the passive acceptance of a standardized cultural product. This logically suggests that the essentially reciprocal functioning of a folk culture is completely erased, as is its ability to mirror in any immediate or vital sense the day-to-day experiences and desires of its listeners. Adorno and Horkheimer stress the absolute lack of true participation by the public in mass cultural production:

The attitude of the public, which ostensibly and actually favours the system of the culture industry, is a part of the system and not an excuse for it. If one branch of art follows the same formula as one with a very different medium and content ... if a movement from a Beethoven symphony is crudely "adapted" for a film sound-track in the same way that a Tolstoy novel is garbled in a film script; then the claim that this is done to satisfy the spontaneous wishes of the public is no more than hot air. We are closer to the facts if we explain these phenomena as inherent in the technical and personnel apparatus which, down to its last cog, itself forms part of the economic mechanism of selection.... In our age the objective social tendency is incarnate in the hidden subjective purposes of company directors. (32)

By this definition, mass culture and folk culture are mutually exclusive; there can be no true "objective social tendency," in Adorno and Horkheimer's words, because original and spontaneous cultural impulses are modified by the purposes of mass-cultural monoliths. There can therefore be no folk voice in mass culture. This means that the pretensions to the folk voice in many fairy-tale films are, as suggested above, "hot air"—their purpose is solely to conceal their commercial manipulations.

This is perhaps too sweeping a judgment, and more recent perception of popular culture as a site of struggle suggest that Adorno and Horkheimer represent only one end of the popular theory spectrum. Noël Carroll offers an opposing voice which explicitly denies the truth of such claims; he maintains that numerous examples of popular art demonstrate clearly the lack of "necessary connection between accessibility and a passive audience response," and that indeed, "in some cases, the very success of the mass artwork presupposes active spectatorship" (38-39). This line of thought is certainly appropriate to the science fiction/fantasy ghetto, in which the highly specific readership may well require active participation in the text—or, indeed, to written narratives generally as Carroll demonstrates (40-41); nonetheless, it is also true to a greater or lesser extent of film. The self-conscious narrative play found in texts such as Disney fairy tales or Dreamworks' *Shrek* may empower a mass-market text, but it is equally able to give the artistic and intellectual pleasure of active reading to the viewer, and indeed would not be successful *without* such narrative pleasures. Theories of a mass-cultural monolith also deny the possibilities offered by the art-house end of the film spectrum, in which films are generally made on a far lower budget, and may be more able to balance their artistic requirements against the need to recoup their costs. A good example of film's potential for self-conscious use of fairy tale is Jordan's *The Company of Wolves*, in which frame narratives and tale-within-tale represent a sustained effort to reproduce the folk voice, and thus allow ongoing metafictional awareness. This is strengthened by the film's attention to the character of the oral storytellers (unlike Disney's disembodied voices), and their association of that oral voice with the readily identifiable grandmother archetype.

However, despite innovative uses such as Jordan's of the folk voice in film, Zipes's characterization is valid in that many fairy-tale films seem to represent an appropriation as much as an exploration or celebration of folk narrative. This exemplifies the uneasy and problematical intersections between popular or folk cultures, and the mass culture of consumerism. Film narrative is dominated by Hollywood, and particularly by big-budget studio films whose economies of scale require appeal to a broad demographic; many recent fairy-tale films represent a process of identifying the kinds of narrative which are currently selling, and reproducing them as closely as possible. Disney's huge successes with fairy tale in the late 1980s and early 1990s could be seen to have prompted later films such as *Ever After* and *The Grimm Brothers' Snow White*, and ultimately *Shrek*, which has itself spawned two sequels and a host of imitators in the knowing fairy-tale parody mode, including *Hoodwinked* and *Happily N'Ever After*. At the same time, the production-by-committee effect of financial oversight on films exists in palpable tension with the impulses of particular directors or screenwriters, who may well see the artistic rather than the commercial potential in recreating a familiar folkloric text. In addition, the construction of a particular text in terms favoring commercial success does not in any way prevent countercultural readings of such a text, representing a very different notion of narrative pleasure from that intended by the producers. Audience-generated responses such as fan fiction demonstrate precisely the kind of active, potentially subversive receptions of mass-cultural texts described by critics such as John Fiske and Henry Jenkins. Even Disney films, perhaps the strongest example of deliberate mass-cultural packaging, are capable of being read on multiple levels which address child and adult audiences separately. Thus, like much of mass culture, fairy-tale film is a site of contestation, with the warping of metafictional play to commercial ends balanced by a wresting back of commercial requirements to artistic and individual purposes. The postmodern cultural environment of modern film also means that at times the two impulses are one: self-consciousness, irony, and the pleasures of recognition are highly saleable commodities.

Works Cited

Adorno, Theodor, and Max Horkheimer. "The Culture Industry: Enlightenment as Mass Deception." In *The Cultural Studies Reader*, ed. Simon During. London: Routledge, 1993. 29-43.

Baudrillard, Jean. "Simulacra and Simulation." In *Jean Baudrillard: Selected Writings*, ed. Mark Poster. Stanford: Stanford UP, 1988. 166-84.

Bazin, André. *What Is Cinema?* Tr. Hugh Gray. Berkeley: U of California P, 1967.

Benjamin, Walter. "The Storyteller." In *Illuminations,* ed. Hannah Arendt. New York: Schocken, 1986. 83-109.

Carroll, Noël. *A Philosophy of Mass Art.* Oxford: Clarendon, 1998.

Fiske, John. *Reading the Popular.* Boston: Unwin, 1989.

Galef, David. "A Sense of Magic: Reality and Illusion in Cocteau's *Beauty and the Beast.*" *Literature/Film Quarterly* 12.2 (1984): 96-106.

Haase, Donald P. "Is Seeing Believing? Proverbs and the Film Adaptation of a Fairy Tale." *Proverbium* 7 (1990): 89-104.

Jenkins, Henry. *Textual Poachers: Television Fans and Participatory Culture.* New York and London: Routledge, 1992.

Lüthi, Max. *The Fairy Tale as Art Form and Portrait of Man.* Tr. Jon Erickson. Bloomington: Indiana UP, 1975.

Ong, Walter. *Rhetoric, Romance and Technology: Studies in the Interaction of Expression and Culture.* Ithaca: Cornell UP, 1971.

Tolkien, J.R.R. "On Fairy Stories." *The Tolkien Reader.* 1964; New York: Ballantine, 1966. 2-84.

Warner, Marina. *From the Beast to the Blonde: On Fairy Tales and Their Tellers.* London: Vintage, 1994.

Zipes, Jack. *Fairy Tale as Myth, Myth as Fairy Tale.* Lexington: UP of Kentucky, 1994.

_____. *Happily Ever After: Fairy Tales, Children, and the Culture Industry.* New York: Routledge, 1997.

_____. *The Oxford Companion to Fairy Tales: The Western Fairy Tale Tradition from Medieval to Modern.* Oxford: Oxford UP, 2000.

BIBLIOGRAPHY

Bacchilega, Cristina. *Postmodern Fairy Tales: Gender and Narrative Strategies.* Philadelphia, PA: U of Pennsylvania P, 1997.

Beckett, Sandra. *Red Riding Hood for All Ages: A Fairy Tale Icon in Cross-Cultural Contexts.* Detroit: Wayne State UP, 2009.

_____. *Transcending Boundaries: Writing for a Dual Audience of Children and Adults.* New York: Garland Publishing, 1999.

Bettelheim, Bruno. *The Uses of Enchantment: The Meaning and Importance of Fairy Tales.* New York: Alfred Knopf, 1976.

Bobby, Susan Redington, ed. *Fairy Tales Reimagined: Essays on New Retellings.* Jefferson, NC: McFarland, 2009.

Boden, Sharon. *Consumerism, Romance and the Wedding Experience.* Basingstoke and New York: Palgrave MacMillan, 2003.

Brantley, Ben. "Gowns from the House of Sincere and Snark: 'Rodgers and Hammerstein's Cinderella' at Broadway Theater." *New York Times,* March 3, 2013.

Broadus, Ray, and Pat Browne, eds. *The Guide to United States Popular Culture.* Bowling Green, OH: Bowling Green State U Popular P, 2001.

Cavallero, Dani. *The Fairy Tale and Anime: Traditional Themes, Images and Symbols.* Jefferson, NC: McFarland, 2011.

Crane, Walter. *Jack and the Beanstalk.* London: George Routledge and Sons, 1875.

Danesi, Marcel. *Forever Young: The Teen-Aging of Modern Culture.* Toronto: U of Toronto P, 2003.

_____. *Popular Culture: Introductory Perspectives.* 2nd ed. Rowman and Littlefield, 2012.

Dawkins, Richard. *The Selfish Gene.* 30th anniversary ed. Oxford: Oxford UP, 2006.

Dickens, Charles. "The Christmas Tree." In *Christmas Books and Reprinted Pieces.* New York: International Book Company, n.d.

Ellison, Harlan, presenter. *The Masters of Comic Book Art.* VHS videorecording. Los Angeles: Rhino/WEA, 1987.

Fiske, John. *The John Fiske Collection: Reading the Popular.* New ed. New York: Routledge, 1989.

_____. *The John Fiske Collection: Understanding Popular Culture.* 2nd ed. New York: Routledge, 2010.

Giroux, Henry A., and Grace Pollock. *The Mouse That Roared: Disney and the End of Innocence.* 2nd ed. New York: Rowman and Littlefield, 2010.

Greenhill, Pauline, and Sidney Eve Matrix. *Fairy Tale Films: Visions of Ambiguity.* Logan, UT: Utah State UP, 2010.

Hallett, Martin, and Barbara Karasek, eds. *Folk & Fairy Tales: Concise Edition.* Peterborough: Broadview, 2011.

Hellekson, Karen, and Kristina Busse, eds. *Fan Fiction and Fan Communities in the Age of the Internet: New Essays.* Jefferson, NC: McFarland, 2006.

Jenkins, Henry. *Fans, Bloggers, and Gamers: Exploring Participatory Culture.* New York: New York UP, 2006.

McAra, Catriona, and David Calvin, eds. *Anti-Tales: The Uses of Disenchantment.* Newcastle-upon-Tyne: Cambridge Scholars Publishing, 2011.

Moen, Kristian. *Film and Fairy Tale: The Birth of Modern Fantasy.* London: I.B. Tauris, 2013.

Orenstein, Catherine. *Little Red Riding Hood Uncloaked: Sex, Morality, and the Evolution of a Fairy Tale.* New York: Basic Books, 2003.

Otnes, Cele, and Elizabeth Pleck. *Cinderella Dreams: The Allure of the Lavish Wedding.* Berkeley: U of California P, 2003.

Parker, Holt N. "Towards a Definition of Popular Culture." *History and Theory* 50 (May 2011): 147-50.

Poniewozik, James. "The End of Fairy Tales? How Shrek and Friends Have Changed Children's Stories." *Time,* May 10, 2007.

Postman, Neil. *The Disappearance of Childhood.* New York: Random House, 1994.

Pullman, Philip. *Fairy Tales from the Brothers Grimm.* New York: Penguin, 2012.

Rankin, Walter. *Grimm Pictures: Fairy Tale Archetypes in Eight Horror and Suspense Films.* Jefferson, NC: McFarland, 2007.

Review. "A Witch, a Wish and Fairy Tale Agony." *New York Times,* August 9, 2012.

Robertson, Chris, and Shawn McManus. *Cinderella: Fables Are Forever.* New York: DC Comics, 2012-present.

Scott, Graham F. "Reads Like Teen Spirit." *Canadian Business* (February 18, 2013): 68.

Spiegelman, Art, and Françoise Mouly, eds. *Big Fat Little Lit*. New York: Puffin, 2006.

_____. *Little Lit: Folklore and Fairy Tale Funnies*. New York: HarperCollins/Joanna Cotler Books, 2000.

Storey, John. *Cultural Theory and Popular Culture: An Introduction*. 5th ed. New York: Pearson Longman, 2009.

Teverson, Andrew. *Fairy Tale (The New Critical Idiom)*. New York: Routledge, 2013.

Tiffin, Jessica. *Marvelous Geometry: Narrative and Metafiction in Modern Fairy Tales*. Detroit: Wayne State UP, 2009.

Weitman, W. *Kiki Smith: Prints, Books and Things*. New York: The Museum of Modern Art, 2003.

Willingham, Bill, and Phil Jimenez. *Fairest*. New York: Vertigo, 2012-present.

Wolf, Matt. "Playing Sondheim in the Woods." *New York Times*, August 24, 2010.

Zipes, Jack. *The Enchanted Screen: The Unknown History of Fairy-Tale Films*. New York: Routledge, 2010.

_____. *Happily Ever After: Fairy Tales, Children, and the Culture Industry*. New York: Routledge, 1997.

_____. *The Irresistible Fairy Tale: The Cultural and Social History of a Genre*. Princeton, NJ: Princeton UP, 2012.

ACKNOWLEDGMENTS

Advertisements

"Cinderella Math Equations," created by Revolve, Bedford, Nova Scotia, for Brain
    Candy Toys, Bedford, Nova Scotia, April 2011.
"Little Red Riding Hood: It's Another Story," created by Miami Ad School/
    ESPM, Sao Paulo, Brazil, for Burger King, Brazil, 2007.
"Little Red Tender," created by Unitas/RNL, Santiago, Chile, for Amnesty Inter-
    national, Santiago, Chile, 2009. Creative Director and Copywriter, Pancho
    González; Art Director, Rodrigo Geisse; Photographer, Javiera Eyzaguirre.
Pantene Anti-Breakage Shampoo promotional event, Toronto, Ontario, 2008.
    Reprinted with permission from Grey Canada, Full Serve Productions, and
    Aristea Rizakos, Photographer.
"Rapunzel: Melissa Bedtime Stories," created by BorghiErh, Brazil, for Melissa,
    Brazil, 2007. Art Directors, Erh Ray and Rodrigo Rodrigues; Creative Direc-
    tors, José Henrique Borghi and Erh Ray.
"Snow White: Anthropologie Catalogue Cover," created by Diego Uchitel for
    Anthropologie, November 2012. Diego Uchitel/Trunk Archive.
"Snow White: An Early Pregnancy Is No Fairy Tale," created by Fuel, Lisboa,
    Portugal, for Ajuda de Mãe, Portugal.

Comics/Graphic Novels/Illustrations

Joe Brusha and Ralph Tedesco. "Hansel and Gretel" from *Grimm Fairy Tales* (Volume 1, 4th edition). Zenescope Entertainment, September 2009.

Adam DeKraker and Jonathan Vankin. "The Stubborn Child," from *The Big Book of Grimm*, copyright © DC Comics. Reprinted with permission.

Sean Dietrich. *Hansel and Gretel: The Graphic Novel*. Copyright © 2008, 2009 by Stone Arch Books, an imprint of Capstone. All rights reserved.

Marlene Dumas. "Snow White and the Broken Arm," 1988; oil on canvas. Collection of the Gemeentemuseum Den Haag.

Will Eisner. "The Princess and the Frog." Copyright © 1999 Will Eisner Studios, Inc. Reprinted with permission.

Camille Rose Garcia. "How did you get to our house?" From *Snow White*, by the Brothers Grimm. Text copyright © 2012 by Harper Design. Illustrations copyright © by Camille Rose Garcia. Reprinted by permission of HarperCollins Publishers.

Shannon Hale and Dean Hale. *Rapunzel's Revenge*, Bloomsbury Children's Books (USA), 2008, Bloomsbury Publishing Inc. Copyright © 2008, Shannon Hale and Dean Hale. Illustration copyright © 2008 by Nathan Hale. Reprinted with permission.

Photograph by RANCINAN. "Red Riding Hood," 2003. Reprinted by permission of Gérard Rancinan.

Paula Rego. "Happy Family—Mother, Red Riding Hood and Grandmother," copyright © Paula Rego, 2003. From "Visualising Little Red Riding Hood" by Sarah Bonner, *Moveable Type*, 2006.

Paula Rego. "Little Red Riding Hood on the Edge," copyright © Paula Rego, 2003. From "Visualising Little Red Riding Hood" by Sarah Bonner, *Moveable Type*, 2006.

Paula Rego. "Mother Takes Revenge," copyright © Paula Rego, 2003. From "Visualising Little Red Riding Hood" by Sarah Bonner, *Moveable Type*, 2006.

Paula Rego. "Mother Wears the Wolf's Pelt," copyright © Paula Rego, 2003. From "Visualising Little Red Riding Hood" by Sarah Bonner, *Moveable Type*, 2006.

Paula Rego. "Swallows the Poisoned Apple," 1995; pastel on paper, mounted on aluminium. Copyright Paula Rego.

Paula Rego. "The Wolf," copyright © Paula Rego, 2003. From "Visualising Little Red Riding Hood" by Sarah Bonner, *Moveable Type*, 2006.

Paula Rego. "The Wolf Chats Up Red Riding Hood," copyright © Paula Rego, 2003. From "Visualising Little Red Riding Hood" by Sarah Bonner, *Moveable Type*, 2006.

Jon Scieszka (text), and Lane Smith (illustrations). "Giant Story" from *The Stinky Cheese Man and Other Fairly Stupid Tales*. Penguin/Puffin, 1993. Reprinted with permission from Penguin Group USA and Penguin Group UK. Text copyright © 1992 by Jon Scieszka. Illustrations © 1992 by Lane Smith. Used in North America by permission of Viking Penguin, a division of Penguin Group (USA) LLC.

Kiki Smith. "Born," 2002. Lithograph, 68 x 56" (172.7 x 142.2 cm). Photograph courtesy of Universal Limited Art Editions and Pace Gallery.

Kiki Smith. "Daughter," 1999. Nepal paper, bubble wrap, methyl cellulose and hair, 48 x 15 x 10" (121.9 x 38.1 x 25.4 cm). Photograph by Ellen Page Wilson, courtesy of Pace Gallery.

Kiki Smith. "Gang of Girls and Pack of Wolves," 1999. Fired paint on glass with brass and lead, 69-3/8 x 53-3/4" (176.2 x 136.5 cm); 12 glass sheets, each installation dimensions variable. Photograph by Ellen Page Wilson, courtesy of Pace Gallery.

Kiki Smith. "Rapture," 2001. Bronze, 67-1/4 x 62 x 26-1/4" (170.8 x 157.5 x 66.7 cm). Photograph by Richard-Max Tremblay, courtesy of Pace Gallery.

Bill Willingham. "As sorry as I am …" page 15 of *Fables: Legends in Exile*, Volume One, copyright © DC Comics. Used with permission.

Literary and Critical Texts

Kim Addonizio. "Ever After," from *The Palace of Illusions: Stories*. Counterpoint/ Soft Skull Press, 2014; copyright © Kim Addonizio.

Sarah Bonner. "Visualising Little Red Riding Hood," from *Moveable Type*, 2006. Reprinted with the permission of Sarah Bonner.

Roald Dahl. "The Three Little Pigs," from *Revolting Rhymes*. Puffin Books, 1982. Reprinted with the permission of David Higham, London.

Gail de Vos. "Storytelling, Folktales and the Comic Book Format." From *Language & Literacy: A Canadian Educational E-Journal* 3.1 (2001). Available at: <http://works.bepress.com/gail_devos/14>.

Alex Fury. "The Fairest of Them All: A Series of Hollywood Films Based on Classic Tales Is Putting Fairy Tale Fashion in the Spotlight," from the *Financial Times*, copyright © The Financial Times Limited, 2012. All rights reserved.

Neil Gaiman. "Snow, Glass, Apples," copyright © 1994 Neil Gaiman. First appeared in chapbook by DreamHaven Press.

James Finn Garner. "Jack and the Beanstalk," from *Politically Correct Bedtime Stories*. John Wiley & Sons Inc., 1994. Reprinted with the permission of James Finn Garner.

ACKNOWLEDGMENTS

Lyrics

Anita Baker. "Fairy Tales," from the album *Compositions*. Anita Baker, Vernon D. Fails, Michael J. Powell. Elektra Records, 1990.

Sara Bareilles. "Fairytale." Words and music by Sara Bareilles. Copyright © 2007 Sony/ATV Music Publishing LLC and Tiny Bear Music. All rights administered by Sony/ATV Music Publishing LLC, 8 Music Square West, Nashville, TN 37203. International Copyright Secured. All Rights Reserved. Reprinted by permission of Hal Leonard Corporation.

from the publisher

A name never says it all, but the word "broadview" expresses a good deal of the philosophy behind our company. We are open to a broad range of academic approaches and political viewpoints. We pay attention to the broad impact book publishing and book printing has in the wider world; we began using recycled stock more than a decade ago, and for some years now we have used 100% recycled paper for most titles. As a Canadian-based company we naturally publish a number of titles with a Canadian emphasis, but our publishing program overall is internationally oriented and broad-ranging. Our individual titles often appeal to a broad readership too; many are of interest as much to general readers as to academics and students.

Founded in 1985, Broadview remains a fully independent company owned by its shareholders—not an imprint or subsidiary of a larger multinational.

If you would like to find out more about Broadview and about the books we publish, please visit us at **www.broadviewpress.com**. And if you'd like to place an order through the site, we'd like to show our appreciation by extending a special discount to you: by entering the code below you will receive a 20% discount on purchases made through the Broadview website.

Discount code: **broadview20%**

Thank you for choosing Broadview.

Please note: this offer applies only to sales of bound books within the United States or Canada.

The interior of this book is printed on 100% recycled paper.